Memory, Myth, and Seduction

Psychological Issues Book Series

Volume 71

PSYCHOLOGICAL ISSUES BOOK SERIES

DAVID WOLITZKY
Series Editor

The basic mission of *Psychological Issues* is to contribute to the further development of psychoanalysis as a science, as a respected scholarly enterprise, as a theory of human behavior, and as a therapeutic method.

Over the past 50 years, the series has focused on fundamental aspects and foundations of psychoanalytic theory and clinical practice as well as on work in related disciplines relevant to psychoanalysis. *Psychological Issues* does not aim to represent or promote a particular point of view. The contributions cover broad and integrative topics of vital interest to all psychoanalysts as well as to colleagues in related disciplines. They cut across particular schools of thought and tackle key issues such as the philosophical underpinnings of psychoanalysis, psychoanalytic theories of motivation, conceptions of therapeutic action, the nature of unconscious mental functioning, psychoanalysis and social issues, and reports of original empirical research relevant to psychoanalysis. The authors often take a critical stance toward theories and offer a careful theoretical analysis and conceptual clarification of the complexities of theories and their clinical implications, drawing upon relevant empirical findings from psychoanalytic research as well as from research in related fields.

The Editorial Board continues to invite contributions from social/behavioral sciences such as anthropology and sociology, from biological sciences such as physiology and the various brain sciences, and from scholarly humanistic disciplines such as philosophy, law, and esthetics.

PSYCHOLOGICAL ISSUES BOOK SERIES

DAVID WOLITZKY
Series Editor

Published by Routledge

71. *Memory, Myth, and Seduction: Unconscious Fantasy and the Interpretive Process*, Jean-Georges Schimek & Deborah L. Browning
70. *From Classical to Contemporary Psychoanalysis: A Critique and Integration*, Morris N. Eagle

Published by Jason Aronson

69. *Primary Process Thinking: Theory, Measurement, and Research*, Robert R. Holt
68. *The Embodied Subject: Minding the Body in Psychoanalysis*, John P. Muller & Jane G. Tillman
67. *Self-Organizing Complexity in Psychological Systems*, Craig Piers, John P. Muller, & Joseph Brent
66. *Help Him Make You Smile: The Development of Intersubjectivity in the Atypical Child*, Rita S. Eagle
65. *Erik Erikson and the American Psyche: Ego, Ethics, and Evolution*, Daniel Burston

Published by International Universities Press

64. *Subliminal Explorations of Perception, Dreams, and Fantasies: The Pioneering Contributions of Charles Fisher*, Howard Shevrin
62/63. *Psychoanalysis and the Philosophy of Science: Collected Papers of Benjamin B. Rubinstein, MD*, Robert R. Holt
61. *Validation in the Clinical Theory of Psychoanalysis: A Study in the Philosophy of Psychoanalysis*, Adolf Grunbaum
60. *Freud's Concept of Passivity*, Russell H. Davis
59. *Between Hermeneutics and Science: An Essay on the Epistemology of Psychoanalysis*, Carlo Strenger
58. *Conscious and Unconscious: Freud's Dynamic Distinction Reconsidered*, Patricia S. Herzog
57. *The Creative Process: A Functional Model Based on Empirical Studies from Early Childhood to Middle Age*, Gudmund J. W. Smith & Ingegerd M. Carlsson
56. *Motivation and Explanation*, Nigel Mackay
55. *Freud and Anthropology*, Edwin R. Wallace IV
54. *Analysis of Transference, Vol. II: Studies of Nine Audio-Recorded Psychoanalytic Sessions*, Merton M. Gill
53. *Analysis of Transference, Vol. I: Theory and Technique*, Merton M. Gill & Irwin Z. Hoffman
52. *Anxiety and Defense Strategies in Childhood and Adolescence*, Gudmund J. W. Smith & Anna Danielsson Smith
51. *Cognitive Styles, Essays and Origins: Field Dependence and Field Independence*, Herman A. Witkin & Donald R. Goodenough

PSYCHOLOGICAL ISSUES BOOK SERIES

DAVID WOLITZKY
Series Editor

50. *Internalization in Psychoanalysis*, W. W. Meissner
49. *The Power of Form: A Psychoanalytic Approach to Aesthetic Form*, Gilbert J. Rose
47/48. *Intelligence and Adaptation: An Integration of Psychoanalytic and Piagetian Developmental Psychology*, Stanley I. Greenspan
45/46. *Hysteria: The Elusive Neurosis*, Alan Krohn
44. *Symbol and Neurosis: Selected Papers of Lawrence S. Kubie*, Herbert Schlesinger
42/43. *Modern Psychoanalytic Concepts in a General Psychology: General Concepts and Principles/Motivation*, Allan D. Rosenblatt & James T. Thickstun
41. *Freud in Germany: Revolution and Reaction in Science, 1893-1907*, Hannah S. Decker
40. *A Structural Theory of the Emotions*, Joseph De Rivera
39. *A History of Aggression in Freud*, Paul E. Stepansky
38. *Schizophrenia: Selected Papers*, David Shakow
37. *Emotional Expression in Infancy: A Biobehavioral Study*, Robert N. Emde, Theodore J. Gaensbauer, & Robert J. Harmon
36. *Psychology versus Metapsychology: Psychoanalytic Essays in Memory of George S. Klein*, Merton M. Gill & Philip S. Holzman
34/35. *Freud: The Fusion of Science and Humanism: The Intellectual History of Psychoanalysis*, John E. Gedo & George H. Pollock
33. *A Consideration of Some Learning Variables in the Context of Psychoanalytic Theory: Toward a Psychoanalytic Learning Perspective*, Stanley I. Greenspan
32. *Scientific Thought and Social Reality: Essays*, Fred Schwartz
31. *Else Frenkel-Brunswik: Selected Papers*, Nanette Heiman & Joan Grant
30. *Psychoanalytic Research: Three Approaches to the Experimental Study of Subliminal Processes*, Martin Mayman
29. *Similarity in Visually Perceived Forms*, Erich Goldmeier
28. *Immediate Effects on Patients of Psychoanalytic Interpretations*, Edith L. Garduk
27. *The Effect of Stress on Dreams*, Louis Breger, Ian Hunter, & Ron W. Lane
25/26. *Information, Systems, and Psychoanalysis: An Evolutionary Biological Approach to Psychoanalytic Theory*, Emanuel Peterfreund
24. *Ego Boundaries*, Bernard Landis
23. *A Psychoanalytic Model of Attention and Learning*, Fred Schwartz & Peter Schiller
22. *Toward a Unity of Knowledge*, Marjorie Grene
21. *Prediction in Psychotherapy Research: A Method of the Transformation of Clinical Judgments into Testable Hypotheses*, Helen D. Sargent, Leonard Horwitz, Robert S. Wallerstein, & Ann Appelbaum
20. *Psychoanalysis and American Medicine, 1894-1918: Medicine, Science, and Culture*, John Chynoweth Burnham
18/19. *Motives and Thought: Psychoanalytic Essays in Honor of David Rapaport*, Robert R. Holt

PSYCHOLOGICAL ISSUES BOOK SERIES

DAVID WOLITZKY
Series Editor

17. *The Causes, Controls, and Organization of Behavior in the Neonate*, Peter H. Wolff
16. *Freud's Neurological Education and Its Influence on Psychoanalytic Theory*, Peter Armacher
15. *Dragons, Delinquents, and Destiny: An Essay on Positive Superego Functions*, Wolfgang Lederer
14. *Papers on Psychoanalytic Psychology*, Heinz Hartmann, Ernst Kris, & Rudolph M. Loewenstein
13. *The Influence of Freud on American Psychology*, David Shakow & David Rapaport
12. *The Formation and Transformation of the Perceptual World*, Ivo Kohler
11. *Ego and Reality in Psychoanalytic Theory: A Proposal Regarding the Independent Ego Energies*, Robert W. White
10. *Topography and Systems in Psychoanalytic Theory*, Merton M. Gill
9. *Activation and Recovery of Associations*, Fred Rouse & Richard O. Schwartz
8. *Personality Organization in Cognitive Controls and Intellectual Abilities*, Riley W. Gardner, Douglas N. Jackson, & Samuel J. Messick
7. *Preconscious Stimulation in Dreams, Associations, and Images*, Otto Potzl, Rudolf Allers, & Jakob Teler
6. *The Structure of Psychoanalytic Theory: A Systematizing Attempt*, David Rapaport
5. *The Developmental Psychologies of Jean Piaget and Psychoanalysis*, Peter H. Wolff
4. *Cognitive Control: A Study of Individual Consistencies in Cognitive Behavior*, Riley W. Gardner, Philip. S. Holzman, George S. Klein, & Harriet Linton
3. *On Perception and Event Structure, and the Psychological Environment*, Fritz Heider
2. *Studies in Remembering: The Reproduction of Connected and Extended Verbal Material*, Irving H. Paul
1. *Identity and the Life Cycle: Selected Papers*, Erik H. Erikson

Memory, Myth, and Seduction

Unconscious Fantasy and the Interpretive Process

Jean-Georges Schimek

Edited by Deborah L. Browning

Foreword by Alan Bass

Routledge
Taylor & Francis Group
New York London

Routledge
Taylor & Francis Group
270 Madison Avenue
New York, NY 10016

Routledge
Taylor & Francis Group
27 Church Road
Hove, East Sussex BN3 2FA

Routledge is an imprint of Taylor & Francis Group, an Informa business

Printed in the United States of America on acid-free paper
10 9 8 7 6 5 4 3 2 1

International Standard Book Number: 978-0-415-87393-2 (Hardback)

Library of Congress Cataloging-in-Publication Data

Schimek, Jean-Georges.
Memory, myth, and seduction : unconscious fantasy and the interpretive process : Jean-Georges Schimek / edited by Deborah Browning ; foreword by Alan Bass. -- 1st ed.
p. cm. -- (Psychological issues book series)
Includes bibliographical references and index.
ISBN 978-0-415-87393-2 (hardcover : alk. paper) -- ISBN 978-0-203-86414-2 (e-book)
1. Fantasy. 2. Subconsciousness. 3. Memory. 4. Transference (Psychology) I. Browning, Deborah L. II. Title.

BF175.5.F36S35 2011
150.19'5--dc22 2010028963

Visit the Taylor & Francis Web site at
http://www.taylorandfrancis.com

and the Routledge Web site at
http://www.routledgementalhealth.com

To Jean's patients, supervisees, and students.

Contents

Acknowledgments

I want to thank, most of all, David Wolitzky, for his longstanding respect for Jean and for Jean's thinking and writing, and for his commitment to helping me work out the best way of pulling these essays together for this volume of *Psychological Issues*. In that regard, *Psychological Issues* could be no better venue. The first volume, in 1959, published Jean's mentor Erik Erikson, and later volumes contained the writings of Rapaport, Gill, Witkin, and Peter Wolff, all highly significant people in Jean's intellectual and personal world and several of whom were connected in one or another way with Jean's first intellectual home, Austen Riggs Hospital in Stockbridge, Massachusetts. This all feels so right.

Kristopher Spring, Associate Editor at Routledge, has been at this project with me from the beginning, even as we were still getting my first edited volume, *Adolescent Identitites*, into print. The idea of my providing introductions to each of the three sections was his. I had wanted to just let Jean speak for himself; it seemed outrageous to me at the time to think I could add anything to my husband's writing. But Kristopher was insistent—and right—and the book, I think, is the stronger for it. Judith Simon, Project Editor, picked up where Kristopher left off and saw to an accurate and carefully proofed copy for production.

I want to thank Alan Bass for his willingness to write the foreword. I don't think anyone understands Jean's approach to Freud better than he. I want to thank Victoria Mills, originally Jean's friend, who has stuck around and helped me not lose sight of the bigger picture. I want to thank David Salvage who joined me in conceiving the title. And finally, I want to thank Diane Sholomskas, not only for her enduring friendship, but also for her critical reading and thoughtful discussion of my introduction to Part II: On the Seduction Theory.

Foreword

Alan Bass

What will be the fate of psychoanalytic theory and practice? Will both die the death they deserve, according to some? Will the theory become solely an object of scholarly interest? Will the therapy disappear? There is no psychoanalyst practicing and writing today who is not haunted by such questions.

And yet some analysts continue to write and to practice with all the vitality of those impassioned by psychoanalysis from its earliest days. Jean Schimek was one of these—a great scholar and a great clinician. The clinician is known only to those he treated and supervised, who tend to speak of him with admiration and love. The scholar is only somewhat better known, a situation that will be rectified by this posthumous collection, assembled and edited by Deborah Browning. Browning's effort here will influence the fate of psychoanalysis. However it survives, that survival is largely in the hands of the scholar-clinicians like Schimek, who chose to meet the standard set by Freud.

Schimek is best known for his prescient, detailed work on Freud's seduction theory. However, that is but one facet in his kaleidoscopic approach to psychoanalysis. The list of topics includes the analytic relationship, transference (from many angles), intersubjectivity, psychic reality, unconscious fantasy, trauma, reflective conscious awareness, unconscious representation, and unconscious fantasy. Schimek does not shy away from the most difficult issues. That is what is so important about this book. It asks the reader to consider the hard questions, the questions psychoanalysis has to answer if it is to remain the most sophisticated integration of theory of mind and clinical practice extant.

Some of Schimek's ideas are startling. He thinks we can do without the concept of unconscious mental representation and that there are no infantile wishes in dreams. He offers an original interpretation of Freud's almost universally dismissed concept of phylogenetic fantasy, seeing it in relation to the question of mental categories. Clinically, he advocates the neutral, abstinent stance associated with "classical" analysis.

The combination of rigorous critique and respect for the resources of Freud's clinical method inevitably reminds one of Loewald. Like Loewald,

Schimek has been influenced by both developmental thinking and the approach to metapsychology associated with Rapaport, but he goes further. Not only is he more familiar with Melanie Klein, about whom he has important things to say, but Schimek is also demonstrably influenced by Jean Laplanche—unusual for an American analyst. The interplay of these influences creates Schimek's distinctive voice: measured and daring at the same time.

The key to Schimek's method can be found in some remarks in "The Construction of the Transference: The Relativity of the 'Here and Now' and the 'There and Then'" (Chapter 2):

> Transference always involves the use of multiple perspectives, both along the horizontal axis of the patient's interpretation of his experience versus the analyst's point of view and the vertical axis of the present versus the past.
>
> It is the interface, the overlap among these various perspectives, which constructs the transference as an ongoing process. The material of the analysis acquires new meanings by being considered simultaneously from the triple perspective of the patient's experience of the analyst, his experience of his current life, and his experience of his past. Each of these perspectives acquires meaning and relevance only in terms of the others. (p. 25)

The important words here are "ongoing process" and "only in terms of the others." If there is a central target of Schimek's criticisms of Freud and other psychoanalytic thinkers, it is the tendency to limit perspectives, to fail to see how psychoanalytic concepts only have relevance in terms of other, often competing concepts, and, above all, to make unjustified claims based on reified and overly simplistic thinking. Thus, Schimek thinks that each psychoanalytic theory has its own construction of psychic reality, which is an attempt to give "coherent meaning to what seems strange, incoherent, or random" (p. 61). Schimek is always thinking about how psychoanalytic theory might have an antipsychoanalytic effect. For him, it is only right that the demystifying stance of psychoanalysis (and of Freud, in particular) should be applied to it—or himself.

Schimek's explanation of why one might avoid multiple perspectives on transference again speaks to how he thinks. He is discussing the dangers of too one-sided a focus on the patient:

> These dangers are quite real because of all the forces that make the quest for simple, unambiguous, and final answers an ever recurring temptation for both patient and analyst. The emphasis on the relativity, the transience, and the multiple perspectives of the here and now is always resisted as a source of anxiety; yet, psychoanalysis is built on

> the hope that, for some, this relativity has a freeing effect and opens the possibility for self-initiated change. (p. 27)

Schimek is always attempting to think against the anxiety generated by multiple perspectives. He performs for himself, and then for his discipline, the "self-initiated change" that will free it from its resistance to itself.

Deborah Browning has provided excellent, insightful overviews of each section of the book, including brief summaries of the chapters. Her tone is that of editor and teacher—explaining, extending, summarizing and is not personal, even though she is Schimek's widow. I will not follow her example. I was very happy to be asked to write this foreword because of my own contact with Jean. I first met him when I was applying to become a training analyst at IPTAR (Institute for Psychoanalytic Training and Research), New York City, the psychoanalytic institute of which we were both members. I had to present a case to Jean over many months. This became a process I looked forward to, when it easily could have been otherwise. At our meetings, I was consistently astonished by Jean's ability to absorb all the detailed clinical material I was presenting. I joked to myself about his having the "ears of an elephant." Later, Jean and I were in an IPTAR study group on French psychoanalysis. No matter what we were reading, it was the same: Jean had absorbed the entire argument and could just talk about it, covering all the bases.

I cite this personal experience to repeat the point already made: For Schimek, psychoanalysis was, and has to be, the capacity to listen, to absorb, to think, to resist the anxiety that pulls for limited perspectives, and then to institute "self-initiated change." He is right that this is the hope on which psychoanalysis is built. Whatever his often sharp criticisms of Freud, he also knew that this hope was Freud's legacy. Through this book, he now legates that hope to us.

Editor's introduction

Deborah L. Browning

> I think that each culture, I mean each cultural form in Western civilization has had its system of interpretation, its techniques, its methods, its ways of suspecting that language means something other than what it says, and of suspecting that there is language elsewhere than in language.
>
> Foucault (1964, p. 60)

This selection of 14 essays by Jean-Georges Schimek represents a lifetime's engagement with Freudian as well as contemporary psychoanalysis. His focus ranges from careful expositions of Freud's texts, and the theoretical paradoxes and inconsistencies which are the inevitable result of such brilliant and creative thinking, to considerations of the implications of both traditional and more modern psychoanalysis for the varieties of work that take place in the contemporary analytic situation. Educated initially in Lausanne and then at the Sorbonne, Schimek has contributed richly to North American psychoanalytic thought while challenging such local views from the perspective of continental discourse.

The book is divided thematically into three sections. The first concerns the analytic situation and the manner in which analyst and patient coconstruct meaning and reconstruct and recover memory. The second section consists of two seminal chapters that provide careful scholarship on Freud's several revisions of his so-called seduction theory. Schimek's purpose is to lay out the data of Freud's writing, allowing one to draw one's own conclusions about the implications of the changes in the theory that Freud made. In the third, more theoretical section, Schimek provides a foundation for understanding many of today's discussions about unconscious fantasy, dreaming, remembering, self-reflection, and interpretation. He clarifies and illustrates Freud's original formulations and their inherent problems through a careful reading of sections of *The Interpretation of Dreams* and a study of Freud's famous motivated forgetting of the name of the Italian painter Signorelli (see the cover of this book for a representative fresco).

Running through virtually all the chapters are two interwoven threads or, differently put, two related questions. What do we mean when we speak of unconscious fantasy—a concept central to psychoanalysis? And what kinds of assumptions influenced Freud and now influence the analyst and patient alike—sometimes in opposition—in the *interpretation* of unconscious fantasy as it is discerned in dreams, conscious fantasies, slips of the tongue, motivated forgetting, and in both the transference of the patient and the countertransference of the analyst? Analyst and patient are both meaning-making individuals, implicitly as well as explicitly interpreting each other throughout the process. Schimek is alert to both the powerful dangers and the curative power of this delicately maintained balance.

Schimek brings a strong sense of history and cultural context to all his thinking about the interpretative processes of Freud, other psychoanalytic writers, and today's analyst and analysand. He maintains this sense—a "suspicion" to pick up on Foucault's word—that the language of the patient's symptoms and spoken story, as well as the analyst's choice of interpretation and mode of intervention, reflect the culture and historical time in which the analysis is taking place, each person's own cultural embeddedness, and the location of that culture in history.

So we know that approaching Freud requires a recognition of the time and place in which he lived, learned, and wrote. Schimek's rigorous study with Egon Brunswick at Berkeley in both perception and the history of psychology prepared him well for his exposition on Freud's nineteenth century understanding of perception, memory, and consciousness and the influence these assumptions had on Freud's theoretical constructs. If perception is veridical and images are stored as exact copies in a container-like unconscious and only secondarily distorted by the primary process, then the role of interpretation is to undo the distortions of the primary process, revealing repressed memories or fantasies just as they once were. This is one side of Freud's thinking.

But when Freud describes primary process as developmentally earlier, he is suggesting something quite different—something chaotic, unformed, undifferentiated, and disorganized. Here, then, interpretation has the implicit role of bringing experience to a higher level of organization, thus creating something essentially new. Schimek shows us in many different ways just how Freud's varying assumptions influenced what he expected from the process of interpretation and also how much Freud struggled with the goal of trying to make scientific the process of interpreting something he had claimed to be unverifiable—that is, the unconscious. Schimek reminds the reader that such phenomena as transference, psychic reality, and unconscious fantasy—essentials of Freudian psychoanalytic theory and clinical work—are unverifiable, hypothetical constructs; as such, they have their first existence in the mind of the analyst as interpreter of the patient's material. There is no such thing as transference, Schimek states with mock dogmatism, only transference interpretations.

Schimek's intellectual mentorship with Erikson also began at Berkeley and later led him east on Erikson's invitation to Austen Riggs in Stockbridge, Massachusetts, for clinical supervision and training. (It was here he studied with Rapaport as well.) This additional time with Erikson further infused Schimek with a sense of the rich, complex ways in which time and place—historical and cultural context—become woven into one's conscious and unconscious fantasy life and influence how we interpret experience. As analysts, our preference for seeing psychoanalysis as a process of uncovering and discovery or of creation and coconstruction (and, of course, it can be both) rests on our assumptions about perception, memory, and trauma—whether our earliest childhood experiences are perceived and recorded intact or constructed and differentiated over time. In the chapters on the analytic relationship, Schimek emphasizes the extent to which the analyst brings her preconceptions, assumptions, biases, "prejudices" to use Gadamer's (1960) term, into her listening, watching, and interacting with the patient. Bion's (1967) invocation to "listen without memory or desire," as Schafer (1994) says, "makes a good deal of sense so long as it is not examined too closely" (p. 428).

Schimek maintains a fairly clear and consistent point of view about the extent to which we always risk interpreting from within the limits of our own personal frame of reference, while his views about unconscious fantasy changed and evolved over the course of his career. In his earlier writings, as he looked at the implications of Freud's assumption of veridical perception and the influence of this nonmotivational and nondevelopmental view of memory and fantasy, Schimek suggested instead that perhaps our earliest fantasy is built upon sensorimotor, affective schema. This more Piagetian perspective reverses Freud's idea that ideation precedes organized action. Schimek extended this hypothesis into the clinical realm, suggesting that it may well be that the therapeutic interaction within the clinical situation sets the stage for new insight, rather than the other way around.

Over time, Schimek moved toward a more traditional notion of unconscious fantasy as some kind of "scene" involving two or more people in interaction of some sort, with accompanying affect and with the patient imagining herself in any of the various roles. What may be unique to Schimek's conception is the idea that these fantasied scenarios, drawing their specifying material from the individual's early life of experience and fantasy, may be built upon a limited set of underlying fantasy structures, functioning much like preorganized Kantian categories. These potential unconscious fantasy scenarios operate within the thinking of both analyst and analysand and have a significant effect on the interpretive process of the analyst. Each version of psychoanalytic theory, Freudian, Kleinian, Winnicottian, Mahlerian, Kohutian, has its own set of assumptions and organizing categories of interpretation, influencing and shaping the interpreting of the analyst, perhaps as much, Schimek (2002) suggests, as organizing unconscious fantasies influence the meaning that the patient makes of her world:

> Unconscious fantasies determine the organization of personal and emotional reality. They are systems of belief which indicate what is to be desired and fought for and what is to be feared and avoided. [They are] known only through their consequences or derivatives. This means that they are constructions or inferences based on a specific psychoanalytic theory; they constitute the basic organizing and interpretive categories of this theory.

In this introduction and in the introductory notes that precede each of the three sections, I have tried to explain, clarify, and explicate Schimek's chapters and his points of view. My introductory notes differ in style and format from section to section because the themes of each section and the nature of the chapters are sufficiently different to call for varying introductions. These notes are clearly my interpretations, prejudiced in myriad ways by my training as a psychologist and psychoanalyst, my personal preference for a particular theory, my past, my feelings about my current and prior analyses—and, of course, my relationship with the author. In these months that I have labored with Schimek's writings, reading them again and again, living with Laplanche and Pontalis' *Language* at my side, checking and double-checking the literature to which Schimek refers to see how the authors might explain themselves to me, I have wondered what Schimek would think of my interpretations of his interpretations of Freud and this whole psychoanalytic enterprise. I can only ask readers to remain suspicious of my thinking, tolerant of my errors, and curious in their engagement with Schimek's ideas. This, I believe, is what Schimek would have wanted.

Part I

On the analytic relationship

Deborah L. Browning

One can discern two interrelated themes running through Schimek's chapters on the analytic relationship. The first is an assumption of asymmetry in the analytic situation and the implications this has for issues related to the enactment of interpersonal power. The second and closely related theme concerns the extent to which the analyst brings her own frame of reference into her listening to the patient. With these two issues in mind, Schimek steps back from the clinical situation and discusses somewhat broadly the topics of transference, countertransference, psychic reality, intersubjectivity, enactment, and therapeutic action. The protagonists in this story of the analytic relationship are Freud, Klein, Winnicott, Schafer, Loewald, Gill, Hoffman, Renik, Ogden, and the Sandlers, whose ideas he uses to clarify the conceptual and theoretical points he wants to make.

Schimek also moves forward to share his stance with respect to his own work as a clinical psychoanalyst and how he thinks it fits within the field as it exists today. I will limit my notes, here, to highlighting Schimek's concern with the asymmetry and power differential in the analytic situation and the way in which the analyst's conscious categories of interpretation and unconscious psychic reality risk taking center stage. Following these comments, I will provide a brief synopsis of each chapter.

POWER AND THE PATIENT'S POINT OF VIEW

Simplifying the history of psychoanalysis rather greatly, one may note that when Freud found that suggestion was insufficient for his purposes, he began to exert pressure. That failing, a struggle broke out between analyst and patient. It was as if the analyst now had a mandate to overpower the patient's mind—and, by extension, her self. (It is called "breaking through resistance.") Today, as medical practice outside the institute has been increasingly required to collaborate with a patient in all aspects of her care, the psychoanalyst is left with the thorny task of figuring out how to be of help and use, without taking over, without misusing the power that the pained and paying patient will likely be inclined to offer.

At the close of his "Dynamics of the Transference" (1912), Freud remarked that "this struggle between the doctor and the patient, between intellect and instinctual life, between understanding and seeking to act, is played out almost exclusively in the phenomena of transference. It is on that field that the victory must be won" (p. 108). Freud was an ineffectual hypnotist, and his forays into the pressure technique failed to yield his hoped-for discoveries of the patient's "hidden and forgotten erotic impulses." It now appeared to him that transference would be a new "royal road."

But what, exactly, is transference? If we think along with one of Freud's criteria of transference as that which is "inappropriate," then one may raise the questions: "inappropriate in what respect?", "inappropriate according to whom?" Schimek suggests rather provocatively that perhaps there is no such thing as transference, only transference interpretations. He points out that different analysts will identify different aspects of the patient's behavior and affect as transference, contingent upon their own frame of reference, beliefs about the purpose of treatment, and personal defensive needs, so that the nature of this victory that Freud would have us win risks becoming the victory of the therapist's point of view over that of the patient.

Schimek assumes that the analytic situation is unavoidably asymmetrical and involves an imbalance of power, but this need not and must not mean that the analyst becomes the final authority on what is true. Even the new perspective that the analyst may hope to provide is not meant to supplant or supersede the patient's, but rather only to enlarge and supplement it. And while he agrees with much that Gill and Hoffman bring to our attention about the influence of the analyst on the patient's experience, Schimek believes that, because the analyst must restrain the revelation of his own private associations in order to protect the patient from undue influence, a "negotiated consensus" about what is actually happening in the interpersonal situation, is most likely an unreachable goal. Schimek suggests that recognition of the asymmetry places particular responsibility on the analyst for self-control, self-discipline, and tolerance of frustration. The rule of abstinence applies as much, if not more, to the analyst as to the analysand. This restraint is all in the service of the analyst's efforts to be an attentive, alert, open-minded listener. It is the patient's point of view that should take precedence, and it is the analyst's task to safeguard this view.

Of what are patient and analyst together in search? Schimek takes a traditional point of view that the goal of analysis should be greater self-awareness and self-knowledge and that the role of the patient's reconstruction of her history is crucial. This construction and reconstruction of the patient's life story, while pursued together, must make some kind of intrinsic sense to the patient. The patient must be allowed to assume first and final authorship in filling out a story where, initially, there may have been only inarticulate and fragmentary elements.

In taking this position, Schimek indicates his view that a person's past is not buried exactly as it once happened, providing clear, veridical memories. The past will have left its imprint, to be sure, but not necessarily in a way that can be remembered in a singular, distinct, and accurate way. And it is this assumption of a real and influential, but largely unrememberable, early past that makes it all the more important that the patient should be the "first author" of her story. This role of first author both respects and supports the patient's sense of identity and self-image, and her way of relating to the world. The understandable urge of many therapists to move in, take over, and fill in the gaps, imposing their own assumptions demands what Schimek refers to as the *rule of abstinence for the analyst.*

While Schimek perhaps privileges the importance of historical construction and reconstruction in the analytic process, he does not dismiss the significance or the reality of the analytic relationship, even if mostly mediated though the interpretive activity of the analyst. His thinking at times is reminiscent of Loewald, and he sees the analytic situation as a staging area where prior relationships are lived out under the stewardship of the analyst as "stage director." What may account for therapeutic change is not so much a new view of the past, but more likely the internalization of the patient's experience of the relationship with the analyst. And, here again, we see the ascendance of the patient's point of view, in that what matters and is potentially internalized is the patient's explicit, as well as unexpressed, opinion of what in that relationship constituted "transference" and what for him or her has been real.

PSYCHIC REALITY AND THE MIND OF THE ANALYST

Discussions of the analytic relationship in clinical psychoanalysis involve issues related to reality and fantasy, self and other, past and present, psychical and external reality. We assume increasingly that these ideas and phenomena cannot be dichotomized, nor should they be polarized; rather each "this and that" is a blend, an "interpenetrating mix-up" (Balint, 1960, p. 39), that can only be worked with, handled, transformed, detoxified, but most likely never fully disentangled. The "truth" of a situation can never be fully known. The concept of psychic reality is particularly useful for its emphasis on something ineffable about the patient—and also the analyst—that, while ultimately unknowable, still requires our full attention. It captures both "inflicted fact and purposeful editing" (Friedman, 1995, p. 27). It is that which gives shape to the neurosis, to fantasy, dreams, slips of the tongue, to the analyst's desire to know, and to the patient's resistance to knowing. In its timelessness, it plays tricks on us, inspires our multiple self states, makes us feel restless during those moments when time seems to stand still.

Definitions of psychic reality abound, and while the concept is made use of in a great many psychoanalytic articles, there remains no consensus as to its meaning—only choices of definitions. In his recent discussion of the topic, Zepf (2006) takes the position that the idea of psychic reality should not be "watered down" from Freud's original conception. Freud introduces the term *psychical reality* in the closing pages of the seventh chapter of *The Interpretation of Dreams* (1900), writing:

> The unconscious is the true psychical reality; *in its innermost nature it is as much unknown to us as the reality of the external world, and it is as incompletely presented by the data of consciousness as is the external world by the communications of our sense organs.* (p. 613)

But this comment is sufficiently ambiguous, and there are few enough other elaborations by Freud that there is still leeway for interpretation of its meaning.

Schimek defines psychic reality first by that which he views it is not. It does not refer to a patient's conscious, subjective experiences. At most, these experiences would reflect, be derivatives of, be shaped by something underlying. Schimek reads Freud's comments on psychic reality to suggest "that unconscious wishes have an autonomous structure, organization, and persistence with an enactive power and causal efficacy of their own" (see Chapter 3). He is thus describing psychic reality essentially as unconscious fantasy, a topic he elaborates extensively in Chapters 9 and 10 on unconscious mental representation and fantasy. As such, Schimek defines a person's psychic reality as consisting of a set of basic, unconscious fantasies that operate in the manner of Kantian categories to organize, structure, and give meaning to experience.

In the chapters on the analytic relationship, Schimek emphasizes the way in which the analyst's own psychic reality as well as her assumptions of certain basic, organizing fantasies in all individuals' psyches can influence both listening to and speaking with the patient. Schimek argues that, to the extent that psychic reality involves a "limited set of primary fantasies" that organize and give meaning to one's experience, the analyst's choice of interpretive category, whether it is that of the "holding mother," "the oedipal father," or "the mirroring parent," reflects an aspect of her own psychic reality taking shape in her theory of mind, which can be imposed upon the patient's material.

Schimek compares the analyst at work, making meaning while listening, with Freud, the "archeologist of the mind," and suggests that, in both cases, this reflects a basic search by the individual for causes and explanations. And it is these theories and the material that gives content to them that constitute an individually created psychic reality. Put another way, our psychic reality is constituted because of our need for causes and explanations, which operates, then, as much in the analyst as in the patient. While not linking it specifically to psychic reality, Blass (2006) elaborated extensively on this desire for knowledge in her paper on Freud's (1910) "Leonardo" monograph. One will see the topic of psychical reality taken up more fully by Schimek in his considerations of Freud's seduction theory (Chapters 7 and 8).

Not only will the analyst bring her own personal history, implicit theory of development, psychopathology, goals of treatment, and "voices" of prior supervisors (Smith, 2001) into the psychoanalytic situation, but each theory of psychopathology, development, and therapeutic change also has built into it assumptions about the presumed psychic reality of the patient. It is this issue about psychic reality at its broadest level that Schimek brings into his thinking throughout the chapters on the analytic relationship. These differing psychoanalytic models of a prototypical past tag along with the analyst in her listening, regardless of whether the material is about the patient's past, current life, or expressed in the here and now of the analytic situation.

Despite the imbalance in the analytic relationship and the vulnerability of many patients toward interpersonal submission, how might we try to limit the imposition of our own frame of reference on the patient? How do we limit the rigidity of our assumptions about what we see or what we expect to see in any next moment? In her extensive writing on analytic listening, Schwaber captures Schimek's advocacy of the patient's point of view when she refers to the "inherent legitimacy" of the patient's experience. She writes:

> We lose sight of the fact that our vantage point, even our view of ourselves, is simply that—ours; the patient may have another, the inherent legitimacy of which is still to be found. We tend, thereby, not to ask, not to take our patients at their word. (2006, p. 17)

Schwaber's writing on analytic listening helps attune the analyst to the possibility that, by carefully following the manifest, the conscious in the patient's thinking and feeling, more unconscious areas will be opened up, and the analyst will be less inclined to impose "assumptions" about the unconscious on the other person.

Pine's (2006) recent plea for a measure of diversity and tolerance thereof offers a different kind of anodyne for the pain of the dissonance between the patient's experience and the analyst's frame of mind. To the extent that we open ourselves to a "multiplicity of ideas about mind" (p. 464) and accept and recognize their intrinsic validity in certain contexts with certain patients, we open ourselves as well to the differing needs of different patients and also, importantly, to the shifting needs of any individual patient at any given moment. In doing so, we offer ourselves, and thus our patient as well, more opportunity to find and employ, if only initially and preconsciously, the least discordant conception until the individuality and originality of the patient and her experience is more fully understood.

CHAPTER SUMMARIES

In Chapter 1, "Psychoanalysis and Transference: Yesterday, Today, and Tomorrow," Schimek reminds the reader that clinical psychoanalysis was never Freud's primary motive or goal and that his writing on technique comprises a fairly small proportion of his total work. He points to the way in which psychoanalysis has become increasingly concerned with treatment issues in the last 40 years and has been applied in ever greater variation to an ever broader range of patients in ever lengthening analyses.

In Chapter 2, "The Construction of the Transference: The Relativity of the 'Here and Now' and the 'There and Then,'" after providing a succinct summary of Freud's criteria of transference as inappropriateness, resistance, and repetition, Schimek proceeds to challenge many aspects of the concept and the phenomena that are labeled as such. He points to the extent to which transference is defined by the analyst in terms of her view of pathology, development, and goals for the treatment. Those aspects of the transference that will serve to facilitate the treatment may well be ignored, allowed to flourish in a *sotto voce* manner, or relabeled as the "real relationship." He considers the writing and theories of Melanie Klein and Gill and Hoffman in order to show that, in two such different approaches to treatment, both work within implicit models, leading to selective constructions influenced by the analyst's frame of reference.

In Chapter 3, "Intersubjectivity and the Analytic Relationship," Schimek discusses Renik's oversimplified caricature of the objective, neutral, anonymous analyst. He points to the pitfalls of the postmodern emphasis on relativity and the idea that an analytic relationship could ever truly be a "collaboration between peers"—unless, perhaps he comments wryly, the individuals took turns paying each other. In his discussion of Ogden, Schimek notes the many ways the idea of projective identification is used, and he questions the assumption that unconscious influence seems to be assumed to be unidirectional, from patient to analyst, and that the analyst could truly function as a "clean container" without the mediating effect of his own psychic reality.

In Chapter 4, "On the Resolution of the Positive Transference: Suggestion, Identification, and Action," Schimek returns to the topic of transference per se, focusing here on the role and fate of the positive transference and the idea that, more than just identifying with the analyst or his interpretations, internalization of the entire relationship with the analyst may be a crucial part of therapeutic action. He also elaborates on the importance of interweaving the patient's experiences from the three different perspectives—of her experience of her past, her experience of her ongoing life, and her experience of the analytic situation—in providing a part of the therapeutic action.

In Chapter 5, "Transference and Psychic Reality: Ideas About the Timeless Past in Psychoanalysis," Schimek explores the concept of psychic reality, extends this discussion to a consideration of the impact of the analyst's psychic reality on the analytic process, and concludes with an emphasis on the centrality of the concept of psychic reality in psychoanalysis.

In Chapter 6, "Further Thoughts on the Contemporary Analytic Relationship," Schimek summarizes what he sees as six interacting trends found within discussions of the contemporary analytic relationship. He considers issues related to countertransference and enactment, and he proposes his own view of the principles and goals of the analytic relationship.

Chapter 1

Psychoanalysis and transference

Yesterday, today, and tomorrow*

It is well known that Freud never saw himself primarily as a therapist and healer; neither did he view psychoanalysis as first and foremost a technique of therapy, nor even a theory of psychopathology. In the most general way, he defined psychoanalysis as primarily a procedure for the investigation of mental processes which are almost inaccessible in any way other than from the special analytic situation. Only secondarily was it defined as a method for the treatment of neurotic disorders based on that investigation. Thirdly, psychoanalysis was a collection of psychological information, gradually being accumulated into a new scientific discipline.

In 1926 Freud stated that "the future will probably attribute far greater importance to psychoanalysis as the science of the unconscious than as a therapeutic procedure" (1926b, p. 265). We may now see that this was more a wish than an accurate prediction. For Freud, psychoanalysis was "the science of the unconscious mind" (1923a, p. 252), a depth psychology. His major interest in psychopathology was that it should make a unique contribution to the understanding of normal mental functioning. He repeatedly stressed the continuum and basic similarity between neurotic and normal phenomena. From the beginning of his writing, he used data not only from the clinical situation, but also from dreams, slips of the tongue, jokes, folklore, and myths. His two major works, *The Interpretations of Dreams* (1900) and *Three Essays on Sexuality* (1905b), deal with the psychopathology of everyday life and are not meant to apply primarily to neurosis.

It is also well known that Freud's writings on treatment technique are only a very small part of his total oeuvre, work which extends to most areas of human endeavor and social institutions. The exploration of the unconscious mind and its place in individual and social processes was not just applied to psychoanalysis, *but at its very core*. It is also clear that the broad influence of psychoanalysis on twentieth-century Western culture has not

* Part of this chapter was presented at the Institute for Psychoanalytic Training and Research (IPTAR) 40th Anniversary Celebration, "IPTAR at the Dawn of the 21st Century," November 2000.

been limited to therapeutic endeavors, but also has been most conspicuous in the arts, psychology, and philosophy, as well as in popular language and modes of thinking. It is not its therapeutic successes which have made psychoanalysis unique and famous.

Freud's emphasis on a general theory of mind was largely shared by many major analytic writers in the first half of the century, Melanie Klein, among others. It extended to the ego psychology of the 1950s, which tried to make psychoanalysis into a general psychology, mostly by highlighting nonconflicted and nonmotivational aspects of functioning, moving into the areas where psychoanalysis actually had little specific to contribute.

The emphasis has gradually changed in the last 40 or so years, particularly in the United States. The emphasis has become mostly clinical, with analysis widening its scope by including an ever greater variety of techniques and types of patients. Likewise, the therapeutic goals of psychoanalysis have changed since Freud's earliest formulations. They have moved from symptom removal to structural change through a lasting resolution of conflicts, leading then to the recent emphasis on the repair of developmental deficits through the creation of new structures. These more recent, and more ambitious, goals have been accompanied by an increasing emphasis on the "real" analytic relationship (acting "beyond interpretation," providing a holding environment, a new object, etc.) as a prime curative agent, rather than as a necessary background support for the interpretation of resistance and transference.

Despite or perhaps partly because of an endless proliferation of theories, their importance intellectually, seems to be decreasing. Theory and concepts have been reduced to tools for communication and organization of thought, more or less equivalent languages, as long as they promote the patient's sense of being understood and facilitate the coconstruction of some narrative. To the extent that many contemporary formulations view the patient as essentially needy, confused, helpless, and infantile, they may attribute an inflated role to the analyst's interventions and to the curative effect of the intrinsic virtues and capacities of the analyst's personality—as a model of a mature, wise adult.

Freud's classical formulation already underestimates the extent to which the transference (particularly the unconscious fantasies underlying its positive "facilitating" aspects) is not and maybe cannot be really analyzed and "dissolved." And an essential aspect of lasting structural change is likely to be an identification with the analyst, or better, an internalization of the patient's changing experience of the analytic relationship. Such a change becomes consolidated through its application and modification in the extra-analytic reality of the patient; the interaction between the analysis and real life is a necessary ongoing process, not limited to "acting out" or a change in symptoms, but including the tangible consequences of the patient's actions, as well as his changed subjective experiences in major life situations.

The reference and perspective of real life, in addition to that of the past, seems essential to maintain the "playground" reality, intense and artificial, of the analytic relationship—thus permitting its lasting, flexible transfer to other life situations. Without minimizing the role of training and experience, we assume that the effectiveness of the analyst largely rests on the special conditions of the analytic setting and the attributes, power, and expectations transferred to him by the patient. The analyst obviously can become only the concrete symbol, not the real substitute, for a holding environment or a good-enough mother.

This process, while facilitated by the analyst's actual behavior, depends essentially on the patient's ability to bring to the situation not only a wish, however faint and conflicted, for such a relationship, but also the capacity to create and use symbolic gratification. In the best case, the analyst probably uses his symbolic transferential powers, not to dissolve the transference, but to facilitate the creation and internalization of a modified, less conflicted, and more realistic version of it.

In much of the analytic literature at present, there has been a marked decrease in the role of interpretation, and there is more emphasis on preverbal attunement and implicit affective communication. The special playground of the treatment situation has become, progressively, less a means to an end (presumably, the analysis of free associations and transference), than an end in itself. It is primarily the relationship, nourished by the symbolically enacted fantasies of both participants, which has become central. This special relationship and the ongoing support and substitute gratifications it can provide may begin to be experienced as more real and lasting, less nasty and brutish, than what life outside has to offer.

The more precise description of these changes in psychoanalysis and their possible causes and consequences would take us far afield. Whether for the better or worse, these are clearly major changes. As the comprehensive review by Sandler and Dreher (1996) entitled "What Do Psychoanalysts Want?" confirms, there is very little consensus about the aims of psychoanalysis and how these aims are to be achieved. And, of course, the relevance and interaction of psychoanalysis with the world at large, with endeavors beyond the couch, is getting more remote and foggy. Theory and practice have become more and more split apart. On the nonclinical side, we see psychoanalytic theory expelled from psychology and psychiatry departments, finding some refuge in literature and the humanities. This has led to some interesting and original contributions, but I think that academic psychoanalysis, devoid of a clinical base, may often become mostly a clever word game.

Where might the boundaries of psychoanalysis be in the future? What might one hope or wish for? I think the boundaries of psychoanalysis could become both more extended again, beyond those of a besieged, therapeutic enclave, and also more narrow and limited, preserving the uniqueness and specificity of psychoanalysis—as a form of treatment, a method of inquiry, and a set of concepts. To start with treatment, psychoanalysis would, ideally, keep increased self-knowledge as one of its primary goals, even if limited to those relatively few who can tolerate it and benefit from it. Otherwise, psychoanalysis risks making exaggerated claims for cure, as it once did in the United States, which may have contributed to disappointment and decline, or becoming only one of the more intensive and interminable brands of psychotherapy.

I believe that psychoanalysis cannot and need not become a definitive and all-encompassing theory. Thus, it is not very meaningful to give it a sharp and lasting definition. As such, it does not serve well as a general psychology, even as a psychology of motivation. Psychoanalysis is a limited and specialized one, dealing mostly with unconscious and conflicted motives. Neither do I think it promising for psychoanalysis to sacrifice its unique aspects and potential by trying to become a natural science, under the cover of brain research or child behavioral observations.

I see the broader and more universal aspects of psychoanalysis as including an emphasis on unconscious, conflicted motives and the role of beliefs and fantasies in shaping them. But such universal aspects cannot be reduced to biology; they acquire concrete reality only through the changes and variations in the language, beliefs, and conditions of a particular period and culture.

Clinical psychoanalysis deals with *individual versions* of experience, twice removed from the universals of any theory. And here we are left with many unanswered questions about the relative contribution of the patient's transference, the analytic technique, and the analyst's personality to the curative potential of the analytic process. Is the analyst's choice of a specific theory more than a matter of personal history and preference? Do we still believe that the choice of a specific theory and its presumed validity makes a major difference in the process and outcome of treatment?

What is most needed and probably hardest to achieve is some integration between clinical reality, in all its compelling ambiguity, and concepts applicable to the world beyond the couch. It may be mostly a question of transfer, transference, and transformation: for the patient, transfer from what happens in the encapsulated analytic dyad to what happens in the real life; for the analyst, transformation of clinical experiences and observations to a view of psychic processes beyond psychotherapy; and for both of them a recognition of the relativity of many aspects of the transference.

Chapter 2

The construction of the transference

The relativity of the "here and now" and the "there and then"*

The gap between theory and clinical practice has remained one of the major problems of psychoanalysis. The concept of transference is a central bridge between these two areas, but it is a rather precarious one. Transference is not a self-evident, clearly delineated, or even directly observable clinical fact. There is little agreement, not only as to the specific origins and functions of transference, but also even as to the clinical observations to which the concept refers. As Laplanche and Pontalis (1967) state,

> For many authors the notion of transference has taken on a very broad extension, even coming to connote all the phenomena which constitute the patient's relationship with the psychoanalyst. As a result, the concept is burdened down more than any other with each analyst's particular views on the treatment, on its objectives, dynamics, tactics, scope, etc. (p. 456)

In this chapter I shall stress the view that transference is always a selective construction based on and relative to specific theoretical concepts and a particular patient–analyst interaction. Psychoanalysis involves the construction of a transference just as it involves the construction of a past (Schafer, 1978), the two being more or less explicitly part of the same process.

With this perspective in mind, let me first briefly review Freud's well-known defining criteria for transference, specifically, inappropriateness, resistance, and repetition of the past. The first criterion, inappropriateness, is a descriptive one based on the "here and now" of the analytic situation; the second is a functional one—that is, the function of transference in terms of the goals and process of the treatment; the third refers to the basic meaning and origins of transference. I would like to highlight two interrelated points. First, these criteria as formulated by Freud have many areas of unclarity and ambiguity—areas that are directly related to elaborations

* This chapter originally appeared in *Psychoanalysis and Contemporary Thought*, 6(3), 1983, pp. 435–456. Reprinted with permission.

and reformulations by later authors and which will be briefly discussed in the second part of this chapter. Second, these three criteria are interdependent, in that each one implies and assumes all the others and rests more broadly on Freud's general view of the process of the treatment and the (oedipal) dynamics and origins of psychopathology.

The first criterion states that transference is those manifestations of the patient's behavior toward the analyst which are inappropriate and unreasonable. To the obvious questions—inappropriate to what? and unreasonable to whom?—the answers would have to be: inappropriate to the present situation and unreasonable from the analyst's point of view. One could say that such reactions are not really inappropriate to the situation because the analytic situation is a special one, an artificial kind of interpersonal relationship in which the whole setting, including the patient's physical position, the analyst's relative neutrality and anonymity, and other aspects of this technique, are aimed at bringing about these "inappropriate," regressive manifestations.

In a more narrow sense, the word *inappropriate* refers to those reactions and behaviors of the patient which cannot be accounted for by aspects of the here and now, by the analyst's input and his contributions to the patient's reactions. The analytic situation is, of course, precisely designed so that the analyst's input will be relatively small and fairly constant, at least in principle. But as many authors have pointed out since Freud (Gill & Hoffman, 1982; Wachtel, 1980), the analyst's contribution is never nil and always plays a role in the patient's reaction.

We all know that when Freud highlighted this criterion of inappropriateness he mostly had in mind the more dramatic example of his early female hysterical patients having strong reactions of love or hate toward the analyst, falling in love with him, fearing him as a dangerous seducer, and the like. In such cases this criterion has some descriptive value, but this value lessens considerably when one is dealing with less dramatic, more ordinary manifestations of transference—less intense, less elaborate, less directly and openly expressed toward the person of the analyst. This is already evident in Freud's discussion of his having overlooked the transference in the Dora case; he makes it quite clear that the transference was not expressed directly and openly, but only alluded to in an indirect fashion, and he concludes that the transference has often to be guessed from "slight clues."

Thus, Freud did not limit the clinical definition of transference to its conspicuous and dramatic manifestations, although he tended to do so in his more general and didactic formulations. Most analysts since Freud have included as an essential component of transference patient behaviors and statements that do not refer to the analyst or the here-and-now situation in a manifest and explicit fashion; thus, their transference meaning rests on the inferences and interpretations of the analyst.

The second criterion is the function of transference as resistance. Freud's first description of transference identifies it as "when the patient's relation to the physician is disturbed and it is the worst obstacle that we can come across" (Breuer & Freud, 1895, p. 301). The function of transference as resistance always remained fundamental for Freud. But resistance to what? The answer is clear when we consider that Freud's (1900) broadest and most clinical definition of resistance is "*whatever interrupts the progress of analytic work*" (p. 517). Whatever its multiple sources and manifestations, resistance is essentially resistance to the goals and process of the treatment as seen by the analyst. Freud makes it clear that the concept of resistance comes from the hypnotic situation (and later on the pressure technique), where it is a question of the patient resisting the will and demands of the analyst instead of being cooperative, allowing the regression to an altered state, and yielding to the memories and experiences which are at the root of the present symptoms.

In his later formulations Freud (1912) described resistance as a "struggle" between patient and analyst, between impulse and intellect—a struggle in which the analyst tries to "compel" the patient to remember the past in the psychical sphere instead of repeating it in action. Negative feelings toward the analyst clearly function as resistance; so do strong erotic wishes insofar as they demand direct gratification or trigger strong inhibitions and avoidance of involvement with the analytic situation. Insofar as the past is experienced as "contemporaneous and real" in the relation to the analyst, it will increase the patient's resistance to revealing his thoughts and impulses to the very person to whom they are directed.

However, transference functions not only as the main obstacle to the treatment but as its indispensable facilitator. I am, of course, referring to what Freud calls the "unobjectionable" positive transference—that is, sublimated, aim-inhibited, affectionate feelings for the analyst, investing him with the authority of a parental figure and wishing for the approval and love of such a parental oedipal figure. It is only through the use of this facilitating positive transference that the analyst can have an influence and can fight the transference as resistance.

It is important to stress (especially in the light of contemporary attempts to separate out this aspect of the transference as some kind of autonomous function, as a working or therapeutic alliance, etc.) that this facilitating transference is just as much a transference, just as much a repetition, a reenactment rather than a memory of the past, as the resistance transference is; it has the same origin in childhood libidinal wishes and conflicts. The only difference is that its manifestations are more toned down, more adaptable, and they make the patient amenable to suggestion rather than resistant to it. The unobjectionable positive transference is the heir to hypnotic suggestion.*

Getting to the third criterion, transference is for Freud, by definition, a displacement and transfer, the repetition of the past in the present. But how does this tell us which of the patient's behaviors is transference unless we have some idea of what kind of past is being repeated? To put it differently, if we already knew the past, this would provide an adequate criterion of transference as the more or less direct repetition of a previously known past. Clinically, we know that this is not the case and that the analyst has to start with a model and a prior expectation of certain general types of past conflict. The breaking of resistances, largely through the use of the facilitating transference, is supposed to make possible the remembering of the past, the ultimate goal of the analytic process.

But is "remembering" really the production by the patient of conscious memories of the crucial events or experiences of early childhood? Only in a very limited sense. Not only are memories of the early years of childhood scarce and incomplete, but Freud assumed also that they were at best what he called screen memories, a manifest content which has to be interpreted and whose real latent content has to be "extracted" through the interpretive activity of the analyst.

In this sense conscious memories have no privileged position and are equivalent to the other products of free association, such as dreams and fantasies—which Freud also used as manifest material for the confirmation and specification of his reconstructions of the past. The main distinguishing characteristic of conscious memories is that their content, unlike that of dreams, fantasies, or transference reactions to the analyst, is located by the patient in the past and is part of his present conscious experience and interpretation of certain aspects of his past. Thus the main difference between remembering and transference material rests on the patient's beliefs about the reality and origins of his mental productions—that is, whether they are experienced as memories, fantasies, or perceptions.

The difference is lessened even more when we take into account the fact that remembering is directly influenced by the present state of the

* This, of course, raises the important question of to what extent this unobjectionable positive transference also needs to be analyzed in order eventually to bring about a true resolution of the transference as the ideal goal of the analytic treatment. This issue is actually bypassed in the contemporary literature by subsuming it under some sort of "primary" transference or therapeutic alliance which should not or cannot be analyzed. The basic clinical paradox, which cannot be discussed here, is using the power of the transference to dissolve this power or, as Ferenczi and Rank (1925) put it, "to get the patient with the help of the love for the analyst to give up this love" (p. 20). Defining certain behaviors of the patient as resistance transference or as facilitating unobjectionable transference depends completely on the judgment of the analyst and, more specifically, on his view of the aims and goals of the treatment. In the case of Freud this ultimate goal always remained the remembering and reconstruction of the pathogenic past.

transference, not only in its occurrence (resistance versus facilitating transference) but also in its content, insofar as it is a communication to the analyst in the analytic situation. Remembering, even in the broader sense of free associations, does not provide an independent source of material to establish the transference as the repetition of the past. In fact, Freud came to acknowledge (1914b, 1937) that crucial aspects of the early past were unlikely to emerge in memory and had themselves to be inferred and reconstructed primarily from their transference manifestations.

The analyst brings to the situation a certain model of the relevant past, a set of selective expectations based on his general theoretical orientation as well as the ongoing data of the analysis. This model will play a crucial role in determining what among the patient's behaviors is transference as the repetition of a particular past. And, in turn, the transference behavior will be seen as one of the main sources of evidence for the specific knowledge and confirmation of this past. The difference between transference and remembering is narrowed even more when we consider how much present perception is organized and mediated by the past—that is, by prior selective schemata—and how much memories of the past are remodeled in terms of the present.

For psychoanalysis, the past is only accessible in terms of its repetition in the present, in the here and now of the dynamics of a particular interpersonal situation. For both patient and analyst, although in different ways, beliefs about the past influence experience of the present; in turn, the changing aspects and meanings of the present influence and modify the experience of the past. As Schafer (1982) has put it, "Reconstructions of the infantile past and the transferential present are interdependent" (p. 77).

In short, Freud's clinical definition of transference depends on the convergent use of multiple criteria. These include the analyst's view of the reality of the analytic situation (which defines what is appropriate and inappropriate to it), his view of the goals and process of the treatment (which defines what obstructs and facilitates it), and, last but not least, prior assumptions and theoretical models of the typical past conflicts that are likely to be reexperienced by the patient in the here and now, in the "playground" of the analytic situation.

A change in the meaning of or relative emphasis on any one of these criteria will drastically change the meaning of transference and thereby the rationale and goals of the whole psychoanalytic process. This is indeed what has happened in many post-Freudian analytic developments, often in an implicit form. I cannot, of course, review all these developments here, and I will merely illustrate this by referring to two fairly typical, although widely different, explicit examples: namely, the approach to transference in a Kleinian framework and, secondly, the *Analysis of Transference* by Gill and Hoffman (1982).

MELANIE KLEIN

While Freud did not always limit transference to its explicit manifestations, Klein's position is indeed a major shift in its meaning and interpretation. The repetition of the earlier stages of development can be "deduced" from "the whole material presented" (1952, p. 437). The here-and-now analytic situation can be interpreted as the reenactment of archaic fantasy scenarios, dominated by the projection and introjection of good and bad internal objects, and the primitive defenses (splitting, idealization, etc.) against the anxiety generated by such fantasies. Even when the patient's material is not explicitly about the analyst or the analytic situation, most of the analyst's interpretations will include a reference to the analyst as a fantasy object, a stand-in for important figures in the patient's life, and, above all, a representation of the patient's internal objects as well as the patient's self-representation.

To give a simplified illustration, when a 10-year-old patient of Klein (1961) makes a reference, during World War II, to his anxiety about Hitler, this is interpreted as Hitler's being a stand-in for the analyst as a sadistic persecutory object, as well as for the patient's father and the patient himself in the same sadistic persecutory role.

Another distinctive characteristic of the Kleinian approach, in contrast to Freud's, is that the role of remembering and reconstructing the specific origins of present conflicts is much decreased. What is being reconstructed is a fairly universal, timeless, quasimythical past for which particular events, repressed experiences, or any kind of narrative sequence no longer seems to play a significant role. Thus, the lifting of repression and the recovering of specific memories, which for Freud remained the primary goal, become much less essential.

The focus of interpretation is on the translation of all the aspects of the patient's here-and-now manifest experience into another language—a deep, archaic, basic language that still regulates the affective meaning of experiences and accounts for the anxiety of the patient in the here-and-now analytic situation as well as in his current life and symptoms. The structure of this language revolves around two basic organizing positions (paranoid and depressive) and a few binary oppositions and combinations between good/bad, inside/outside, part/whole; its vocabulary and specific content are mostly limited to a few interchangeable part-objects (e.g., breast, penis).

Kleinians emphasize that interpretations should address whatever aspects of the patient's material are at "the point of urgency" (Strachey, 1934, p. 352)—that is, show evidence of direct or indirect manifestations of anxiety. This recommendation is hardly controversial and would seem to apply to any interpretation, not being specific either to Kleinian theory or to transference interpretation. For the Kleinians, interpreting the transference does not mean systematically interpreting the patient's explicit references to the analyst or the analytic situation, but systematically including the analyst in the formulation and language of all interpretations. Kleinians stress that such transference interpretations are the most, if not the only, effective and "mutative" ones. It cannot be argued that this is so because such interpretations are close to the manifest content of the patient's conscious, immediate experience of the analyst because the content is often very far removed from the immediate here and now.

What makes the Kleinian interpretation a transference interpretation is not its starting point in the material of the patient, but the inclusion of the analyst in the content of the interpretation. The rationale for the mutative value of such interpretations is that the analyst does not merely point to unconscious impulses and defenses but also makes himself the target or the object of the impulses and conflicts interpreted by him. The analyst is both the interpreter and the content of the interpretations, so to speak. This is supposed to give more impact and immediacy to the interpretations, and it will certainly influence the transference, in the sense of the patient's image and experience of the analyst. The overall aim of such interpretations is to allow the patient to differentiate more clearly between the analyst as a conflicted fantasy object and the analyst as a real, presumably benign, external object, thus reducing anxiety in the immediate and, in the long run, lessening the influence of primitive fantasies and defenses on the patient's experience of others and himself in his actual life.

The Kleinians also stress the importance of the analyst remaining neutral and limiting his activity to the giving of interpretations. Strachey suggests that, through the use of such transference interpretations, the analyst may function as a new, more benign auxiliary superego for the patient and thereby ultimately modify the patient's harsh and primitive superego. I understand this to mean that the patient is confronted with the reality of the analyst as a new object, who, while attributing to the patient all kinds of primitive, frightening fantasies and impulses directed toward the analyst, remains benignly nonjudgmental and nonretaliatory. The analyst is implicitly communicating to the patient the attitude that it is permissible to have such impulses, safe to experience them in the here and now of the analytic situation, and possible to reassess them as fantasies rather than as threatening realities.

One may wonder whether this contrast between the content of the analyst's interpretations (for instance, in terms of primitive, sadistic, and sexual fantasies) and the analyst's attitude toward them is not one of the main factors in their effectiveness—a factor that may not depend primarily on their accurate fit with the patient's experiences. It may function more as an overall encouragement to the patient to express, explore, and accept what he only feared and dimly experienced as the darker side of him.

The assumption that the point of urgency in the patient's material, the sudden emergence of increased anxiety and resistance, may frequently be triggered by suppressed or unconscious thoughts and fantasies about the analyst in the here and now is a clinical hypothesis that is useful and often valid. But, as many critics have rightly pointed out, there is likely to remain a wide gap between the patient's conscious experience and the analyst's interpretive language at a "deep" level. Although Kleinians seem aware of this gap and state programmatically that it has to be slowly bridged, their main assumption seems to be that deep interpretations, if properly timed, can give direct access to the patient's unconscious and allow it to surface through shared verbal representations never available before.

One gets the impression that deep interpretations are supposed to function like paratroop commandos who seize key enemy positions behind the lines, thereby drastically shifting the balance of forces; the rest, linking up with the main body of troops—that is, the bulk of the patient's conscious everyday experience and behavior—is nothing but a necessary and often protracted mopping-up operation (working through).

These few remarks have been sufficient, I believe, to highlight how much the Kleinian concept of transference is different from Freud's and rests on the whole of Klein's view of development, the role of fantasy, and the rationale of the psychoanalytic process.

GILL AND HOFFMAN

The central role given to transference interpretations also characterizes the approach of Gill (1982) and Gill and Hoffman (1982). This approach shows several similarities to, but also marked differences from, the Kleinian view of transference. Here, too, transference has to be inferred from the whole material of the analysis. The analyst should give the highest priority to dealing with the patient's "resistance to awareness of the transference" (Gill, 1982, p. 15)—that is, to indirect allusions to the transference in the patient's description of experiences and interactions which are not manifestly about the analyst or the analytic situation.

Transference, for Gill, is synonymous with "the patient's experience of the analytic relationship...[particularly] the conflicted and resisted aspects of that experience" (Gill & Hoffman, 1982, p. 5). The main rationale for the primary, if not exclusive, role given to such transference interpretations is similar to that of the Kleinians—namely, that interpretations in order to have impact and to be "mutative" have to address the meaning of the patient's experience in the here and now, even though this experience is often not the direct manifest content of the patient's communication. However, Gill and Hoffman, unlike the Kleinians, stay closer to the "surface," at the level of the patient's conscious experience. They do not suggest a translation of the patient's material in the language of primitive fantasy scenarios, with the analyst as primarily a fantasy object. The patient's description of an interaction in his current life or in the past is interpreted as an indirect communication about his experience of the analytic relationship.

Such an interpretation is based on a relatively small amount of transformation, essentially substituting patient and analyst in the here and now for the protagonists in the more remote interaction that the patient is describing. Thus, there is less of a gap between the content of the patient's material and the analyst's interpretation. Both stay in the here and now of the analytic situation and thus presumably have more impact, and they can more readily be validated, modified, or refuted by the patient's comparing them with his immediate experience of the ongoing interaction.

In this framework, Gill also stresses the importance of searching for those aspects of the analyst's actual behavior which may have contributed to the patient's experience and made it plausible for him. Gill and Hoffman assume—rightly, I believe—that the analyst always has a significant input on the patient's experience of the immediate situation. Ultimately, of course, it is assumed that the patient's experience of the analytic situation, while plausible in part, is largely his subjective interpretation—what he has brought to the situation—and thus is "probably governed by relatively rigid schemata associated with childhood wishes and childhood attempts to deal with early conflicts" (Gill & Hoffman, 1982, p. 5). But this last step, the crucial one for the classical view of the interpretation and resolution of the transference, seems relegated to a minor and optional role for Gill and Hoffman. For them, the essential aspects of the analysis are the unearthing of the hidden aspect of the patient–analyst relationship, the delineation of the actual contribution of both of them to this interaction, and the ongoing comparison, if not confrontation, of the patient's and analyst's views of this relationship.

The therapeutic effects depend partly on the patient's increased cognitive awareness of the attitudes and expectations he brings to the analytic situation (and presumably to other situations and interactions in his life) and partly on "the new experience" of a special interaction—namely, the analytic situation, where it is possible to acknowledge and express negative and childlike feelings and attitudes toward the other without losing this person's acceptance, respect, and sympathy. But Gill (1982) adds that this positive, new experience will usually remain dependent to some degree "on the gratification of the unanalyzed and persisting transference" (p. 119).

Gill stresses that the analyst's interpretations become themselves part of the patient's experience of the relationship and that their effect on it must in turn be analyzed. The particular type of interpretations that the analyst uses is a prominent part of the actual reality to which the patient is reacting. Furthermore, the content of the interpretation will itself be understood in terms of the patient's own point of view and transference schemata (for instance, the interpretation that the patient takes the analyst's interventions as a seduction may itself be reacted to by the patient as a seduction). There is, as Gill admits, the possibility of an infinite regress. But, I would ask, within the here and now, how can this regress be ended except by an ultimate appeal to the judgment and authority of the analyst? When we keep telling the patient how we think he is perceiving and judging us, we are also thereby telling him how we are perceiving and judging him—and in a much more direct manner than when we interpret attitudes and motives toward people in the past outside the analytic situation.

Gill is well aware that a constant emphasis on the interpretation of the here-and-now aspects of the analytic interaction may tend to heighten the confrontational atmosphere of the analytic situation and lead to an unresolvable power struggle. He is particularly critical of the analyst in the role of the arbiter of reality who makes occasional Olympian pronouncements in the context of a lofty silence. Gill (1982) seems to be aiming toward the ideal of "a consensually validated concept of the actual situation arrived at by discussion and 'negotiation' between the two participants in the analytic situation" (p. 96). But does not such an ideal require moving outside the transference and resolving or denying the inequality of the role of the participants created both by the transference and by the reality of the analytic situation (however benign and egalitarian a particular analyst's style may be)?

Maybe acknowledging this inequality and asymmetry as an intrinsic part of the transitional reality of the analytic relationship and taking it into account in any transference situation are all that we can aim for. Although these issues need more extensive consideration, the point I want to emphasize here is that transference interpretations in terms of the disguised unconscious aspects of the here and now are selective constructions, just as classical interpretations of the manifest transference in terms of the past are. In both cases, we start with prior models and expectations: in one case, as to the nature of the past and its manifestations in the present and, in the other, as to the nature of the analytic situation and the underlying dynamics of the patient–analyst relationship.

The tendency to view the core of the patient–analyst interaction as transference, as the direct repetition and reliving of early preverbal stages of development, has been a characteristic of various "object-relations" authors (Winnicott, Balint, etc.), all more or less influenced by Melanie Klein. But, in contrast to Klein, these authors tend to shift the emphasis from the role of internal objects and conflicted fantasy scenarios to viewing present psychopathology as the lasting effect of defects or "faults" in the actual interaction with early caretakers. More or less explicitly, this trend seems to involve a return to an environmental, traumatic origin of psychopathology. The hypothetical traumas are now cumulative and insidious rather than single traumatic events and tend to stress failures on the part of parental figures rather than direct assaults or injuries to the child.

The clinical rationale here is less on the resolution of the transference through the interpretation of its fantasy aspects than on a regressive reliving of the early stages of object relations under better circumstances; the analyst's real "holding" or "primary love" allows at least a partial correction of the consequences of the original developmental defect (usually presumed to be in the preverbal mother–child relation). The relevant early past has not been repressed but cannot be remembered; it can only be relived in the analytic relationship where the analyst's attitude and interpretations may give it meaning and an articulation that had always been lacking.

It is obviously not my intent to discuss here the specifics of these various approaches (among which Kohut's theory could be included) in any detail. I only want to suggest that analytic approaches, starting with Ferenczi and Rank, that focus primarily on the patient's here-and-now experience of the analytic situation often end up playing down the role of interpretation and reconstruction in favor of the "reality" of the affective relation with the analyst as a "new object."

CONCLUSIONS

There is little doubt that "an intense emotional relationship between the patient and the analyst which is not to be accounted for by the actual situation" (Freud, 1925c, p. 42) refers to an empirical phenomenon often occurring in the analytic situation. Identifying this phenomenon already requires agreement on what is "intense" and what is "actual"; however, aside from this problem, such a description does not provide an adequate and sufficient definition of transference.

I have highlighted how the definition of transference involves not only the analyst's view of the actuality of the here and now and his own contribution to the analytic relationship, but also his ideas as to the goals of the treatment and the origins of psychopathology. Specifically, any clinical definition of transference requires the use of several dimensions, each of which refers to a continuum rather than to sharp dichotomies as to what is transference and what is not. Different analytic schools and different individual analysts vary considerably in their—usually implicit—definitions of transference, the relative weight they give to these dimensions, and the end of the continuum within each dimension on which they focus.

The first dimension ranges from direct, explicit references to the analyst and the analytic situation to indirect, disguised, and implicit ones (which can only be made explicit by the analyst's interventions). Freud deals mostly with the explicit end of the continuum and Klein and Gill, among others, with the implicit one. As I indicated earlier, when one is referring primarily to the disguised, unconscious aspects of the patient's reactions to the analyst, it is the analyst's interpretation, not the patient's manifest experience, which addresses the immediacy of the here and now.

The second dimension ranges from realistic, "appropriate" reactions to the analytic situation to unrealistic and inappropriate ones. This corresponds roughly to the relative influence of the present situation and the analyst's contribution to it versus the influence of the past, what the patient brings to the situation and repeats there. Freud and most analysts stress the inappropriate repetitive aspects of the patient's experience and tend to assume that the analyst's influence is constant and minimal—a point of view that has been most explicitly challenged by Gill.

The third dimension deals with the degree to which the transference functions as an obstruction (transference resistance) or an essential facilitator (unobjectionable positive transference, alliance, etc.) of the process and goals of the analysis. What has been emphasized here is that these are not different and clearly separate transferences but variable effects of the same transference. For instance, the positive transference, as the patient's intense emotional involvement or libidinal cathexis of the analyst, can function both as a resistance and a facilitation at different times and in different contexts. In both cases fantasy elements and a repetition of the past are involved. There is no reason to believe that the more conscious and realistic the patient's attitude toward the analyst is the more it will facilitate the treatment; indeed, if a patient stayed only at this reasonable, realistic level, the analytic process would never get started.

The unobjectionable positive transference is the sublimated expression of it insofar as it does not demand concrete, openly sexual, immediate gratifications, but feeds on symbolic and fantasy gratifications, which are often built on unrealistic assumptions about the analyst and what he and the analysis have ultimately to offer. Whether the expressions of the transference are sublimated or crude, they may involve the same infantile wishes and conflicts; the unobjectionable, sublimated transference may well express itself by subtle and insidious forms of resistance, particularly in seemingly ideal patients, which, if left untouched, can lead to interminable analyses and unresolvable transferences.

The last classical dimension is the degree to which the transference involves a repetition of the past, how much it is an identical repetition, and what kind of past is being repeated. The question is not only whether we are dealing with an oedipal or pre-oedipal level, but also whether one assumes a concrete repetition of behavior patterns, of early object relations, or mostly the repetition of unconscious fantasy scenarios, providing some symbolic equivalence between present and past. Without going into this complex issue, one can agree that a patient's behavior in the here and now will often be considered transference primarily on the basis of its apparent fit with certain known or presumed aspects of the patient's past, even when the patient's reactions are not particularly intense or inappropriate to the present situation.

Finally, one should at least mention another dimension of transference, which deals with the patient's rather than the analyst's point of view. I am referring to the kind of reality that the patient attributes to his experience (from direct perception to fantasy) of the analytic situation and, more broadly, what he will "interpret" as transference. This involves the clinically crucial question of the fluctuating conditions under which a special transitional "playground" reality can be maintained—so that the transference may eventually both be dissolved and have a lasting effect.

One sometimes forgets the obvious fact that the concept of transference in psychoanalysis involves the "transfer" from somewhere to somewhere—a shift of frame of reference. Transference cannot be defined or interpreted along one perspective and with a focus on only one area, be it that of the patient's experience of the analytic relationship, his current life, or his past. Transference always involves the use of multiple perspectives, both along the horizontal axis of the patient's interpretation of his experience versus the analyst's point of view and the vertical axis of the present versus the past.

It is the interface, the overlap among these various perspectives, which constructs the transference as an ongoing process. The material of the analysis acquires new meanings by being considered simultaneously from the triple perspective of the patient's experience of the analyst, his experience of his current life, and his experience of his past. Each of these perspectives acquires meaning and relevance only in terms of the others. Strictly speaking, there is no such thing as transference—only transference interpretations, that is, patient behaviors which are selectively perceived, labeled, and interpreted as transference.

What Loewald (1971b) said about transference neurosis can also be applied to transference in general: "The transference neurosis is not so much an entity to be found in a patient but an operational concept...it functions as an organizing principle which is gradually distilled out of the events when investigated in a certain perspective" (pp. 61, 64). No behavior, in and of itself, is transference; it becomes transference only by the formation of relations and transfers of meaning with other areas of experience and other perspectives. Defining transference, interpreting it, and trying to resolve it through interpretations are inseparable parts of the same process. Thus, the very definition of transference is part of a changing, ongoing process—both within the clinical reality of the psychoanalytic situation and within the evolution of psychoanalytic theory.

It is obvious that all the material of the analysis is experienced in the here and now, in the context of the analytic situation. The analyst does not have and does not want independent access to data about the patient's past or current life; these are not independent variables whose influence and causal relationship to the here and now can be proven and demonstrated. Accounts of the present as well as of the past are selective constructions, expressing a particular and changeable point of view always based on incomplete and ambiguous data, whether they be perceptions or memories.

The perspective of the patient's present memory experience and of his past cannot be left out; even if it is not the past "as it once happened" or a past that can give a full explanation of the present, it is a past that is an integral part of the patient's identity and self-image and of his relatedness to the world in the present. The sometimes neglected perspective of the patient's current life is ultimately the arena where his conflicts and any changes or improvements in them have lasting and decisive consequences. To paraphrase what Freud said already in 1912, "From the point of view of recovery, it is a matter of complete indifference whether the patient overcomes this or that anxiety or inhibition in the treatment setting [Freud refers specifically to "institution"]; what matters is that he shall be free of it in his real life as well" (p. 106).

None of these perspectives (here and now, current, and past) can be considered as the basic underlying cause or the ultimate reality of which the others are nothing but partial and distorted expressions. The same is true for the ongoing comparison of the analyst's with the patient's point of view. Each perspective has to be considered in terms of all the others (for instance, the present in terms of the past, the past in terms of the present, etc.). Through this process the experiences of the analytic situation, of current life and of the past—are all given a broader context and new or changeable meanings, instead of just remaining things as they are or as they were, in a fixed and inexorable necessity.

In the psychoanalytic situation, the patient, through the use of the analyst's organizing concepts and perspectives, may discover how all areas of his experience are influenced and mediated by his own unconscious, conflicted organizing fantasies, and schemata in manifold yet repetitive ways. This process requires the creation of new organizing schemas and perspectives, a new way of perceiving one's relation to the world, which may open the possibility of new ways of interacting with it. Interpreting the here and now as transference is precisely going beyond the single perspective of the limited, transient, and highly specialized analytic situation. An interpretation of the past is unlikely to be effective unless it is anchored in its specific manifestations in the here and now, but any delineation of this here and now is likely to be of little value unless it includes the broader perspective of the "there and then."

Psychoanalysis reopens for the patient the strict and fixed boundaries that he had established between past and present, between fantasy and reality. Clinically, we know that the immediacy, intensity, and vividness of the patient's experience in the analysis are not limited to material about the analyst, to the transference, but apply equally to memories and accounts of current events, as they are told and relived in the analytic situation. In this experience the content becomes present and real in the here and now, with the analyst experienced not only as a listener but also as an implicit participant in the relived event, and an intrinsic part of the new meaning and experience of it.*

Psychoanalysis cannot and need not reconstruct an objective, biographical narrative in a linear time sequence; rather, it deals with the mythical time of the unconscious and the sameness and variety of its recurrent manifestation in the present. As Schafer (1982) has put it, "Here and now becomes a condensed, coordinated and timeless version of past and present" (p. 78).

Such a multiple perspective is, of course, difficult to attain both in theory and in clinical practice. A one-sided emphasis on the reconstruction of the past brings the danger of making the analysis a kind of intellectual, biographic, or literary exercise. An exclusive emphasis on the transference in the here and now leads to the danger of the analysis becoming an encapsulated, self-contained process, divorced from the rest of the patient's life or an intractable artificial illness swallowing up most of it. And an overemphasis on the patient's present life may make the analyst into the real parent or guru who teaches the patient how to lead his life by advice and example.

These dangers are quite real because of all the forces that make the quest for simple, unambiguous, and final answers an ever recurring temptation for both patient and analyst. The emphasis on the relativity, the transience, and the multiple perspectives of the here and now is always resisted as a source of anxiety; yet psychoanalysis is built on the hope that, for some, this relativity has a freeing effect and opens the possibility for self-initiated change.

* What is a transitional regression for analytic patients is a constant and disorganizing phenomenon for patients who have severe difficulty with self/other, past/present, and reality/fantasy boundaries. Such patients find it almost impossible to report an event from outside the analytic situation with any affect without reexperiencing the situation as if it were happening now and as if the analyst were the other protagonist in the situation (e.g., feeling immediately humiliated or threatened by the analyst when they recount an incident where they have felt humiliated or threatened by another person).

Chapter 3

Intersubjectivity and the analytic relationship*

In the 1926 *Encyclopedia Britannica,* Freud stated that the term *psychoanalysis* came to have two meanings: "1) a particular method of treating nervous disorders"; and "2) the science of unconscious mental processes, which has also been appropriately described as 'depth psychology'" (p. 265). In the last 35 years or so, psychoanalysis has become primarily a clinical and therapeutic technique; elaborations of the concept of the unconscious and a theory of mind have become increasingly secondary, if not irrelevant. The majority of contemporary, particularly American, writings deal chiefly with clinical technique and the interactive aspects of the psychoanalytic situation. And, within these topics, there has been an increasing emphasis on the role and experiences of the psychoanalyst, whose mental processes, once unduly neglected, have almost taken center stage.

We hear much of psychoanalysis as a healing relationship, meeting some presumed primary relational needs. This focus on the relational, interactive (subjective, dyadic, intersubjective) aspects of psychoanalysis is shared by many authors, expressing a wide range of approaches. I cannot here review this broad literature and do justice to its variety and complexity. Furthermore, many of these authors are difficult to evaluate because they are often quite ambiguous about how much they reject the traditional goals and rationale of psychoanalytic treatment, and they are as well rather vague and inconsistent in translating their arguments into actual clinical practice.

I shall discuss first the challenge to the ideal of the objective, neutral, and anonymous analyst, as expressed most forcefully by Renik (1992, 1993, 1995, 1996). I will then briefly examine Ogden's (1979, 1994) use of the concepts of intersubjectivity and projective identification. At the end, I shall touch upon some general issues about the nature and rationale of the analytic relationship.

* This chapter was originally given as the Edmund Weil Memorial Lecture, Institute for Psychoanalytic Training and Research (IPTAR), May 1998.

RESPONDING TO RENIK

Renik has an easy time attacking the rather caricatured picture of the analyst as the lofty embodiment of reason and objective reality, overcoming the patient's resistances and subjective distortions. Such a picture has some reality in the writings of Freud, Klein, and many others, although we know that Freud and Klein were far from impersonal in their actual attitudes toward patients. But it has become clear that the analyst's specific theory, what Schafer (1992) calls his master narrative, predetermines his answers to most basic questions. Renik was hardly the first to point this out. The issue was already raised just about 100 years ago by the 4-year-old Little Hans: "Does the professor speak to God, as he can tell all beforehand?" (Freud, 1909b, pp. 42–43). We don't speak to God, and we hardly speak to Freud anymore!

Complete neutrality and anonymity have always been impossible, if even desirable. Every intervention of the analyst is an expression of his point of view, his theory, his rationale and goals of treatment, as filtered through his own style and personality. In that sense, his interpretation is always relative, subjective, and changeable. Renik's arguments are clearly valid, if fairly obvious.

In a narrow sense, Renik can be seen as advocating a change in the analyst's attitude and manner, essentially a corrective to some of the excesses of the past. I am referring to the times when some analysts believed that to be silent most of the time and never to answer a question or even a greeting was to be neutral and anonymous. Instead, it probably made them appear stilted, pompous, and uncaring rather than neutral. Quite a few older analysts were subjected to this form of anonymous neutrality in their own analyses and maybe are getting even now. So we may know better now and try to be more natural, open minded, and willing to have some dialogue with our patients.

But Renik (1996) goes much further than pointing out the limitations of neutrality and anonymity. He tends to claim that because *complete* neutrality and anonymity are impossible, there is no point in trying to maintain them *at all* and he further indicates why the "pursuit of neutrality as a technical ideal is *counter*productive" (p. 497). Yet there is obviously a wide range in the use of personal self-disclosure and the amount of suggestion and explicit guidance toward specific goals and values. And much of this does remain under our conscious control. Such control is facilitated, although by no means ensured, by features of the setting and frame (lack of face-to-face interaction, avoidance of outside session contacts, etc.).

The patient does get to know his analyst firsthand, but rather, primarily if not exclusively, as functioning as an *analyst in a special setting,* what Schafer has called the "analytic self, " endowed by the setting and his training with all sorts of qualities—tolerance, forbearance, clear vision—which may not be conspicuous in the rest of his life. Of course, this analytic self, especially at a more unconscious level, is bound to reflect extra-analytic aspects of the analyst's personality; but it also has a large degree of autonomy. And what the patient knows about the "real" analyst beyond the sessions usually consists of small isolated bits of information, serving as fodder for transferential fantasies.

It shouldn't need restating—but it obviously does by now—that the attempt to maintain some neutrality, boundaries, and objectivity is an intrinsic feature of the psychoanalytic situation. It is essential not only for the interpretation of transference, but also to protect the patient from undue indoctrination and from what may be considered the intrusive interference of irrelevant aspects of the analyst's personality. That this protection is never complete and that it is hard to draw a line between what influence is helpful and what is distracting and intrusive do not make the goal of neutrality unnecessary and impossible.

I think that under the so-called rule of abstinence, the analyst may need to withhold undue gratifications from himself even more than from the patient. For the analyst, self-control, self-discipline, and tolerance for frustration are required at all times, even if lapses are unavoidable. It is hard for me to conceive of a situation which would still resemble analysis if the analyst freely gives advice, makes moral judgments and teachings, and is ever ready to talk about himself, offering his own experiences as examples or models for the patient.

This is what Renik seems to endorse, if not advocate, although he is more ambiguous when it comes to specifics. Thus, after having recommended the rejection of anonymity, he gives as an example of free self-disclosure: sharing with the patient the reasons underlying his thoughts and interpretations in a specific context. I think many of us, myself included, have been doing this frequently, without needing to invoke a change of technique or theory. And, at times, Renik admits that the analyst's self-disclosure should be "selective" and subordinated to the goal of increasing the patient's self-awareness.

With the postmodern emphasis on the relativity of analytic theories and analytic knowledge, any dogmatic, inflexible position has become harder to justify and rationalize, if it ever were justifiable. Analysts are also influenced by a social climate where any open display of an authoritative attitude has become unpopular. This, in general, may have more to do with the display style of authority and power than with their actual use, and a premium is put on appearing sincere, spontaneous, warm, and so on. In this context, Renik (1995) and many others see the optimal analytic interaction as a "collaboration between peers" (p. 492) exchanging opinions on an equal footing and comparing freely their separate experiences of the interaction.

This may sound appealing, but I think it is rather unrealistic and deceptive, given the nature of the analytic situation. For nobody actually denies that this situation is uneven and asymmetrical, with the two participants in very different roles. The interaction is supposed to be centered around the patient and his psychological reality, particularly in its unconscious aspects. If the psychoanalytic interaction allowed the analyst equal opportunity to express his personal concerns and interests, to take turns free associating, it could easily become an exploitation of the patient, psychologically and practically. Nobody has yet suggested that, for the sake of equality and mutuality, the two participants alternate in paying the bill.

But one should be reminded that asymmetry need not mean that the analyst becomes the authority and the repository of truths to which the patient must eventually acquiesce. The situation is not an adversarial legal court battle as to whose version of the facts will be accepted (this seems to be the model which Gill and Hoffman, 1982, assume and then try to repudiate so forcefully). It is precisely the analyst's role and position in an asymmetrical and structured interaction that allows him not to see the truth, but to contribute a different perspective, possibly more broad, objective, and detached than the more direct, intense, and narrowly centered experience of the patient.

However, it is not a process of the analyst's supposed superior knowledge or wisdom superseding the patient's self-deception and ignorance. An interpretation does not basically challenge or disown the patient's experience as mere manifest content (the "real" meaning of *a* is *b*). Rather, it points to some connections and patterns, which were missing or only background for the patient, and suggests additional and alternate meanings to the patient's experience—expanding rather than negating and superseding it. How the analyst handles the authority given to him by the transference and how he uses it and/or challenges it remains, of course, a major issue.

More generally, as Friedman (1996) has remarked, the believers in an open collaborative relationship are not without their own predetermined ideas of what the treatment should be and their own, at least implicit, theory of pathology and development. And dogmatism or arrogance is not the attribute of any theory, relational or other, but of individuals.

The seeming respect for the patient's equality and autonomy can sometimes lead in the opposite direction; for instance, Hoffman argues that because we are bound to influence our patients in ways which we cannot control, we might as well express our opinions firmly and directly and exercise explicit influence. Does he believe that this will diminish our covert influence?

So with Renik, what seems at first a mere correction of past distortions of the analytic attitude is really more than that, even more than a change in technique, as Renik claims. It amounts to a change in the rationale of treatment and the understanding of psychopathology—what some authors have somewhat grandly labeled a paradigm shift. While Renik (1995) tries to remain within a classical model, he does state the main conclusion quite clearly: "If an analyst places primary emphasis on the importance of healing interactions within the treatment relationship, as opposed to the pursuit of insight, there is no reason for the analyst to strive for a posture of anonymity" (p. 475). Indeed, that would be undesirable and interfere with the goal of generating new experiences, presumably as intense, spontaneous, and authentic as possible, with a new object.

Renik (1993) states that there is nothing wrong with the analyst enacting personal motives, such as a wish to compete with or punish a patient—although his actual example is very mild and hardly objectionable—as long as the patient is given a chance to explore his reactions to such behavior (p. 563). I suspect that such a position is likely to discourage a disciplined reflective attitude in the analyst and legitimize the most immediate subjective reactions, gut feelings, and such in the name of spontaneity and "authentic candor" (1995, p. 493).

Renik's (1993) analogies between the experience of the analyst and surfing, skiing, or good sex as situations where one "allows himself or herself to be acted upon by powerful forces, knowing that they are to be managed and harnessed, rather than completely controlled" (p. 570) may sound appealing to many, but can make one wonder about the limits and aims of an analyst's behavior. So does his recommendation to be "passionately and irrationally involved in our everyday clinical work" (p. 570). Renik even writes:

> It is the ethical norms we establish...rather than our theories that prevent us from taking advantage of our patients. We do not have sex with our patients or borrow money from them for the same reasons that internists and surgeons refrain from doing these things with their patients (because responsible care givers do not want to trade on the hopes and fears of people who rely upon them), not because we conceptualize that enactment of fantasies interferes with the analysis of transference. (p. 566)

I would suggest that it is for both reasons. The engagement in certain behaviors precludes any constructive analysis of them. Renik is fully aware of the need for the analyst to avoid a self-indulgent exploitation of the analytic situation; however, one could certainly wonder whether his recommendations do not increase the danger of such an exploitation and can even provide a rationalization for it.

For Renik implicitly and for many authors explicitly, the basic model seems to have become that of psychoanalysis as a healing relationship. Then one must ask: What kind of a relationship? What does it heal and how? These are basic and familiar questions which I will briefly touch upon in the last part of my discussion. I think the term "relationship," unless further specified as to type and purpose, has little meaning except as a kind of buzzword or partisan label. All human relationships have more or less explicit purposes and rules: They involve a power balance between the participants and serve as a framework for the expression and enactment of complex mixtures of narcissistic, aggressive, and libidinal desires and scenarios.

Strangely enough, many contemporary authors who constantly talk in relational terms seem to have little to say about the actual variety and dynamics of human relationships, and they tend to reduce them to some narrow basic models—usually built around the gratifications of presumed primary relational or object-seeking attachment needs. The specific aspects of the analytic relationship have also become blurred, except for statements that it should be genuine, spontaneous, mutual, authentic, and the like. It sounds at times like the description of a perfect friendship or maybe a sublimated love affair, but it is some ideal mother–infant model that is usually invoked.

Here, one must give Renik and also Mitchell (1988) credit for mentioning at least in passing what I consider to be a very important and usually ignored point: namely, that the mother–infant model is hardly compatible with an analytic relationship that stresses equality and the patient's autonomy. Hidden behind concepts of empathy and symbiosis is the fact that the mother–infant relationship is probably the most fundamentally *unequal* human relationship. One can get around this problem by invoking different coexisting levels of interaction in both analyst and patient, but this does not dispose of this basic paradox.

OGDEN, INTERSUBJECTIVITY, AND THE ANALYTIC THIRD

Another aspect of the new look at the analytic relationship is the popularity of the concept of "intersubjectivity." This originally philosophical expression has acquired multiple connotations, and you will find it hard to discover a clear-cut, agreed-upon definition. Intersubjectivity stresses that the analytic situation is the interaction of two subjects rather than a subject taking the other for an object. The experience of each subject is shaped by the presence and influence of the other as a set of reflecting and distorting mirrors, in ways which are hard to isolate and pinpoint. For instance, the analyst's picture of the patient is partly his construction, a reflection of his subjectivity, as well as the result of the effect of his presence on the observed behavior of the patient.

Intersubjectivity highlights the *unconscious* aspects of influence and communication and the constant interplay of transference and countertransference. Much of the ongoing data of an analysis are the product of a unique interaction, a *shared new creation* coauthored by both analyst and patient. Thus, at least at the initial level, it may be hard to tell where things start and who is doing what to whom. Ogden (1994) has called this dimension of analytic experience the "analytic third"—an intermixed, merged creation which interacts "dialectically" with the two separate subjectivities of analyst and patient. For Ogden, the intersubjective data are only part, and not the whole, of the analytic interaction. Clinically, with Ogden and others, the emphasis has been primarily in one direction: namely, on the unconscious influence of the patient *on the analyst* and how the analyst can make use of his awareness of this influence to help his understanding of the patient.

Here the Bion version of the concept of projective identification plays a major role. The Ogden/Bion model assumes a greater permeability of boundaries in the mutual regression of the analytic situation; thus, dissociated aspects of the patient's unconscious will become projected into the analyst's unconscious and influence him. Projective identification becomes a way of unconsciously communicating and influencing the analyst. The analyst's unconscious becomes a container for some of the patient's unconscious projections as communications. In terms of technique, the analyst will be able to capture some aspects of the patient's unconscious by paying attention to their derivatives in his own mind—in other words, to the derivatives from his own unconscious as they surface to awareness—for instance, in the form of peripheral, unfocused thoughts and reveries.

This is vividly illustrated by Ogden in several extensive clinical examples. In one of the most dramatic ones, he began having various physical symptoms (difficulty breathing, etc.) during the hour and became worried about illness and death. The patient suddenly turned around from the couch to look at him, thinking he may have had a heart attack. Ogden then interpreted his symptoms and her enactment as the expression of an unconscious fear that she would kill him if she let herself be fully involved in the treatment (she had kept a strained emotional aloofness). Ogden claims that this fear/wish of his death was unconsciously projected into him and registered through his psychosomatic symptoms and fantasies of death and illness.

Other variants of Ogden's approach have been evident in the contemporary literature under the concept of enactment—the enactment being mostly the analyst's enactment of the patient's unconsciously expressed desires and projections. That much communication occurs at an unconscious level has always been assumed. And the belief that some of our intrusive unexpected thoughts or sudden strange moods may reflect the influence of the patient and the atmosphere of the session is hardly controversial for analysts. But attributing them to direct projections from the patient's unconscious seems to me at best a promising hypothesis, to be used with caution.

There may be little direct resemblance between our reaction (a peripheral or somatic expression of anxiety) and what in the patient may have triggered it (e.g., an unconscious hostile impulse or fantasy). Our reaction is bound to be selectively registered and reinterpreted by our own unconscious and conscious concerns. Here I would agree with Renik (1995) that projective identification assumes that the analyst can be a clean container for the patient's unconscious in a direct and uncontaminated way (a Kleinian heir to the blank screen).

Besides Klein and Bion, Ogden refers to Winnicott's mother–infant model and the presumed direct communication and intuitive unconscious attunement existing there. But he also has to assume a separate observing analytic self who can accurately retranslate the manifestations of the intermixed, intersubjective third and trace them back to their original form in the patient. We should add that Ogden (1994) sees no need to challenge the need for neutrality and for an asymmetrical relationship. We are not dealing with "a democratic process of mutual analysis" (p. 17), and the goal remains a better understanding of the analysand's experience.

It seems far from clear what status is to be given to this kind of intersubjective communication and to projective identification in general. Are we assuming unconscious messages and signals from the other, which are unconsciously and automatically registered, processed, and interpreted in ways yet poorly understood? But unconscious preverbal and mostly presymbolic communication is likely to be rather global, diffuse, and affective rather than cognitive. The direct transmission of specific thought and contents seems a rather dubious assumption. So are we dealing with a powerful shared fantasy of extra sensory thought transmission, a literal merging of the boundaries and contents of two minds, a quasimystical union, or something of that sort? Psychoanalysts should be the last to dismiss the power and psychic reality of shared fantasies. The interpretation of unconscious aspects of communications and their reverberating influence is an important and fascinating issue, both clinically and theoretically—but an issue full of risks and complexities.

A VIEW OF THE ANALYTIC RELATIONSHIP

The issues mentioned so far all imply different views of the analytic relationship. Let us go back to a few basics. The analytic interaction is obviously a two-person relationship. But what kind of a relationship? What is specific and special about it? What are its purpose and aims? The answers to such questions are always tied to a more or less explicit particular theory of treatment, of psychopathology, and of mental functioning and human relations in general. Different approaches differ in their readiness to acknowledge and articulate their goals, premises, and theoretical assumptions. There is also no doubt that, in any particular analytic interaction, the specific individuality of the two participants shapes the relationship; however, the importance attributed to this factor is quite variable.

So let me briefly restate what I would consider some of the minimal defining features of an analytic relationship. Its minimal actual reality includes the physical features of regular scheduled meetings in a private setting and the duality of roles, with the analyst first and foremost an attentive, alert, and open-minded listener—and the asymmetrical focus on the patient, who, whatever else, is paying for a professional service. Behind these rather strict, narrow, and protective rules, the relation as experienced can become whatever the patient makes of it (transference in the broad sense), but also how the analyst experiences it. The psychoanalytic situation in its concrete reality offers a very limited range of actual gratifications and frustrations. Within the classical framework of a kind of protected playground, it aims at maximizing the expression of the patient's transferences—but also at minimizing the expressions of the analyst's countertransferences.

Within these special limits, the analytic situation can provide a range of expression much wider than the events of daily "real" life. The narrow but secure base of the analytic relation functions as a stage on which an unlimited number of scenarios with a multiple cast of characters can be enacted—while keeping what has been called its fantasy character as playground or transitional reality.

The analytic situation is more than an ordinary two-person interaction, but one where many selves, many voices, and introjects become present and can be identified. This involves more than the familiar dual roles of the analyst as participant and also more detached observer, and the split in the patient between the experiencing and observing ego. With the patient, the voices and presences of all the central figures of his life, present and past, real and imagined, are given the opportunity to come out of hiding and his unconscious scenarios to find some symbolic but partly shared and externalized enactment (ghosts tasting blood, Loewald, 1960).

And the analyst, for his part, may, in addition, feel the presence of his own analyst(s) and various patients, colleagues, supervisors, and family members looking over his shoulder. As Loewald put it, the analyst is a codirector and somewhat of a coactor on the special analytic stage. The patient needs to be fully involved in the play, yet remember that it is a still a play. When Strachey already in 1934 wrote that "the analytic situation is all the time threatening to degenerate into a 'real' situation" (p. 146), he was referring to a blurring of the patient's sense of reality. I think that the analyst's highly personalized intrusive presence can have the same effect.

Another relevant, well-known, but usually minimized factor is the enormous lengthening of the average analysis. A 10- or 15-year relationship is likely to acquire a very different and more concrete, self-sustaining reality in a patient's life than the 1- or 2-year analysis of yore—the time when much of the main theory and rationale of treatment was formulated.

All of this touches upon the long-standing debate about the relative primacy as mutative agents of interpretation and insight or the "relationship with a new object." The issue has a long history and was already central in the wild and original experiments of Ferenczi. Freud is supposed to have said, "We treat our patients with interpretations but they cure themselves with transferences." Of course, both factors are involved because interpretations can only occur in the context of a relationship and provide the most direct and powerful material, and this relationship is manifested primarily through interpretations, in the broad sense of verbal speech of some kind. But the emphasis is different: In one case, the relationship is used to give power to interpretations; in the other, interpretations are used to enhance the power of the relationship.

The issue of the intrinsic importance of the actual relationship seems also linked with two different images of the analyst. At one extreme, we have what may be called the classical view: the analyst as expert, defined by his training, technique, and his role and function in the special analytic situation. Such a model downplays individual differences in analysts. In principle, there would be only variations on the theme of the well-analyzed and well-trained analyst.

At the other extreme, there is the romantic model of the healer or guru who acts through his intense charismatic presence and offers his individual wisdom. This model, of course, emphasizes the crucial importance of the individual analyst and the unique, specific relationship; it is more narcissistically gratifying. And, in general, it downplays the role of theory and technique in favor of improvisation and creative spontaneity. Most analysts in their attitude and self-image are probably some combination of both these models.

Broadly speaking, relational approaches claim to be more, natural, experience-near, and theory-free. I think this is largely an illusion. Patient and analyst experience the relationship through their own theories and interpretations. Try to banish theory and it will sneak back under the guise of spontaneous intuition and receptive, unbiased openness. For the analyst, his very subjectivity is shaped by his theory, just as his choice of theory is an expression of his subjectivity. His theory will preselect the type of transference he anticipates and finds in the patient, as well as the aspects of it that he is likely to accept, leave uninterpreted, and help enact as part of his countertransference, whether he sees himself as knowledgeable wise father, holding empathic mother, or other prototypical imagined role.

And the patient, for his part, interacts with an analyst that he has constructed himself out of fragments of the analyst's actual behavior, amplified and fitted within his transference scenarios. It is with this custom-made analyst that the patient has his primary analytic relationship, which is usually continued as a more or less vivid presence and dialogue in between the sessions. I think this relationship beyond the actual 4 or 5 hours may play an important role in the course of the analytic relationship and its eventual internalization. But this would be a whole topic in itself.

Let me add that the analyst may at times feel rather left out in this process, somewhat displaced by yet another "analytic third" as a rival in whom he finds it often hard to recognize himself. Not being acknowledged as a full partner and given a unique and dominant role may be hard to bear for the analyst's narcissism and sense of identity; it may lead to such enactments as premature transference interpretations and inappropriate self-disclosures which preconsciously are meant to express, "pay attention to the unique, real me!"

I want at least to mention one last issue. Stressing the unique, specialized, and intersubjective aspects of the analytic interaction increases a conceptual problem always present. How do we generalize from unique and limited data? How representative are they of the patient's behavior, conflicts, and assets in most of the other situations and relationships of his ongoing life? And how are changes going to generalize and endure beyond termination? On what grounds do we build a general theory of mind and of psychopathology from such limited, specialized, and unique data?

These are fundamental issues, not to be taken for granted or to be disposed of by some vague concepts of structural change, relearning new ways of relating, or whatever. Classical psychoanalysis has tried to manage with various modified versions of Freud's model of a narrow, standardized situation, providing limited special data (such as the manifest dream) from which an interpretive road to broader and lasting aspects of the unconscious could be built. In all cases, the narrow analytic situation is expanded and interpreted as the partial expression or symbolic reliving of whatever basic and lasting issues a particular theory views as crucial and determining.

It is not difficult to see why it is the relationship aspect of the analytic process which would come across to the patient as most immediate and central. Most patients do not have greater self-knowledge and self-understanding as their most compelling need and primary treatment goal. They want to feel better, and in the process they mainly seek a person to help them, implicitly a relationship that they hope will fulfill some of their desires, disprove some of their worst anxieties and, at the very least, give them the recognition of a reliable, attentive, and understanding listener.

Most analysts have become skeptical about the mutative power of insight and the truth value of any particular theory. Thus, a relationship of some sort may be the most immediate and concrete reality that we offer our patients. The relationship aspect of psychoanalysis is probably its most tangible, positive aspect for the greatest number of patients, but it may also be its least specific contribution and the lowest common denominator, shared with most psychotherapies. Yet I believe that psychoanalysis can be *more* than an endless attempt to fulfill some presumed primary relational needs and a shoring-up of sustaining illusions. But this belief itself may be only a subjective illusion.

Chapter 4

On the resolution of the positive transference

Suggestion, identification, and action*

If psychoanalysis is called one of the impossible professions, transference may well be one of its impossible concepts. The concept of transference has acquired a wide variety of meanings and connotations. It is certainly not a clearly delineated or self-evident phenomenon. In any clinical context, singling out a particular behavior of a patient as transference, giving it that label, is an interpretive judgment resting on multiple and ambiguous criteria. This applies as well to our judgment as to how inappropriate to the here-and-now reality of the analytic situation a particular behavior is, or how much it has a dominant transference component, uninfluenced by the immediate situation.

In principle, we would readily agree with Fenichel (1941), who stated that every behavior in psychoanalysis has a transference component and that no behavior is pure transference. Furthermore, the analyst brings to the situation his theory and judgment as to what kind of past is being repeated as transference and how much this involves a direct or modified repetition—what Freud called an identical or a revised edition of the past.

In addition, the analyst's handling of the transference is largely determined by the way in which he sees it as an obstacle or a help to his conception of the goals and process of the treatment. More specifically, this involves an attempt to separate out different components of the transference in terms of their resistance or nonresistance functions. Is there a substantial part of the transference that cannot or should not be interpreted and, ideally, dissolved? If so, what does this imply for the process of the resolution of the transference neurosis, the termination of the treatment, and its lasting effects as internal or structural change?

This touches directly upon an issue very much alive in contemporary psychoanalysis: namely, the meaning and handling of the various therapeutic alliances and, more broadly, the relative importance of the analyst's role as interpreter and as acting "beyond interpretation" for the technique and therapeutic efficacy of psychoanalysis.

* This chapter was originally presented at the New York Freudian Society, January 1983.

To what degree is the therapeutic alliance used only as a necessary tool for the primary task of interpretation? Or is the purpose of interpretations mostly to enhance the effectiveness of the therapeutic alliance, as a new curative object relation, as the main agent of change? I do not plan to replay here the battle of the therapeutic alliances in our literature. This chapter will have three parts: on positive transference as resistance and suggestion, on identification and the resolution of the transference, and, finally, on the transfer back to real life. Because the same issues keep recurring, often in only slightly different terminology in the contemporary literature, I shall limit myself mostly to some of Freud's formulations.

POSITIVE TRANSFERENCE AS RESISTANCE AND SUGGESTION

It is the patient's resistance that made Freud aware of the phenomenon of transference and it remained for him one of its dominant characteristics. Psychoanalysis originated from hypnosis and the pressure technique; to the extent that the patient was willing to submit to the authority, suggestion, or pressure of the analyst, this did not require any particular explanation—at first. It was only after discovering transference as an enemy of the treatment that Freud turned his attention to transference as an indispensable ally—hence, the need to separate out different components of the transference and to handle them differently. The descriptive distinction between positive and negative transference as temporary dominance of overt positive or negative feelings was not very useful, given Freud's recognition of the ambivalent nature of all such feelings.

The distinction between positive and negative, therefore, came to refer more and more to the positive or negative effects of the transference on the process of the analysis on what Freud (1912) called "the struggle between the doctor and the patient, between intellect and instinctual life, between understanding and seeking to act" (p. 108). The positive transference as libidinal wishes and feelings was more or less divided into two parts, depending on the criteria of it being a resistance or, on the contrary, an ally—indeed, the main motive force of the treatment. Here we have the familiar distinction between positive transference as either resistance or as what has been often referred to as the unobjectionable or facilitating transference. Such adjectives are rather misleading euphemisms for what Freud describes as the main vehicle of success and the main motivating force of the treatment.

Descriptively, the resistance transference expresses itself by crude libidinal wishes and demands in an unrealistic and rigidly repetitive fashion. Insofar as such wishes are objectionable and conflicted for the patient, they will lead to increased resistance; insofar as they express themselves openly, they are bound to be met by frustration in the analytic situation and turn into hostile feelings. The positive motivating component expresses itself by affectionate, trusting, friendly feelings, as a tamed, aim-inhibited, sublimated version of the objectionable erotic transference. This aim-inhibited transference is more flexible and adapted to the realities of the present situation with a capacity for delay of gratification and for accepting substitute symbolic gratifications instead of more concrete tangible ones. Freud makes it entirely clear—and this is my main point here—that both types of manifestation have the same source in childhood libidinal wishes and conflicts.

The distinction between the two levels of expression of these wishes is essentially that between the dominance of the pleasure principle and the primary process and the greater dominance of the reality principle and the secondary process. In "Dora" (1905b), where Freud first makes the distinction between these two types of expression of the erotic transference, he calls the aim-inhibited version a revised edition of the past, one more adapted to the present, rather than a mere repetition. One can note in passing that at that time he does not directly associate this distinction with the distinction between the resistance and the motivating aspects of the transference. In any case, we are dealing with gradients, more or less modified and transformed manifestations of the same impulses and feelings, not two different transferences.

The relationship to resistance versus motivating force is also a highly relative one. The more intense and unmodulated the positive transference is, the greater its potential to be both a resistance and a motivating force for the treatment (usually at first strong motivation and then disappointment and resistance; Freud, 1938). The tamer affectionate transference is less likely to be an obstacle and a nuisance, but also a weaker, if more reliable, motivating force and ally of the analyst. Furthermore, the reasonable, tamed aspects of the transference can readily become a hidden and insidious form of resistance, covering over more primitive and conflicted wishes and thus a significant contributor to unresolvable transferences and interminable analyses.

Let me concentrate for a moment on the positive transference as the main motivating force of the treatment. Freud readily admitted that it was the heir to hypnotic suggestion and that the use of the patient's potential for suggestibility was and remained an essential and indispensable part of the analytic treatment. But from the beginning to the end of his writings, Freud struggled against the specter of suggestion and the related accusation that psychoanalysis was essentially a form of suggestion therapy or transference cure. Admitting the essential role of suggestion meant for Freud and his critics that the therapeutic results as well as the findings of psychoanalysis remained dependent on and limited to the analytic situation and the effects of the power and authority that the patient attributed to the analyst—and the analyst's use of this power.

Freud subsumed suggestion under transference and its infantile libidinal sources. As is well known, Freud's general and theoretical answer to the role of suggestion in psychoanalysis and the difference between psychoanalysis and primarily suggestion-based therapies was that (a) the power of suggestion is not used for the unreliable goal of symptom removal but rather is used to remove resistances to the search for the basic roots of symptoms and thus the possibility of lasting inner change, and (b) the power of suggestion as transference "is itself subjected to treatment and is dissected in all the shapes in which it appears. At the end of an analytic treatment the transference must itself be cleared away" (1917, p. 453).

This point of view has been restated many times, particularly in the classics on psychoanalytic technique by Fenichel and Glover. But, except for a few programmatic statements, Freud's clinical answer seems to have been more that the positive transference, insofar as it is useful to the treatment, is to be left alone and strengthened. Only the resistant part is interpreted and dissolved, precisely in order to make more effective use of the positive transference as the main motivating force:

> In psychoanalysis we act upon the transference itself, resolve what opposes it, adjust the instrument with which we wish to make our impact. Thus it becomes possible for us to derive an entirely fresh advantage from the power of suggestion. We get it into our hands. The patient does not suggest to himself whatever he pleases. We guide his suggestion so far as he is in any way accessible to its influence. (1917, p. 452)

Thus, the positive transference as suggestibility, as affectionate trust and belief in the authority and superiority of the analyst (Freud's words) is somehow put off limits for interpretation and tends to become part of the real relationship. For instance, in the paper on the dynamics of the transference, Freud (1912) stated that "if a 'father imago'...is the decisive factor in bringing this [the transference] about, the outcome will tally with the real relations of the subject to his doctor" (p. 100).

This trend has been dominant in much of contemporary psychoanalytic literature, which has essentially segregated off a part of the transference by labeling it therapeutic or working alliance, real relationship, or by contrasting a mature transference, a basic capacity for positive object cathexis and human relatedness, with the transference neurosis to be dissolved.

Yet within Freud's conception of the transference—and, I think, within clinical reality—it is hard to draw a sharp and stable demarcation between the aim-inhibited and the less inhibited, more primitive expressions of the transference. In principle, to the extent that the transference is not dissected in all the shapes in which it appears, psychoanalysis remains open to the suspicion of being "a particularly well disguised and particularly effective form of suggestive treatment" (1917, p. 452). Glover's (1931) classical paper stressed that the effects of incomplete interpretation are primarily due to suggestion; this can readily be extended to the effects of incomplete transference interpretation and the results of unresolved transference.

There is little doubt that the aim-inhibited transference-as-alliance can act as a defense, a resistance particularly hard to pinpoint and interpret. It can be only the manifest content, the outward expression of repressed, conflicted wishes, fears and fantasies, both erotic and hostile (Stein, 1981). The aim-inhibited or alliance-transference may feed on the small, sublimated gratifications provided by the reality of the analytic interaction, while the patient holds on to the hope of the ultimate fulfillment of secret fantasies and magical rewards, earned by years of good, dutiful analytic work. Seemingly good analytic work can cover up a reluctance to relinquish the image of the analyst as an idealized omnipotent and all-knowing parent who may provide fantasy gratifications and be an object of narcissistic identification.

It is particularly with respect to the seemingly more reasonable aspects of the transference that Gill's (1979) emphasis on resistance to awareness of the transference and the need to ferret out its hidden, disguised manifestations may be particularly relevant. Such resistances and unresolved aspects of the transference can be important contributors to interminable or repeated analyses, often accompanied by little if any real changes in the patient's outside life.

It is often only major external events and accidents, such as the prospect of unavoidable termination or a change in the analyst's actual status or condition (e.g., marriage, divorce, illness), which will bring to the surface and possibly shatter such secret hopes and fantasies. Both analyst and patient may collude in resisting the awareness of the defensive and unrealistic aspects of the positive transference. For the analyst, a positive, facilitating transference makes the work easier and can provide pleasant narcissistic gratifications.

In the paper on transference love, Freud (1915a) stated that it is relatively easy for the analyst not to give in to a patient's "crudely sensual desires," but he adds, "it is rather a woman's subtler and aim-inhibited wishes which bring with them the danger of making a man forget his technique and his medical task for the sake of a fine experience" (p. 170). This "fine experience" seems to refer to the danger of the analysis turning into an interminable, mutually gratifying, aim-inhibited love affair. In any case, the more the resistance to these aspects of the transference is aim inhibited and seemingly reasonable, the harder it will be for the analyst to detect them and for the patient to acknowledge them.

Furthermore, to the extent that the analyst succeeds in interpreting some of the motives and resistances hidden by the aim-inhibited transference, his influence on the patient for dealing with further resistances will decrease.

For both theoretical and clinical reasons, the goal of a complete resolution of the transference can only be an ideal, and not a workable criterion for termination. Even Gill (1982), who puts such an absolute priority on the interpretation of the transference in all its hidden aspects, had to conclude:

> One must recognize that however expertly one analyzes the transference, the effect of an analysis will still, to a certain extent [and I wonder whether it isn't to a *large* extent] be dependent on the gratification of the unanalyzed and persistent transference. (pp. 119–120)

One can hardly expect that a patient's basic wishes, fantasies, and characterological conflicts as expressed in the transference will simply be dissolved. It is more likely that, through the analytic process, their expression will be modified precisely in the direction of becoming more aim inhibited, adaptive, and flexible. The capacity for sublimated, unobjectionable transferences may be more the *outcome* of treatment than its prerequisite and main motivation.

But let me add that just as the difference between the two aspects of the positive erotic transference has been overplayed, the negative transference is too often considered as all of one piece and as being only resistance. Aggression can be expressed on many levels. Intense, global, and repetitive expressions of hostility and mistrust toward the analyst are obviously a major obstacle to the treatment. But more tamed, aim-inhibited, reality-attuned manifestations can be a positive factor—for instance, in the form of a certain challenging, questioning, critical attitude, with a reluctance to accept interpretations on faith and a need to transform and remold them before they can be effectively assimilated. Such an attitude, if flexible and modulated and not systematically dismissed by the analyst, may protect and increase the patient's autonomy and self-reliance, counteract the regressive pull of suggestion and dependency, and even become an important contributor to the resolution of the transference.

IDENTIFICATION AND THE RESOLUTION OF THE TRANSFERENCE

In the first part of this chapter, I have tried to argue that the aim-inhibited, seemingly rational components of the transference cannot be readily and conveniently separated out from a presumed transference neurosis. I have further suggested that these components often function as a false ally and an insidious form of resistance, which ideally should also be interpreted and analyzed—even though this is a very difficult task which can have only limited success. I would like now to approach the issue from a somewhat broader perspective and raise some questions as to what we mean by the dissolution or resolution of the transference. Again, I will stay primarily within Freud's framework and formulations.

Psychoanalysis suffers from what has been called a developmental lag between theory and clinical technique, with sometimes the one, sometimes the other lagging behind. As we all know, Freud frequently changed his views, and once he had done so, he not infrequently reverted back to older ones. Furthermore, after roughly 1920, Freud kept changing his theoretical, but not his clinical, formulations. All this had several consequences for the evolution of the concept of transference. First, the concept of the transference neurosis—as a new, artificial illness, the only one that the analyst has access to—was never fully developed and clinically illustrated by Freud. Transference seems to have remained for Freud primarily an indispensable tool or a major obstacle to the main task of analysis as the reconstruction of the past through memories, dreams, and free association. Second, clinically, Freud seems to have stayed at the level of his earliest formulation of the transference as a false connection, a displacement of a specific, unconscious mental representation or imago, and the affect connected with it, onto the person of the analyst. Transference was to be treated like any other symptom—namely, to be dissolved by tracing it back to its original object and to the primary conflicts of which it is a disguised manifestation.

Third, Freud viewed the transference as essentially the repetition of oedipal conflicts and fantasies. Yet it was only in 1923 and later that he gave a formulation of the complete Oedipus complex, of the mechanism of its dissolution, and, more broadly, of the role of introjection and identification in the formation of the basic structural components of the personality—superego and ego ideal, but also the character of the ego. Would we not expect some parallel between the dissolution of the Oedipus complex and structure formation, on the one hand, and the dissolution of the transference and the analytic goal of structural change on the other? Yet, to the best of my knowledge, Freud never integrated these two sets of ideas, and even the post-Freudian analytic literature has done so only in a limited and one-sided fashion. I have no comprehensive integration to offer either, but I would like to follow up this idea a little bit, possibly in the hope of offering a slightly different perspective on important if familiar issues.

My main point is that Freud's formulations of the 1920s remain quite relevant to the views of the origins of the different components of the transference, their interpretation, and their resolution. The complete Oedipus is ambivalent and bisexual; that is, it involves conflicts between positive and negative feelings and wishes toward both parents and attempts to integrate identifications with each of them. The Oedipus complex is thus a system of conflicted unconscious fantasies and scenarios with shifting roles and identifications, some dominant and mostly conscious, some repressed and disowned. Insofar as the transference is a repetition of such oedipal scenarios, the patient will put the analyst in many different roles (including father, mother, or child). Each transferential representation of the analyst corresponds to a self-representation of the patient, and these roles and representations can readily be reversed or operate simultaneously—with the patient, for instance, putting himself in the role of the parental authority who criticizes or has to protect the analyst as child.

It is not my point here to elaborate these clinical issues, which I will summarize by a quote from Loewald (1975): "The psychoanalytic situation and process involves a reenactment, a dramatization of aspects of a patient's psychic life history, created and staged in conjunction with, and directed by, the analyst" (p. 278). I only want to remind us that identifications are an integral part of the Oedipus complex and, in more or less reexternalized forms, an integral part of transferences in the analytic situation.

But identification is even more centrally involved in what Freud calls the dissolution of the Oedipus complex, through introjection of the parental authority and the idealized parent, as superego and ego ideal. Even more generally, Freud (1923b) came to view identification (what we would now call internalization) as the main, if not only, way in which important object cathexes could be given up: "the character of the ego [what we would now more often call the self or identity] is a precipitate of abandoned object cathexes" (p. 29). Identification is the basis of structure formation. And for Freud, this process involved a change in the expression of drives—namely, that they become desexualized, aim inhibited, and more reality attuned. Here Freud uses some of the very same adjectives that he uses to describe the tamed, cooperating aspects of the transference in contrast to its more crude expressions, which mostly serve resistance and repetition.

Now does not the analyst become a strongly cathected object which has to be given up, with the aim of the process, not simply symptom removal but some structural change? Is not a partial identification with the analyst, the analyst as perceived by the patient as a mixture of both reality and fantasy, likely to be an essential part of the resolution of the transference—a transference which has been modified through being reexternalized and reenacted in the analytic process, leading then to a new internalization? And thereby, the transference is not dissolved but changed from its repressed, rigid and primitive manifestations to more aim-inhibited, unobjectionable ones.

One might consider that this is both obvious and dubious: obvious in the sense that identification with the analyst and the idea of the analyst's taking the place of the patient's superego are hardly new concepts; dubious in the sense that structural change in adult life is certainly not identical with structural formation in the oedipal period. There is a good deal of truth in both these points, but it is worth taking a somewhat closer look, if only briefly.

It is no coincidence that after 1921 Freud made frequent references to the patient putting the analyst in place of his superego and ego ideal. Through this process, the analyst, as well as initially the hypnotist, acquires power and authority over the patient. This, rather than libidinal wishes, becomes the basis of what Freud calls suggestion. Under the pressure of this protective authority, the patient can temporarily give up some of his resistances and can acquire, presumably through identification with the analyst's attitude, a more conciliatory attitude toward his own primitive wishes and fantasies. Let me add that, clinically, seeing the analyst as the superego authority, as judge and protector, is more likely to induce a compliant and placating attitude in the patient than inducing him to make unrealistic demands for erotic gratifications—in other words, in expressing itself as aim-inhibited transference rather than as open resistance.

This kind of transference is for Freud absolutely necessary for the success of the treatment and is not to be analyzed or dissolved. This would be hard to do in any case because for Freud, at least, such an attitude of the patient corresponds to what he sees as the reality of the situation, the role he readily attributes to himself as being the representative of intellect, understanding, and the necessity of instinctual renunciation. It becomes a part of the real relationship or at least a necessary part of the therapeutic alliance rather than a transference to be removed.

Let me return then to the point I made in the beginning. What we select as transference to be analyzed as opposed to desirable and acceptable attitudes of a patient depends, to a large extent, on the effect of these attitudes on what we see as the goals of the treatment and on the image of our role as a real object in that interpersonal situation.

Identification with the analyst as an objective observer and interpreter is a familiar concept through Sterba (1934). Identification with the analyst as a kindly and accepting superego is central in Strachey's famous 1934 paper. This could be extended to Loewald's stressing, in his 1960 paper on the therapeutic action of psychoanalysis, the role of (the patient's) identification with the analyst's image of the patient's growth potential, with a more mature and integrated representation of the patient. And, of course, one has to mention Kohut and his assumptions about the internalization of the analyst's actual empathic mirroring.

With these last two authors, we can see that it is not only the superego but also the ego ideal and various ego identifications which are assumed to be expressed and internalized in the analytic relationship. As different as they are, all these authors seem to have in common a certain view of identification which stresses the passive copying, imitative aspects of it in contrast to the patient's active role in the process. To the extent that identification has the connotation (as does suggestion for Freud) of passive copying and simple imitation of an external model, identification with the analyst has acquired a questionable status—especially if one sees it as an essential aspect of the resolution of the transference and the lasting effects of the treatment. It smacks of suggestion therapy, manipulation of the transference, corrective emotional experience, and all these other dirty words.

Kohut is, of course, the most recent and famous example of this trend and its controversial consequences. It is the patient's perception of the analyst and, more broadly, his experience of the analytical relationship—with an inseparable mixture of fantasy and real elements—that provide new identifications and internalizations. The patient takes back and reinternalizes a modified version of what he has projected or transferred out in the first place—in other words, something that is not purely an external influence, an outside stimulus, a foreign body, but something which, to begin and to end with, is in large part his own creation. Identification is always to a large extent projective and selective, without this implying all the Kleinian connotations.

Just as transference, at least theoretically, is often described as based only on the patient's subjective fantasy (the transfer of an unconscious representation or imago on the analyst as a blank screen), when identification with the analyst is mentioned, it is often primarily the objective "real" aspects of the analyst's behavior which are highlighted. Yet we all know that there is no purely subjective transference and no identification which is the simple imitation or copying of an objectively perceived reality. The analyst's behavior and interpretations influence the patient, but only on the basis of the meaning, interpretation, and selective assimilation that the patient provides for them.

This is obvious clinically, but conceptually we are still bedeviled by Freud's sharp dichotomy between fantasy and reality—between objective and subjective—as applied to a process which constantly challenges this dichotomy and keeps redrawing the boundaries between internal and external. Are not both patient and analyst constantly learning about the reality behind what seems only subjective fantasy and the fantasy aspect of much of what was held as fixed and given reality?

But let us briefly go back to the role of identification (or, more generally, internalization processes) in the formation, modification, and resolution of the transference. Ideally, the analytic situation, through the protective pressure toward controlled regression, provides the setting for at least a partial reversal of the developmental change from object investments to identifications and internalized structures.

Structures and patterns are partially reexternalized and allowed a more undisguised, interpersonal expression—a partial melting down into their component parts which may allow for some rearrangement and transformation before a new structure is formed and re-internalized. The past is likely to have survived, not so much as images of primary parental objects but as introjects, as "presences," as Schafer (1968) would say, and as various, usually conflicted and disowned ego identifications. It is all these that get transferred and more or less symbolically reenacted in the analytic situation. The separation of the libidinal, aggressive, or narcissistic origins of the transference is always rather difficult, if not arbitrary—more anchored in the preferences and language of a particular theoretical system than in clinical phenomena.

I will not launch into a specific discussion of the analysis of the transference, especially because what I may have to say has already been said better, particularly in papers by Loewald and Schafer. Let me just express the main point, using Freud's classical metaphor. To the extent that the analysis is able to create a transference neurosis, it becomes a new artificial illness, a revised edition, and not simply a reissue of an old text. To continue with Freud's metaphor, I would add that it involves more the creation of a coherent text where only fragmented and inarticulate pieces existed before. This new version is then continuously and progressively updated and revised through the joint work within the analysis; however, only to the extent that the patient assumes final authorship is the final revised construction likely to be of use to him. Loewald (1971b) put it well when he wrote:

> The transference neurosis is the creation of the analytic work done by analyst and patient, in which the old illness loses its autonomous and automatic character and becomes reactivated and comprehensible as a live responsive process and as such changing and changeable. (p. 17)

Insofar as the transference is based on the patient's characteristic ways of loving and hating which form his individuality and identity, it is not likely to be dissolved or removed like a malignant growth. Its resolution will involve a re-internalization of a hopefully modified version of what the patient has been gradually able to transfer to the analytic situation and rework in it. I have limited myself to the oedipal model of transference; let me only add that if one stresses pre-oedipal aspects of development and pathology, the role of identification processes in the transference is even more prominent.

THE TRANSFER BACK TO REAL LIFE

I have been describing the transference and its resolution as if it were a self-encapsulated process involving only the repetition of the past in the special, artificial reality of the analytic situation. Therefore, I want to conclude with a few familiar, though sometimes neglected, comments on the role of the patient's ongoing life outside the analysis. The transference, as an artificial illness, can only be worked through and resolved if it involves a controlled regression, if it stays at an intermediate level of reality from which the transition has to be made to real life. And I doubt that this transition can wait for the termination of the treatment and the presumed resolution of all major intrapsychic conflicts.

Yet there is a tendency, at least in the clinical literature, to neglect what may, after all, be for many patients the bulk of the manifest content of their communications—namely, references to ongoing life outside the analysis. This may be due to a fear of distracting from the necessary regression and intrapsychic conflicts or of playing a counseling, advice-giving role. Already nearly 70 years ago Fenichel (1941) found it necessary to give the following reminder: "We must never forget the existence of this life outside; we must always draw it into the treatment" (p. 96). And I think that drawing it into the treatment means interpreting the patient's reports of life outside in terms of the here and now of the transference and in terms of the past. But it is also important to view the transference and the past in the light of present outside life.

An interpretation has ultimately to be anchored in all three areas. This convergence among these three areas is essential for maintaining the immediate reality of the transference, for showing that it is not simply the product of the analytic situation, real or imagined, and also importantly for allowing an ongoing transition between the analytic situation and life outside. Despite what seems sometimes to be a cult of fostering regression and interminable analyses, keeping the perspective of ongoing outside life in one's interpretation is necessary to prevent the transference from becoming too real and "swallowing the whole of the patient's life," to use the apt expression.

On the patient's side, symptomatic improvement and changes in the patient's behavior in life during the analysis have been viewed traditionally with often justified suspicion. There is little doubt that symptomatic improvement can lead to resistance and flight into health and that changes in outside behavior can often be a destructive form of acting out. But are most symptomatic improvements flights into health and most changes in behavior negative acting out? I doubt it very much. I would even suggest that an ongoing effect of the analysis on the patient's outside life is a necessary part of the eventual transition from the intermediate and temporary reality of the analysis to outside life. This is especially true once we move beyond the realm of the so-called classical neuroses limited essentially to private, encapsulated symptoms.

Patients will tend to enact in life not only the repressed part of what is being stirred up by the analysis, but often also whatever changes, insights, or new attitudes that they feel are acquired in the analytic situation. After all, the specific conditions of the analytic situation cannot be duplicated in real life; indeed, when some patients attempt a direct transfer from one to the other (try to behave outside as if they were with their analyst), this invariably leads to disastrous consequences and can be seen as a form of acting out.

A complex translation and transformation is always required for the transition from analysis to real life. This happens probably mostly unconsciously, but patients do a good deal of more or less deliberate testing, checking, and experimenting to see to what extent they can now behave or react differently in actual life situations, experience less anxiety, inhibition, self-defeating behavior, and the like. Such outside actions are often accompanied by the imagined presence of the analyst as watching, encouraging, criticizing, and so on, or at least with an anticipation of how the event will be reported and reacted to by the analyst. The usually mixed results of such attempts will constantly influence the patient's motivation and resistances in the analysis and bring necessary live material about the ongoing current status of his conflicts.

Most of the issues I have touched on are clinically complex and perhaps controversial. My aim here was only to suggest that the resolution of the transference involves not only the internalization of the patient's experience of the analytic relationship but also an appropriately transformed and ongoing process of change in the patient's self and object representations and their expressions in his behavior in external reality. This is probably necessary for the benefits of the analysis to become lasting and truly internalized, rather than hanging on to the analytic relationship either literally or as a kind of isolated magical introject—a talisman for bad days.

Let me underscore this point with the famous quotation from Freud (1912): "From the point of view of recovery, it is a matter of complete indifference whether the patient overcomes this or that anxiety or inhibition...what matters is that he shall be free of it in his real life as well" (p. 106). Most of the issues I have raised are familiar. Stressing the desirability of analyzing even the aim-inhibited positive transference and its resistance potential makes ones think of Brenner, among others. Emphasizing the projective aspects of identification brings in echoes of Melanie Klein, and considering the possibility that an internalization of a patient's experience of the analytic relationship may be an essential part of any structural change has a Kohutian flavor. Maybe so, although I do not think it is necessary to follow any of these approaches in order to develop the points I have touched upon.

Bringing the concept of transference in line with the central role of identification and thus the interpersonal basis of structure formation and the individuality of the ego or "I" does not commit us to a new self psychology or to the rejection of drive and conflict theory. Clinically, I think, it does not imply a need for special displays of benevolence and warmth toward our patients, nor any attempt to offer ourselves as a real-life model of wisdom and maturity. Such a role would add an unrealistic burden to the already formidable demands of the analytic situation and may not be quite compatible with the most distinctive, if lofty, goal of psychoanalysis—namely, the search for a somewhat greater truthfulness.

Chapter 5

Transference and psychic reality

Ideas about the timeless past in psychoanalysis*

One can make a rough contrast between classical psychoanalysis, which tries to reconstruct the early past, and the contemporary emphasis on the here and now, which tries to relive it, hopefully in a better version. I will claim that in both approaches the analyst uses a theoretical model of a prototypical past as a key to the individual past of the patient—or rather to the unconscious constructions and beliefs about his past that the patient is enacting in the present. With what kind of past are we dealing? How do we infer it and how does it relate to the present? These are some of the underlying questions.

I think these questions are not only of theoretical and historical interest. They also directly influence our clinical interventions and rationale, though often in an implicit and unexamined way. In terms of broader present issues, I need only mention the fanatical recovered (or rather reconstructed) memory movement, often masquerading as a caricature of psychoanalysis. In a different register, the ongoing controversy about the relevance of infant observations as an empirical basis of the past unconscious is also involved.

The past in psychoanalysis always starts with Freud. So I shall start with some comments about Freud, the mental archeologist trying to dig up the past, if only the past as psychic reality. I will then talk about transference and its relation to the analyst's particular theory about the past and its manifestations. I shall use Klein and Winnicott as primary examples. Then, I will offer some conclusions about the centrality of the concept of psychic reality for psychoanalysis.

FREUD AS MENTAL ARCHEOLOGIST

We all know that Freud kept using archeology as his prime metaphor. He surrounded himself in his office with artifacts of the early past. One of his

* This chapter was originally presented as part of the Friday Night Lecture Series at the Austen Riggs Center, June 1995.

ideals for psychoanalysis was as an archeology of the mind, digging for the remnants of a primal past still buried and preserved in all its essentials in the unconscious—the unconscious conceived as a container. He often referred to Pompeii, recovered almost intact, and to the remnants of Troy found and located after millennia. The basic postulate, with a few qualifications, was that what is deeper, more removed from the manifest surface, is also earlier. One gets the impression that this belief and the urge to recover and restore the past in its primal original form was a compelling obsession for Freud—quite beyond any therapeutic goal and rationale, although obviously linked to it.

Ideally, the past would be recovered by retrieving repressed memories. But while Freud never abandoned this ideal in principle, he had to admit early on that the crucial past could not be accessed directly through the recovered memories of the patient. It had to be reconstructed through the interpretation of its disguised manifestations in dreams, fantasies, and transference enactments. But interpretation can never be a simple decoding. It has to be guided by the selective categories and expectations of a particular theory—which for Freud soon became the primacy of the Oedipus complex as a system of organizing fantasies.

In his interpretations, Freud was prone to equate and merge three levels of inference—as is already clearly evident in *The Interpretation of Dreams* (1900). He went from the manifest to the present unconscious—of the latent dream thoughts as day residues, present life concerns, and conflicts. Then, these aspects of the present unconscious were treated as modified replicas or derivatives of the past unconscious, of infantile wishes in their original form. Further, he initially believed that these wishes, as fantasies and memories, could reveal the objective contents of actual scenes and deeds from the primal past. At this last level, Freud had to give ground, and he reluctantly, but not consistently, admitted that only the psychic and not the material reality of the past could be restored.

Now Freud did not elaborate the concept of psychic reality. It has remained the source of much confusion and controversy, as well as of a broad all-purpose use. It is clear that psychic reality does not simply refer to an arbitrary dichotomy between objective memory and purely subjective fantasy, as in "Did trauma occur or was it only imagined?" Psychic reality is not the reality of our conscious subjective experience, perceptions, and memories, as is often assumed. In his most explicit definition, Freud (1900) refers to psychic reality as "the most fundamental and truest shape of unconscious wishes" (p. 620). This assumes that unconscious wishes have an autonomous structure, organization, and persistence with an enactive power and causal efficacy of their own. They are not simply a reflection of contingent external, material events or of the demands of somatic needs.

Of course, such an ultimate psychic reality can never be directly accessible or completely knowable. For Freud, psychic reality involved a limited set of primary fantasies, functioning as a set of categories (in the Kantian sense) which organize and give personal meaning to basic aspects of experience. They can be seen (and this is going beyond Freud's terms) as a system of symbolic meanings, a construction of personal reality which, again, cannot be reduced to or accounted for by external constraints or somatic demands.

In a broad sense, psychic reality, in all psychoanalytic theories, functions as a limited set of basic scenarios with a specific cast of characters (oedipal father, good or bad mother) and prototypical actions. The individual keeps trying to enact such scenarios within the contingencies of his present life, in multiple unpredictable ways—even and especially when these unconscious scenarios have become consciously repudiated and partly superseded. But here I have already anticipated some of my concluding comments.

TRANSFERENCE AND THE ANALYST'S PSYCHIC REALITY

Now let me shift to transference, viewed as the here-and-now manifestation of core unconscious psychic reality. We know these days the clinical emphasis is very much on the ongoing immediate process of the unique patient–analyst interaction. So-called "genetic," "deep" interpretations and reconstruction of the specifics of the early past are rather out of fashion. As mainstream analysts Sandler and Sandler (1994) have put it:

> Analysts are to an increasing extent aware of the importance of self-observation and of the interaction between the patient and themselves. The analytic point of view is less and less a strictly intrapsychic one, limited to a consideration of what goes on in the mind of the patient. Rather, it is one which moves, without the analysts being aware of it, between intrapsychic and interpersonal frames of reference. (p. 1004)

And as the emphasis on reconstruction has lessened, so has the meaning of transference changed. Briefly, the Sandlers, in this interesting but politically cautious paper, view the transference as primarily the manifestations of the present unconscious within the experience of the analytic situation and in patterns of object relations in the patient's present life. What they call the past unconscious becomes primarily "a structuring organization that gives form to the intrapsychic content that arises in the depths of the present unconscious—in particular unconscious wishes and wishful phantasies" (p. 1004). Further, "internal object relations can be placed in the category of structures in the past unconscious which we have referred to as 'templates'" (p. 1008).

Thus, the past unconscious becomes essentially an organizing language influencing the experience of the present. I would essentially agree with this view, while noting that this language is only directly available as that of the analyst's theory. We must hope that it provides some fit, some approximation to the unconscious language of the patient. Specific reconstruction of the distant historical past is problematic for the Sandlers and has the relatively secondary role of providing "a temporal dimension to the patient's view of himself" (p. 1007).

Returning to the concept of transference, it is important to keep in mind the obvious and often bypassed fact that the transference is not simply a clinically given, clearly delineated observational fact, which we can then interpret in various ways. It is already defined by the categories and expectations of our particular theory, including our view of the dynamics of the patient's pathology, the goals of the treatment, and our model of the ideal analytic relationship—especially so because the definition of transference is not limited to explicit references by the patient about the analyst or the analytic situation. Anything that the patient tells or does in the session can rightly be seen as part of the transference or having a transference component. One could make an exercise of going through a session and singling out what could be considered transference.

The analyst makes constant implicit judgments about his contribution to the patient's reactions, as he decides what in the patient's behavior reflects broader unconscious scenarios, conflicts, desires, and anxieties which the patient has brought to the present situation. The analyst is bound to have certain theory-based expectations as to what the main aspects of the transference of a particular type of patient are likely to be; he will thus give selective emphasis and interpret as transference those aspects of the patient's behavior that fit these expectations. The analyst's theoretical model will determine which aspects of the transference are to be interpreted, questioned, and put in a broader context and which are left unchallenged and implicitly confirmed, if not explicitly encouraged. The analyst tries not to respond to the patient's pull to enact a specific transference scenario, to fit with a role assigned to him, although we know that despite his neutrality, he cannot always avoid this pull.

But, based on his theory and personality, the analyst also has a certain image of his fantasied role in the interaction, beyond that of neutral observer—a role that he will attribute to himself, identify with, and enact within the constraints of his theory and technique. He will tend to consider this as part of the reality of the analytic interaction and thus will obviously influence the patient's reactions. Freud already was ready to state that, when the patient experiences him as a "parental imago," this fits with the reality of the situation. In many passages, he takes for granted his function as the ultimate parental authority, benign but stern, educating the neurotic part of the patient to the demands of reality. We can see something similar with Winnicott and the image of the empathic, good enough mother and with Kohut as the mirroring parent who lets himself be idealized.

My point here is that the analyst's definition and handling of transference, his view of the analytic interaction, and his role in it are always influenced by his assumptions of the core unconscious conflicts or deficits being expressed in the here and now. And this is true even, or maybe especially, when the reconstruction of the past is deemphasized.

Let me backtrack a bit. Freud already gave a central role to the interpretation of the transference as a way of confirming the reconstruction of the past, but more in theory than in his actual practice. The emphasis of the here-and-now analytic relation as the most direct expression of the archaic past was much expanded after Freud. We see it clearly with Klein—maybe in its purest form. For Klein, the core of the here and now is the direct expression of the most archaic preverbal past—rather than the starting point of an archeological reconstruction through layers of less and less distorted derivatives, as with Freud.

And Klein is, in many ways, the primal mother of all later object relations theories, in the broadest definition. The Kleinian past is essentially ahistorical: the translation of all aspects of the present into a primitive language of archaic fantasies. Kleinian interpretations assume a kind of direct access to the unconscious in its primal form, ignoring all intermediate levels of disguise and transformation. Much of Kleinian theory sounds like an imaginative, evocative modern demonology, clinically useful if not taken too literally. It can give a language to symbolize and tame some of the patient's profound anxieties and magical thinking, particularly for schizophrenic and borderline patients, as Herbert Rosenfeld has brilliantly illustrated. It deals with part objects as ghosts and demons by which one is haunted and possessed or by which one tries to control others: Some of the mechanisms are projection, introjection, and various magical exorcisms (Fairbairn).

In Kleinian practice, there is no reconstruction of specific individual events or experiences of the first year of life (how could there be?), though this is, in theory, the formative year of these core unconscious fantasies. Thus, one can hardly call it a developmental theory—beyond a hierarchical sequence of the two basic positions. Clearly, with Klein, the psychic reality of unconscious primitive fantasies is supreme, while external reality serves mostly as the material and trigger for fantasies.

With Winnicott, the etiological focus is on actual maternal failures at preverbal levels, early deficits which were never conscious and part of the repressed. Thus, the emphasis is not on recovery or reconstruction, but on some symbolic reliving in the relation with the analyst. The therapy situation is supposed to provide the right holding environment, presumably missing or defective in early childhood, with the analyst "playing mother to the patient's infant." The holding environment is anchored on the reality of the reliable, scheduled availability of the analyst as an empathic nonintrusive listener. But at its core, it is created by the patient as a necessary fantasy or "illusion," unchallenged and at least implicitly fostered by the analyst. It becomes the symbolic enactment (a toned down version of what Sechehaye called "symbolic realization" in the case of Renee) of an idealized mother–infant relation—a fantasy probably present in some form in both patient and analyst.

The fantasy of an ideal mother anticipating all our needs, giving us the illusion of being the omnipotent center of the world (and then slowly fostering our autonomy and initiative) is indeed a powerful and appealing one. It is a fantasy that all of us are likely to share in some form (in the active and the passive mode, having or being such an ideal mother) and that we may keep seeking in various modified and disguised forms as the unreachable goal of our dreams and the secret unconscious motive of some of our actions. In what form, if at all, such a fantasy is actually present in the preverbal infant becomes a moot and basically irrelevant issue. Such a fantasy has a broadly shared psychic reality.

My main point here is that even when the focus is on the ongoing analytic relationship, with little or no explicit reconstruction and interpretation of the early past, a particular model of infant–mother relationship is constructed by the theory and seen as the core of the analytic relationship.

A close reading of Winnicott shows that while the transference of the regressed patient is viewed as the reliving of a mother–infant relationship, his understanding of the core of the adult transference is the prime source of the empirical basis for the infantile model, rather than the other way around. In other words, a certain conception of the patient–analyst relationship is the model of the mother–infant one. Basically, the same is true for the views of Kohut, who explicitly acknowledges that his construction of the present transference (as mirroring, idealizing, etc.) provides the key to the early origins and determinants of the self.

Let me add that when the analyst sees the interaction as the reliving of some mother–infant model, with a mutual preverbal attunement and a merging of boundaries, he may come to believe that he can have a direct, unmediated access to the patient's unconscious. What he experiences in a receptive way is what the patient put in him, unmediated by his own beliefs and selective assumptions. The concepts of empathy and projective identification sometimes tend to be used in this way in present literature. Such a direct translation from what we experience to the patient's unconscious can be dangerously misleading when not used with caution.

THE CENTRALITY OF THE CONCEPT OF PSYCHIC REALITY FOR PSYCHOANALYSIS

In our attitude toward our patients, in our interpretations or lack of them, we always carry and enact some model of the unconscious past. But this is not a biographical past—an account of what parents specifically did or did not do or even of what the infant experienced at the time. The analyst, in fact, does not work like an historian, a detective, or a biographer, who aims at a reconstruction of the past as it once was. His data, obtained only from one biased witness, are not adequate for such a task (which is not his actual goal anyway).

The underlying psychic reality of such a leap into the past may be basically a need for simple, causal explanations, preferably in terms of specific external dramatic events and the search for the ultimate origins and beginnings so dominant with Freud. Such a need and motive are very real and pervasive. It is evident in many of the beliefs, customs, and myths of our social and individual world. (Natural science can be seen as one of its specialized limited expressions.) Freud already described how children construct sexual theories about the mysteries of birth, death, and gender and that such theories shape some of the later expressions of sexuality and human interactions. And one could add that such theories and explanatory systems are not limited to sexuality, but reflect our need to keep a sense of coherence and purpose in our experience. Such theories constitute our individually created psychic reality. But they also contain and maintain a version of the belief systems, myths, and symbolic systems of our primary caretakers and social environment, which then become a core part of internalized self and object representations.

I think that, as analysts, we are trying to estimate and articulate the image and construction of the past which the patient, however unwittingly, keeps enacting in various ways as part of his experience of the present. But the psychic reality of the patient remains an inference and a selective, approximate, and partial reconstruction. Each psychoanalytic theory has its own construction of psychic reality, its own selection of crucial basic issues and beliefs. Such constructions function as an organizing language, a limited set of interpretive categories providing coherent meaning to what seems strange, incoherent, or random. These categories are applied to the understanding and the construction of recurrent themes in all the data provided by the patient, whether they refer to the immediate analytic interaction or the patient's accounts of his current life or of his more remote past.

We can readily refer to the basic scenarios of the oedipal system, of the Kleinian positions, or the good-enough or mirroring mother. While such categories imply some hierarchical order and are endowed with some loose chronology, they refer essentially to a timeless aspect of the present. They evoke more the past of "once upon a time..." or "in the beginning there was..." as we find in myths and tales.

Nor is the early past an individualized one. In our case formulations, we have practically no knowledge of the patient's early history, especially of the earliest preverbal months or years. We provide the patient with the past required by our understanding of the present, by the "logic of the neurosis," as Freud wrote. And this logic is determined by what our theory considers as logical and required. Whatever early events reported by the patient from what he has been told later in life are selectively reinterpreted to fit the overall pattern.

This can be easily verified in our clinical literature. If we know the author of a case formulation, his theoretical orientation, and his description of a patient's present pathology, it is not hard to predict the core conflicts or deficits of early childhood—without even reading the details of the case history. The deepest interpretations tend to be the least specific and most theory-derived ones.

None of this minimizes the role of the patient's remembered individual history. Such a history usually starts with the later years of childhood and includes many external biographical events that we take as essentially factual. An important aspect of the treatment is that the patient revises his personal history—adding some memories, but mostly creating new perspectives on past experiences and their relation to the present. The past as it once was is not thereby revealed or changed. But unconscious and conscious beliefs about one's past, about the origins and meaning of present desires and anxieties may be changed and may reshape the present.

We all know that such revisions of one's history are often strongly resisted by the patient. We all cling to our explanations, as part of our need for understanding, justification, and self-validation. We can only give them up in favor of new or modified ones. It is striking how often patients will pick a major past event, such as the illness or death of a parent, and make it a central explanatory theme of many of their present symptoms and disowned motives. A new formulation constructed with the help of the analyst, once accepted and internalized, will often be cherished as a symbol of the analytic bond and the continued internal presence of the analyst—the primal scene of the Wolf Man, as a classical extreme example. As analysts, we are presumably more open to ongoing revisions—at least until we have published our case formulations.

Chapter 6

Further thoughts on the contemporary analytic relationship*

Much of the analytic writing of the last decades has focused on the analytic relationship, with special attention to the role and experience of the analyst in this interaction. In looking at some of the main dimensions of this relationship, its specific features, and its purpose, I would like to highlight some salient and controversial issues.

DEFINING DIMENSIONS OF THE ANALYTIC RELATIONSHIP

The analytic relationship has at least three main defining dimensions. First, it requires a very unusual, fixed, and well defined setting with clear rules and limits. Second, this setting provides the stage for the interplay of transference and countertransference as an ongoing process. And last, this interplay has a particular make-believe and symbolic character, shared in varying degrees by both participants. This gives it a greater freedom from the constraints of daily life, but also makes its effects difficult to translate directly into concrete behavior and actions. I plan to explore these three dimensions successively, although they are, of course, intrinsically interlinked. A more or less explicit comparison between a classical position and the more contemporary relational, interactive position will serve as a backdrop throughout. I think this is a meaningful polarity for purposes of discussion and sharpening of the issues—even though there is a wide range and diversity within each position.

Let me first mention the physical features—the material reality of the setting of the analytic situation. It is a two-person relationship. It takes place frequently, at fixed times, for a variable but usually quite long period, counted in years—and increasingly so. The physical setting and the spatial arrangement remain basically the same from session to session. The interaction between the two participants occurs at several levels but is carried out, primarily if

* This chapter was originally presented to the Rapaport-Klein Study Group in June 2000.

not exclusively, through speech. The relationship is basically asymmetrical, with different roles and functions for each participant; it is a paid professional relationship, a service provided for the benefit of the patient, with the patient as the main speaker and the analyst as primarily a listener. The use of the couch need no longer be considered an essential defining feature. All this is taken for granted and not directly challenged by any of the contemporary authors, although reading them one sometimes needs to be reminded that this is still the analytic situation to which they are referring.

The classical view tends to maximize the asymmetry of the situation and minimize the interactive, especially nonverbal aspects. In recent years there has been an increasing trend in the reverse direction—stressing, among other things, the participation and involvement of the analyst and minimizing the atypical, limited, and symbolic nature of the analytic interaction. These contemporary trends are evident in many authors from many different persuasions (neo-Freudians, neo-Kleinians, as well as various interpersonal, intersubjective, interactional, and relational groups). These authors state their positions in more or less strong and explicit fashion and often in indirect and inconsistent ways. In their milder form, much of the present view can be considered as a useful corrective to some one-sided and exaggerated aspects of the classical position, particularly prevalent in the United States in the 1950–1970 period; in their more extreme and outspoken form, they seem quite problematic and would require a thorough reconsideration of the assumptions and goals of psychoanalysis.

It is no longer simply a question of differences in technique, but of differences in the rationale of treatment, in the theory of psychopathology, and of normal development, and probably also in basic beliefs and values about mind and human existence. Such differences reflect not only the subjectivity of a specific author, but also a changing context and outlook on social, political, and intellectual beliefs, values, and fashions.

CONTEMPORARY TRENDS CONCERNING THE ANALYTIC RELATIONSHIP

Let me briefly survey some of the contemporary, overlapping trends, indicating for each its range from mild to extreme expressions. In the first trend to be mentioned, many present authors stress the obvious fact that the analyst can never be completely neutral, in the sense of being devoid of any selective point of view and assumptions, or emotionally indifferent. In some writings this extends to an almost righteous rejection of any kind of neutrality being possible or desirable, even when neutrality is seen as a need for the analyst's "disciplined subjectivity" (Erikson, 1958, p. 68) or for his "continuously self analyzing his countertransference and its effects on the analytic situation" (Gill, 1994, p. 51).

In a second trend, while it is taken for granted that speech is the primary, if not exclusive, medium of the analytic interaction, there has been increasing recognition of the importance of the nonverbal and unconscious aspects of communication. This has led to giving an almost exclusive primacy to the affective, the implicit, the unintended, and the unthought in the analytic situation—at the expense of a striving for increased awareness, truthfulness, and higher mental organization. In a third trend, there is increasing acceptance that analysis is not an archeology, not an attempt to dig up the past as it once happened, either as an objective event or as a subjective experience. Only presently active memories and fantasies about the past can be reached and put in a new context, which may change their meaning and influence. A useful emphasis on the new and coconstructed aspects of the analytic experience has led some to the extreme claim that nothing relevant preexisted the analytic interaction, as if everything then started anew on a blank slate.

A fourth trend, highlighting the constantly interactive nature of the analytic situation and the fact that much of this interaction may be unwitting and unconscious, has led to an emphasis on intersubjectivity, defined by Dunn (1995) in his review article as "an inextricably intertwined mixture of the clinical participants' subjective reaction to one another" (p. 723). But such a view sounds at times as implying a kind of merging of minds, a spontaneous telepathy which makes the sorting out of the experiences of the two participants a goal hardly possible or even desirable.

In the fifth trend, most people would now agree that the personality and individual style of the analyst makes a difference. However, this has led to a tendency to give the individual "subjectivity" of the analyst a primary and decisive role, somewhat at the expense of his choice of theory and concepts and of their possible relevance and validity. And, finally, in the broadest sense, the emphasis on the interactive, two-person model, with influence and communication going in both directions, has led to a tendency to minimize or ignore the essential asymmetry and the special, atypical, and "symbolic" nature of the analytic relationship. Instead, it almost becomes a regular social relationship, only better and more meaningful than most.

FROM TRANSFERENCE TO COUNTERTRANSFERENCE

Major changes in the view of the role of the analyst are expressed in an expanded and modified use of the concepts of transference and countertransference. The classical concept of transference stresses the unintended repetition of mostly unconscious and conflicted aspects of the past in the present. Recent formulations have stressed how the transference is always influenced by the here and now of the analytic interaction and is not simply a repetition of the past. Indeed, Freud already had spoken of "new, revised editions" of the transference. The analyst is bound to play a role in the shaping of the transference, a point that Gill, in particular, has heavily emphasized. Exploring the specifics and fluctuations of the here-and-now interaction, as the medium for all the manifest contents of the analysis, is a useful and probably necessary step. It can remain well within the traditional goals of transference interpretation: namely, to get to the underlying long-standing patterns and conflicts of the patient.

But in many of the contemporary approaches, the analysis of the present interaction has become a primary, if not exclusive and self-contained, goal. The emphasis is not on recalling the past but on reliving it in the present, in a symbolic and presumably better way. Yet, even when explicit reconstruction and remembering of the past is downplayed, the analysis of the present is still bound to be carried out from a particular point of view, usually including some template version of the core aspect of the interaction—typically as a parent–child or even mother–infant interaction.

Here it may be useful to restate a fairly obvious but often neglected meaning of transference. Everyone, from Freud on, agrees that transference is not limited to explicit references to the analyst and the analytic situation. The transference can be expressed in all of the patient's material (current life incidents, memories, fantasies, dreams, etc.). Patients may show particular resistance to awareness and direct expression of feelings and thoughts about the analyst—a clinical fact which, again, Gill (1982) has pointed out. Thus, the transference has to be inferred and interpreted by the analyst, not only with reference to its presumed past origins but also as displaced and disowned aspects of the present. Whatever its reference, past or present, transference is a construction of the analyst from selected clinical data. It is a construction which will express his theory, his concepts and assumptions, and even his countertransference.

If one takes the extreme, but now fashionable, position that the present relationship, as a new coconstructed intersubjectively merged process, is the only knowable or relevant reality and that the reconstruction of what the patient brought to the interaction is impossible or useless, then it becomes difficult still to assign a meaning to the term *transference* or a purpose to its interpretation and analysis. After all, transference does assume some kind of transfer and continuity between different realms of experience; interpretation of transference aims at establishing a convergence of repetitive patterns in the here and now with accounts of life outside, present and past. Without such an assumption, the term ends up referring to anything that happens in the office which the analyst considers significant.

Still, the dynamics of the transference imply that it is felt by the patient as a desire (or fear) and by the analyst as a demand, inferred from pressure to play a specific role in an interactive scenario. Classically, the analyst becomes aware of this demand, and interprets it to the patient rather than comply with it, even symbolically. But recent writings have pointed out that the analyst usually cannot help but give some response, however muted and symbolic, to the patient's transference demands.

This phenomenon is often viewed as some form of projective identification and has led to major modifications of the concept of countertransference. The analyst is unconsciously influenced by the patient (by what has been projected into him, to use the Kleinian language). Once the analyst becomes aware of his reaction (as sudden affect, intrusive thought, reverie, etc.), he may trace it back to the patient and thus make use of it to get a better understanding of the patient's unconscious. Some authors write as if this mechanism can give a direct, unbiased access to the patient's unconscious. But, as others (Gabbard, 1995; Gill, 1982; Sandler, 1976) have reminded us, the analyst, too, has an unconscious; he is not a clean container (heir to the blank screen) for the patient's projections.

The patient's projections have a selective effect on the analyst when they resonate with and intensify some of his own unconscious tendencies; there is always an interaction, and it is not easy to separate the relative contribution of each participant. This process has been used as a major argument for assuming a merged intersubjective condition, the creation of an "analytic third," and so on. The modern countertransference has become mainly the analyst's reactions to the patient's transference, rather than the analyst's transference on the patient or, more particularly, the influence of the analyst's unconscious, including the analyst's projective identifications on the patient (a topic rarely mentioned). Just because the earlier meaning of countertransference has been expanded and turned around does not imply that this older meaning of countertransference as the analyst's uncontrolled influence on the patient has become irrelevant.

Modern discussions of countertransference do not provide much clarity or agreement on several important points. How much is the countertransference primarily unconscious? Should the analyst's deliberate interventions, conscious beliefs, theories, and rationale of treatment be considered part of it? They are bound, to some extent, to be an expression of the analyst's subjectivity; but must this imply that they can have no objective validity? An even more important question concerns when the countertransference response to the patient should remain purely internal and private—as a source of information for the analyst's interpretations (Heimann, 1950)—and when it should be expressed outwardly and registered, consciously or not, by the patient.

ENACTMENT

This brings us to enactment, a term used widely, but with such broad meaning that it lacks much specificity or clarity. It is no longer bad "acting out" and breaking the rules and boundaries of the analytic frame. When enactment refers to motor acts, they are usually minor ones, mostly significant because of the symbolic meaning given to them by the context of the special analytic situation. Even verbal behavior can be considered as enactment. Thus, the only specific meaning left for the term enactment would be any behavior which is unintended and the meaning and purpose of which are unclear or ambiguous—at least initially. Or, as Schafer (1997) has written, the term is "sometimes used in relation to the analysand as though it applies to any analytic material that can be interpreted as having transference significance. [As such, it can become]...a synonym for being in analysis" (p. 126).

Enactments of some kind are inevitable, and some, like Renik (1993), claim they are beneficial and even necessary for the genuineness and spontaneity of the relationship. Furthermore, many see most enactments as harmless because they can be retroactively analyzed and interpreted. But this argument is only partially true. Retroactive mutual observations and disclosures cannot really undo the original exchange or get outside the transference–countertransference interaction. They become part of it, adding another layer, at a level once removed; the analysis of the interaction may become a kind of ping-pong game, with the patient at some disadvantage.

THE FATES OF THE TRANSFERENCE: PARTLY DISSOLVED AND PARTLY CONFIRMED

Some aspects of the transference will be interpreted, others ignored, and yet still other aspects will find various levels of confirmation and symbolic gratification. Many aspects of the transference remain uninterpreted, if only because they are kept hidden and not directly expressed. And what is not explicitly questioned or reinterpreted will often become implicitly confirmed for the patient. Besides, we all know that many interpretations fail to dissolve transference beliefs and may even be used by the patient to confirm them; that is, they can be heard as the analyst's attempts to hide his "real" feelings.

A patient will also often give a special confirmatory meaning to small, accurately perceived details of the analyst's behavior (tone of voice, movement in the chair, facial expression at the end of the session), to the setting (as having some actual though limited similarity with some aspect of the patient's life experience), or to the analyst's general attitude, such that acceptance and sympathetic interest can be taken for muted signs of love and total understanding.

Confirming or gratifying selective aspects of the transference has traditionally been considered a major analytic sin, yet it is probably something that has always occurred to some extent, under one guise or another. Obviously, within the analytic frame, only symbolic, mostly verbal, token gratifications are possible. Even the most classical analytic patient may need some support and gratification from the ongoing treatment to keep it going. Aspects of the transference which are seen as desirable or even necessary for the treatment are deliberately not interpreted (dissolved) or are even promoted and validated. But they are then usually renamed as something other than transference, such as analytic alliance or analytic trust, or at least separated from the rest of the transference (neurosis) by such terms as unobjectionable or primal.

Thus when transference fits with the analyst's view of his role in the real relationship—already a rather subjective notion—the transference scenario will not be challenged and may even be fostered. Freud (1912) already remarked, in the "Dynamics of Transference," that "if the 'father imago' [he was still using Jung's term in 1912]...is the decisive factor in bringing this [the transference] about, the outcome will tally with the real relations of the subject to the doctor" (p. 100). Not a few present-day analysts could share such an attitude, provided the mother imago has replaced the father.

Nowadays, when analysts want to be a new object for the patient in a reparative relationship, this is likely to increase a tendency to go along and even share some aspects of the patient's transference fantasies (actually, the analyst's construction of these fantasies); the analyst may identify more or less consciously and deliberately, at least for a while, with parts of the transferential role in which the patient has cast him. However, one then no longer talks of gratifying infantile wishes but of fulfilling necessary developmental needs (for holding, mirroring, attachment). Thus, a degree of shared enactment may become a major factor within the transitional reality of the analytic relationship.

Let us take as an example the concept of the holding environment, often considered to be an indispensable prerequisite for effective treatment. The holding environment is not actual physical holding, and it requires more than the concrete aspects of a stable, protected setting with a sympathetic listener. It seems to include the patient's ongoing fantasies and fantasied experiences of being held and protected by the analyst's presence, attitude, talk, and tone of voice—maybe as a symbolic enactment of some infant–mother situation. I think it may also require the analyst's sharing in some ways such a fantasy scenario, giving it an effective immediacy within the actuality of the relationship. Many modern analysts may welcome such a holding scenario (or some other version with the role of mirroring and/or idealized parent) and be willing to play their version of the role demanded—demanded not only by the patient's transference, but also by their own theory, beliefs, and countertransference.

Obviously, the gratification of transference wishes or needs (such as a wish for an ideal, powerful, and nonintrusive parent who provides direct understanding and unconditional love) can only be symbolic and partial. Frustrations and disappointments are unavoidable. Where, then, does the negative transference fit in? Let me say just a few words on this big topic. The transference has many negative elements; however, these will be the focus of the analyst's attempts at interpretation (deflection) and are not likely to be confirmed by him, at least not deliberately (projective identification would make some unwitting hostile enactments by the analyst unavoidable).

It is likely that the negative reactions of the patient can only be dealt with in a setting where the positive transference predominates, even if temporarily overshadowed and in the background. This may require that a patient have at least some good internal object, some capacity for trust and hope to bring to the treatment. The treatment may strengthen them but not create them without some prior basis. In 1982, Gill wrote that "however expertly one analyzes the transference, the effect of an analysis will still, to a certain extent, be dependent on the gratification of the unanalyzed and persisting transference" (pp. 119–120). This was still a cautious statement; many present authors seem to believe that the effect of an analysis depends to a large extent on selectively confirmed and strengthened transference beliefs.

LOEWALD AND THE CREATION OF AN ILLUSION

I would like to deal further with two related questions: the special reality of the analytic interaction and the analyst's participation in it. I shall turn briefly to Loewald and his 1975 paper, "Psychoanalysis as an Art and the Fantasy Character of the Analytic Situation." Freud (1914a) had already stated that the analytic situation offers a safe "playground" for the unfolding of the transference neurosis:

> We admit it [the compulsion to repeat] into the transference as a playground in which it is allowed to expand in almost complete freedom and in which it is expected to display to us everything in the way of pathogenic instincts that is hidden in the patient's mind...The transference thus creates an intermediate region between illness and real life through which the transition from the one to the other is made. (p. 154)

Loewald (1975) has expanded this idea, emphasizing the special intermediate, play-like actuality of the analytic situation. He wrote, "Analyst and patient conspire in the creation of an illusion, a play" (p. 279). The play is enacted symbolically (mostly in speech) on a special stage with the participation of the analyst. It carries strong feelings and can be a compelling experience; it acquires a transitional reality beyond that of more private fantasy or memory but without the character of real action.

For the patient, at the same time, being author, actor, and spectator in a play with an improvised and changing plot is a difficult and paradoxical attitude to maintain. We know that the patient's level of belief in the transference and the kind of reality he experiences in the analytic situation are likely to vary widely at different times and for different individuals. There is a delicate balance, the dynamics of which are far from clear, between too much distance and detachment ("it's not for real, only a game") or too much concrete and narrow immediacy ("the way I experience it is the way it is"). Both attitudes can function as forms of resistance and defense, but this does not greatly enhance our understanding of their dynamics.

What about the analyst's role and involvement in the play? Loewald writes that the analyst participates in the play mostly as the director who organizes the material provided by the patient, takes the lead in helping to articulate it, and reveals parts of it as an illusion. Loewald states that the analyst's involvement and identification with the action of the play requires sufficiently similar life experiences. I think some shared beliefs and values may be equally or even more important.

Loewald stresses the participation of the analyst in the performance of the play but maintains the traditional view that the analyst does not assume the roles in which he has been cast by the patient, but reflects them back to the patient in highlighted form. Loewald is rather vague as to how much the analyst is also an actor in the play and assumes, deliberately or unintentionally, some of the roles in which the patient's transference has cast him. But even if the analyst remains a minor actor in the play, he is usually a major coauthor, constantly helping to rewrite the play and his own part in it—choosing from among his preselected repertoire of plots, scenarios, and outcomes.

Loewald (1975) also hints at a broad and somewhat grand role for the analyst who,

> "at times, mediates another dimension to the patient's experiences, raising them to a higher, more comprehensively human level of integration and validity while also signaling the transitory nature of human experience. The chorus in Greek tragedy, some soliloquies in Shakespearian plays, or, in a different way, certain commentaries on the action of the play by Shakespearian fools, for example, may give an idea of this function." (p. 282)

In his earlier, 1960 paper, Loewald spelled out the image of the analyst as an ideal parent who has a vision of the child's future that is, "ideally, a more articulate and more integrated version of the core of being which the child presents to the parent. This "more" that the parent sees and knows, he mediates to the child so that the child in identification with it can grow"

(p. 20). Thus, the patient's transference fantasies about the analyst in some parental role would be matched by the analyst's (countertransference?) fantasies of playing his version of a parental role toward the patient.

TRANSFER AND THERAPEUTIC ACTION

Psychoanalysis takes place in a special, artificial setting; when, in addition, it is seen as the intersubjective interaction of a unique dyad, this intensifies a major long-standing problem. How can we generalize from such data? How representative are they of a patient's experience, actions, conflicts, and capabilities in the broader arena of his ongoing life beyond the analytic interaction? And how do changes within the analytic process carry over to life outside and persist after termination? These questions are as old as psychoanalysis itself, and each theory has had its set of answers, usually very broad and nonspecific as to details.

Here, too, Freud set the example by devoting about a single paragraph to the concept of working through. The question of the therapeutic action of psychoanalysis always emerges anew. Clear evidence as to what has changed, and why, is hard to come by. It is wise to assume that multiple factors are involved and that their relative importance varies greatly with each individual case. But each theory selects one crucial factor, somewhat exclusively, based on a particular view of development, psychopathology, and rationale of treatment.

The classical Freudian model seems still to provide the most logical and coherent rationales, with its ideal goal of getting at the unconscious roots of a circumscribed neurosis (via the transference neurosis and the infantile neurosis). The specific manifest contents of the analysis are only important insofar as they provide a road, through interpretations, to the underlying repressed unconscious conflicts—whether the road is royal or plebeian is secondary. The unconscious core always extends much beyond the here and now of any particular analytic relationship. But most analysts have concluded that such a model may at best apply only partly in some cases and hardly at all in many others.

In contrast, a very different, increasingly popular, but by no means new model is built around the ideal of a new relationship with a better object, which will have the power to repair (or at least mitigate) the effects of early traumas and deficits—allowing arrested growth to resume. This model, sometimes labeled romantic (in contrast to the classical, more cognitive one), highlights the affective, ineffable, implicit, and unthought aspects of the interaction. The many theories that follow this model usually rest on a particular view of the mother–infant relationship, for which the analytic interaction becomes a kind of symbolic analogue.

This approach often includes some at least implicit shared belief in a new beginning (Balint), as a kind of rebirth fantasy. It also carries a certain mystique of the relationship and of the magical power of empathy and attunement. To be fair, one may also feel that the classical approach, in its heyday and in its Kleinian version, was not devoid of some belief in the magical power of interpretations, as if naming the demons of the unconscious would exorcise them.

These remarks are not meant to minimize the relevance, the power, and the shared psychic reality of such beliefs. However different, all these rationales of treatment imply that the relationship acquires meaning beyond the concrete here and now and becomes like a play, which can symbolically represent multiple scenarios and evoke the presence of many characters. In what matters, there are always more than two people in the room.

In some cases, the relationship itself can become hyper-real, often as the most important relationship in a patient's life. It then becomes an end in itself, with no natural or desirable termination. This may be increasingly true when patients no longer spend years but rather decades in what is still called an analysis. But for most patients, the relationship does provide at least the possibility of a steady, open-minded listener as ongoing support and an outlet through the crises of daily life. This element is no doubt an important aspect of any analysis, and it is the primary one in quite a few.

INTERNALIZATION

The ongoing relationship in a psychoanalysis includes more than the three to five times a week of actual interaction with the analyst. The analyst is usually active as an inner presence in most circumstances of the patient's life—present as a listener, adviser, questioner, and the like. I think not a few patients spend more time in an inner dialogue with their analyst than during the actual sessions. In other words, internalization of the relationship does not wait for the end of treatment, but is usually an integral part of it. I would tend to see it as a major factor in its lasting effects. And I am referring to more than an identification with the analyst as listener and observer, resulting in an increased capacity for more tolerant and objective self-reflection and observation. This aspect has been long familiar in the analytic literature and its latest reappearance is with Fonagy (1999) and increased mentalization as a major goal of psychoanalysis.

A broader view of internalization involves more than any actual aspect of the analyst's behavior and, indeed, more than just some identification with the actual analyst. What gets internalized would be the patient's construction of the whole relationship, including not only his image of the analyst but the image of himself that he attributes to the analyst, his self-image through the eyes of this Other. In many ways, this process could be seen as a reinternalization of a transference which has been modified by being interpreted and in part symbolically enacted in the analytic interaction. The analyst that the patient interacts with and partly internalizes is, to a major degree, the analyst he has created and that the actual analyst has helped him create. Positive results would presuppose, at least as a potential, the prior presence of some good internal object. This kind of internalization, while not the only mutative factor, is likely to be an important aspect of most analyses and a primary factor in many.

Let me conclude by indicating that I think the role of the relationship in psychoanalysis is essential, and it may be primary, even when mediated largely through interpretations. But the relationship extends beyond the reality of the concrete here-and-now interaction. Its power comes from what the two participants bring to it at many levels—their beliefs, fantasies, goals, and ways of acting. One may see it as a mutual coconstruction shaped by both participants, but, I would hope, in a very asymmetrical way, with the patient having the first and the last word, providing the first and last meaning.

The most important aspect of the analyst may be what the patient makes of him and how he uses him while struggling against the repetition of self-defeating scenarios. And the analyst's main function may be to facilitate this construction selectively and give it some anchoring in shared actuality. By restraining the intrusive and controlling side of his narcissism—or, more nicely stated, of his "subjectivity"—and thus allowing the patient to make a selective use of him as a stand-in for many presences in the patient's psychic reality, the analyst may become not less but more. Giving a primacy to the relationship, but one shaped by and for the patient, need not lessen the goal of greater self-knowledge and less self-deception.

Part 2

On the seduction theory

Deborah L. Browning

I remember reading Freud's "Constructions in Analysis" (1937) in a study group with a psychoanalyst/Freud scholar, many years senior to the oldest of us. As we approached the end of the paper, we were asked to provide examples from our own clinical work of recent constructions we had made for our patients. The strangest muddle ensued, so we had to stop and figure out what was going on. Our much esteemed professor took for granted that we took making constructions in our work for granted. Was this a generational difference in how we approached psychoanalysis? A difference in our training? As we talked about our thinking and our groping for examples, each of us began to state our own position on "telling" patients something about their past that they had not already, on their own, remembered. Around the same time I read "Screen Memories" (1899), where the question for the analyst is the reverse: When do we believe what our patients have told us, memories emerging from their own process, and when do we remain skeptical, seeing the memory as a screen for something else more painful? Are there really only memories "relating to" our childhood, not *of* it?

These questions about analysts' belief versus skepticism, about restraint versus spontaneity in expressing hypotheses of a patient's unremembered (and perhaps unrememberable) past go to the heart of much of the controversy around Freud's so-called seduction theory. The common (mis) understanding of Freud's presumed repudiation of it is that, having come to the conclusion that his patients had experienced sexual abuse as children and adolescents, he then reversed course over time and reinterpreted their reports of seduction as mere fantasy reflecting oedipal sexual wishes, conceived during acts of masturbation. The "quick and dirty" documentation for this point of view is two quotations, one from the famous letter to Fliess of September 21, 1897—"I no longer believe in my *neurotica* [theory of the neuroses]"—and then another, much longer quotation from 1933:

> Almost all my women patients told me that they had been seduced by their father. I was driven to recognize in the end that these reports were untrue and so came to understand that hysterical symptoms are derived from phantasies and not from real occurrences. It was only later that I was able to recognize in this phantasy of being seduced by the father the expression of the typical Oedipus complex in women. (p. 120)

The evidence for Freud's disbelief and disconfirmation of his patients' experience seems confirmed. But is it really? Do these two quotations, taken out of context, really tell the whole story of Freud's 40-year journey through the wilderness of unconscious memory and fantasy?

The two chapters that comprise this section, "Fact and Fantasy in the Seduction Theory: A Historical Review" (Chapter 7) and "The Interpretations of the Past: Childhood Trauma, Psychical Reality, and Historical Truth" (Chapter 8), examine Freud's seduction theory from two different perspectives, documenting his struggle to reconcile the reciprocal influence of reality and fantasy in the etiology of neurosis. Each of the chapters shows that careful scrutiny of Freud's early texts indicates, as best one can tell, that his women patients never told him or ever remembered *infantile* sexual abuse. They did report, in many cases, unwanted sexual encounters from latency and adolescence, which Freud never, even later, disputed or disbelieved. But Freud's assertion of infantile seductions (between 3 and 5, but not later than 8) came from his own inferences, interpretations, and reconstructions based on his observation of his patients' affect and behavior during analytic sessions, combined with other material that they reported.

Both chapters carefully trace and document Freud's writing on seduction and infantile sexual abuse as it evolved from his 1896 "Aetiology of Hysteria" through the previously mentioned 1933 quotation in the "New Introductory Lectures" to important comments in his 1937 "Constructions" paper. Schimek shows us that there is a "wide gap" between the seduction theory as Freud referred to it in 1933 and the model that he originally proposed in 1896. And between 1896 and 1933, there were five modifications (1897, 1905b/1906, 1914b, 1916, 1925c), each one reflecting a shift in Freud's understanding of the relationship between fantasy and reality.

With these two chapters, Schimek provides a more complete view of Freud's public and private (with Fliess) writing on the subject of unremembered infantile sexual abuse, showing the extent to which Freud continuously changed his views and how it was never a settled issue for him. (See Ahbel-Rappe, 2009, for how this operated just within in his "Dora" essay [1905a].) In them, one will see Freud's oscillation from his assumption, despite his patient's denials, of a real but repressed sexual assault to his emphasis on psychical reality and fantasy, to an overt denial and externalization of responsibility onto his "female patients" and, then, in

"Constructions" (1937), back to the proposition that real experiences in infancy are both "remembered" and forgotten. Freud conveys this latter conviction most clearly when he writes,

> Often enough, when a neurotic is led by an anxiety-state to expect the occurrence of some terrible event, he is in fact merely under the influence of a repressed memory (which is seeking to enter consciousness but cannot become conscious) that something which was at that time terrifying did really happen. (p. 268)

Those familiar with Winnicott's "Fear of Breakdown" (1974) will recognize this idea.

The two different perspectives of these chapters on the seduction theory reflect their relative emphasis on Freud's concern with fantasy versus reality. In Chapter 7, Schimek emphasizes Freud's relationship to the psychological, meaning-making aspect of symptom formation, even while he (Freud) was assuming the infantile sexual seductions to have actually occurred. This is seen clearly in Freud's concept of deferred action, elaborated in his 1896 "Aetiology," of which Schimek provides a detailed exposition. In contrast, in Chapter 8, Schimek focuses on Freud's "persistent hope" in identifying a past that was rooted in "factual reality." This focus leads to a discussion of psychic reality, primal fantasies, and Freud's under-recognized affinity for phylogenetic fantasy (see Perron, 2001, for more on Freud and phylogenesis). The different emphases of these chapters also reflect their having been written with different purposes in mind.

Chapter 8 was written as an extension of the conclusions Schimek drew in his study of Freud's assumptions about perception and mental representation (see Chapter 10, "A Critical Reexamination of Freud's Concept of Unconscious Mental Representation"). In that chapter, Schimek shows that many of Freud's metapsychological and clinical concepts were built on the false assumption that perception—regardless of age and internal motivation—provided a veridical impression, camera-like in its accuracy, and that these impressions or images were stored, unchanged, in an unconscious that was thought of as a container. This meant that the unconscious mind could be mined for treasures of the past—exactly as things once happened—as in an archeological dig. Freud's assumptions about perception and memory had important implications for his understanding of psychical versus external reality and for the analyst's process of reconstruction of the patient's past. What would be the implications of this, then, for Freud's original exposition of the seduction theory, and might this help clarify some of Freud's inconsistency on the role of actual seduction in neurosis? These were the fundamental questions addressed in "Interpretations."

To start, because Freud assumed that the contents of a patient's unconscious included actual and accurate memories of external events, it was then just a matter of getting to them. Thus, those patients who had been the victims of even very early childhood sexual assaults would somehow have a memory of them stored in their unconscious. The problem was that his patients had no memory of such early, infantile events. Among the various problems this posed for Freud, intellectually, was that it created a significant "scientific" problem. Schimek explains in Chapter 8 that, from Freud's scientific position, fantasies alone were not suitable causal agents in neurosis. He points out that Freud's hypothesis of primal fantasies, derived from a phylogenetic past, may have reflected his continued search for the reality of a traumatic stimulus; however, unable to find it in the actual past of the patient, he pushed it into the hypothetically real past of mankind.

Modestly titled, "The Interpretations of the Past..." was not generally picked up for its contribution to the literature on Freud's seduction theory. Rather, it was recognized for its place in the discussion of historical truth, a topic dominated at that time by Spence (1982) and Schafer (1983). But neither was the seduction theory on everyone's radar, as it would be only a few years later. As is well known, Jeffrey Masson's *Assault on Truth* (1984) claimed that Freud, in his abandonment of the seduction theory, had suppressed the reports of sexual abuse told to him by his patients. (See Lothane, 1999 and 2001, for details of the stories of both Masson and Crews, whom I will mention later.) Schimek had already made clear in "Interpretations" that the so-called reports that Freud later disavowed as fantasies had in fact been his own reconstructions and interpretations. It was this need to re-set the record straight that stimulated Schimek's writing of Chapter 7.

In counterpoint to his first exposition on the seduction theory, focusing on Freud's search for the external bases for the etiology of neurosis, in "Fact and Fantasy" Schimek shows the extent to which, even in Freud's first presentation of the seduction theory, fantasy components were involved by virtue of his model of "deferred action." Deferred action involves a "complex and lengthy process of symptom formation." It assumes a real sexual trauma, occurring before the age of 8, but most likely between ages 2 and 5, which *by definition* is unremembered and thus unconscious. It is only later (i.e., the "deferred action"), in puberty, in response to some perhaps less overt sexual stimulus, that sexual meaning is unconsciously assigned to the prepubertal events, triggering repression of the current event as well with the subsequent development of symptoms.

It was this unremembered, prepubertal sexual trauma that Freud was wrestling with his patients to recover and that they continued to assert they did not remember. It is this which Freud interpreted and reconstructed without confirmation and then, much later, forgetting the "source" of the material (e.g., his own interpretation), progressively assigned responsibility to his patients for telling him. Freud never questioned the veracity of their conscious memories of later sexual molestation; he merely thought this material was not sufficient to cause the onset of the hysteria. (See Blum, 1996, for the problems with the idea of deferred action and the traumatic impact of early childhood abuse.)

The stories of these two chapters do not quite end here. Schimek was successful in making clear that the initial reports of infantile sexual abuse were Freud's reconstructions, but now this success was used by a Freud "basher," Frederick Crews (1993, 1995), to suggest that Freud, out of political "drivenness," had essentially "faked" his data. He had made up the stories of infantile seduction in order to prove a hypothesis. The very foundation of the reconstructive process, an activity at the heart of analytic work, was being held up to ridicule. Having devoted his life to critical Freud scholarship, that reflected his own belief in the imperfections as well as the brilliance of Freud, Schimek was shaken at the idea that his work would be used to discredit Freud. Should he engage with Crews in a rebuttal? Would that not give him more credibility than he deserved? In the end, Schimek wrote a brief rebuttal, dissociating himself from Crews' intent. This rebuttal letter appeared, along with those of many other Freud scholars and researchers in a subsequent *New York Review of Books* (where the original article appeared) and then was the first in the set included in *NYRB*'s hardback publication (1995) of the original Crews article, which also contained two other articles Crews wrote on the recovered memory movement (1994a, 1994b) with their rebuttals.

Having witnessed Schimek's pained alarm in recognizing the possible misuse of his scholarship on Freud's intellectual tangles and having heard him express his worry about the fate of subsequent papers he might wish to write, I believe that Schimek's leaving "*The Interpretation of Dreams* Revisited" unpublished reflected his concern that his challenge to some of Freud's reasoning about dream work, primary process, and the interpretive process in dream analysis might again be used to undermine Freud's credibility. It is published in this book, for the first time, as Chapter 14.

The seduction theory continues to invite and incite controversy as well as to inspire important reconsiderations with thoughtful contributions. The recent publication of a 1998 symposium (Good, 2006) attests to the continued interest, not only in the seduction theory but also in all types of trauma experienced at all ages. Concerns around Freud's seduction theory continue to circle rather consistently around three main questions. What was his motive for abandoning the seduction theory? Did he actually abandon it? How important is it, clinically, to attempt to distinguish real acts of abuse and seduction from fantasies and to confirm and validate them?

A fourth question has been raised recently as well. What were Freud's motives for his conception of the seduction theory in the first place? With regard to this, Blum (2008) has revisited Freud's highly complicated relationship with his physician friend Fliess, the letters to whom have been central in considerations of Freud's apparent abandonment of the seduction theory. Blum takes us back to a time before the October 21, 1897, letter to view the triangle: Freud, Fliess, and Emma Eckstein, the patient of Freud's whom Fliess nearly killed with a botched nasal surgery. Blum suggests that one aspect of Freud's interest in seduction was his own struggle with the mutually seductive relationship with Fliess, as well as the need to focus on *sexual* abuse as an avoidance of the aggressive component of what had taken place with Eckstein.

Makari (2009), in his *Revolution of Mind,* offers a view of this time through a different lens. He shows us how Freud's theory evolved out of his attempted synthesis of bio- and psychophysics, French psychopathology, and the study of sexology. Thinking like the physician that he was and inspired by the fact that the search for specific causes of disease (germ theory) had led to the isolation of tuberculosis and cholera by Robert Koch in the 1880s, Freud was trying to identify single causes in neuroses. His knowledge of sexology and forensic medicine meant that he was well acquainted with the extent of child sexual (and physical) abuse in the nineteenth century. The linking of infantile incest with the development of hysteria was as perfect (in theory—or fantasy) as the idea that masturbation led to neurasthenia. Makari (1998a, 1998b, 2009) takes us carefully through all the twists and turns of Freud's theory making and theory breaking, as well as the pivotal role of masturbation in the transitions of the seduction theory.

In his recent book on primary process, Robert Holt (2009) warns the reader when thinking about Freud's metapsychological writing not to get caught in reifying concepts. Holt characterizes Freud this way: "It is important to take note of Freud's characteristic procedure of becoming so accustomed to his theoretical constructions that he tended to lose sight of their hypothetical nature and to speak as if he had empirically discovered them" (p. 6). This observation can help us recognize a similar process in Freud's approach to his original seduction hypotheses. Having come to a conclusion, he seems to have forgotten it was his idea in the first place; thus, as he revised his thinking, he progressively externalized responsibility for his reconstructions onto the women whom he treated. Henry Smith (2006) enlarges this point when he suggests, somewhat speculatively, that Freud's protracted search for external causes of psychic and sexual trauma was part of "the natural human inclination to externalize, to look for external causes and external solutions" (p. 91).

This brings us to the crucial and thorny question of whether, if the material of childhood incest is unconscious in the first place, it matters to distinguish fact from fantasy. Cannot the notion of psychic reality and the respect for the patient's experience be sufficient? Ahbel-Rappe (2006) suggests the answer should be "no." It does matter. Following a line of reasoning elaborated somewhat differently by Chasseguet-Smirgel (1975), Ahbel-Rappe points to the problems for reality testing that ensue when fantasies of sexual seduction become actualities. She says that, for the very reason that children are capable of having sexual fantasy reflective of their age and conceptual capacity, the actuality of incest is particularly destructive to processes of thought, fantasy, and reality testing. It leads to a "loss of confidence in the difference between wish and reality and in the safety of dreaming" (p. 195).

As Ahbel-Rappe points out, she is not alone in making this observation, but what I think is important in her presentation is that the threat to reality testing that comes with the breeching of the boundary against incest also implicates the *interpersonal* aspect of the development of that crucial process. There is a powerful other—an older sibling or adult—who engages in an act that is simultaneously denied. The very person that the child relies on to help him or her construct a real world has proven to be duplicitous and untrustworthy in the most intimate realm of all—the body. "The loss of confidence in the difference between wish and reality and in the safety of dreaming is often accentuated in incest by the disavowal of the perpetrator" (Ahbel-Rappe, 2006, p. 195).

Laplanche (1997) suggests that our mistake, our "going astray" in our considerations of Freud's seduction theory, is not in our struggle over whether seduction is real or fantasy, but rather in our failure to recognize the universality of psychic seduction of the infant by the other, that "the driving force of all scenes of seduction is a universal fact: the intervention of the adult other, with his sexual unconscious" (p. 660). To the extent that we accept Laplanche's conception, then actual incest is all the more violating of the child's nascent mind. "In this abuse, the signifier stops being enigmatic, because it is excessively over-loaded by a significance that comes from outside" (Bodner, 2002, p. 505).

And, if, as Laplanche (1987, 1992b, 1997) suggests, the analyst and the analytic setting rekindle the original, primal seduction of the mother and her milk-filled and erogenous breast, then I suggest that in all of this we are left with the need to be mindful of the assumption that the therapeutic relationship is built around some kind of interpretation within the context of some form of imbalanced relationship that is charged with some mix of realistic and fantastic hope and fear. Keeping this process and the relationship from becoming a perverse seduction, while attending to the real and elaborated traumas of the past, is the daunting work of the psychoanalyst.

Chapter 7

Fact and fantasy in the seduction theory

A historical review*

Freud's first systematic theory of neurosis, the so-called seduction theory, and its later revisions are considered landmarks in the development of psychoanalysis. Many basic issues are involved, including most directly the relative importance of external traumas versus internal factors (conflicts, fantasies, drives) in the causation and explanation of neuroses. Equally important, if less conspicuous, are the kind of evidence and the degree of inference involved in the reconstruction of the early past. What kind of truth (material or psychical, causal or narrative—to use more contemporary terms) is expressed by such a reconstruction?

The standard version of the seduction theory and its revision is based on the last summary given by Freud in 1933:

> In the period in which the main interest was directed to discovering infantile sexual traumas, almost all my women patients *told* me that they had been seduced by their *father*. I was driven to recognize in the end that these reports were untrue and so came to understand that hysterical symptoms are derived from phantasies and not from real occurrences. (p. 120; italics added)

This makes it appear as if the seduction theory had been primarily based on a fortuitous clinical discovery: namely, the patients' direct reports of seduction by the father in early childhood. It also suggests that Freud had to change his conclusions because he had been misled by his patients, who presented their fantasies as memories. Such a version of the seduction theory has remained essentially unchallenged (see, however, Laplanche & Pontalis, 1968; Schimek, 1975b). Some authors (Blamary, 1979; Levenson, 1981; Masson, 1984) have even implied that Freud, by abandoning the seduction theory, chose to ignore or suppress the strong and compelling evidence provided by his patients. But did Freud really have such evidence? Did

* This chapter originally appeared in the *Journal of the American Psychoanalytic Association*, 35(4), 1987, pp. 937–965. Reprinted with permission.

his patients provide him with direct reports and explicit stories of seduction by the father in early childhood?

The major part of this chapter will be devoted to an examination of Freud's original presentation of the seduction theory of 1896. My main argument will be that Freud's conclusion that hysteria always requires the occurrence of sexual abuse in early childhood was not based directly on the patients' reports and conscious memories, but involved a great deal of selective interpretation and reconstruction. The reconstructions presupposed a complex set of hypotheses and assumptions and were based on a wide variety of not clearly specified data, ranging from thoughts, images, displays of affect, and gestures to specific memories from later childhood. By changing the original seduction theory, Freud did not suppress clear and unambiguous evidence; he only changed some aspects of his interpretation of the data—namely, their ultimate origin in an internal fantasy rather than an external trauma.

I shall also emphasize two generally known and accepted, but often ignored, facts about the seduction theory. First, the father is not even mentioned in any of Freud's presentations of the seduction theory in 1896. Even by inference from Freud's reported findings, the father could only have been included among several possible categories of seducers—and not the most frequent one at that, a place reserved for the older sibling, not the father.

Second, actual seduction in early childhood played only a limited, though indispensable, role in the complex and lengthy process of symptom formation. This early trauma was significant only to the extent that its unconscious memory had a "delayed" action at puberty and then induced conflict, repression, and symptoms. It is only when the unconscious memory has acquired a new meaning in a different context at a later age that it becomes a psychic trauma. Internal psychological processes and transformations already play a central role in the seduction theory. Thus, Freud's later shift of emphasis from reproductions of real events to fantasies (which contain at least fragments of actual past experience) did not represent such a radical break in the continuity of his thought.

In the second part of the chapter, I shall survey Freud's successive revisions of the original seduction theory, stressing that one does not see a sudden and definitive change, but rather a progressive one, with earlier views often coexisting with later ones. Finally, I shall point out the relevance of this clarification of the seduction theory for the broader, still ongoing, issues of the meaning of fact and fantasy in the reconstruction of the psychoanalytic past.

ETIOLOGY OF HYSTERIA: REPRODUCTION OF EARLY TRAUMAS

Freud presented the seduction theory in three papers in the spring of 1896 (Freud, 1896a, 1896b, 1896c). The most thorough of them, "The Aetiology of Hysteria" (1896c), was based on the lecture that Freud had just delivered to the Vienna Society for Psychiatry and Neurology—where it had been very poorly received. It is this major paper that I shall examine in some detail.

Freud begins by stating that questioning patients directly about the history and origin of their symptoms yields very little. Nor can he accept Charcot's theory, which stresses purely hereditary factors. Freud is looking for a method that is less dependent on the assertions of the patients themselves. To introduce his method, he uses the metaphor of an archeological excavation:

> [T]he numerous inscriptions, which, by good luck, may be bilingual, reveal an alphabet and a language, and, when they have been *deciphered and translated,* yield undreamed-of information about the events of the remote past...If we try, in an approximately similar way, to induce the symptoms of a hysteria to make themselves heard as witnesses to the history of the origin of the illness, we must take our start from Josef Breuer's momentous discovery: "The symptoms of hysteria are determined by certain experiences of the patient's which have operated in a traumatic fashion and which are being reproduced in his psychical life in the form of mnemic symbols." (1896c, pp. 192–193, italics added)

Thus, Freud starts out with the assumption that the hysterical symptoms are the symbolic reproduction of past traumatic experiences. Such events must have "suitability to serve as a determinant" (i.e., be linked to the content of the symptoms) and sufficient "traumatic force." Freud had already concluded earlier that the traumas were always of a sexual kind (Breuer & Freud, 1895; Freud, 1894).

What the patients spontaneously revealed did not meet these requirements and was frequently "innocuous and unrelated to the character of the hysterical symptom" (Freud, 1896c, p. 194). So Freud kept urging the patients to produce more material and go back further into the past:

> If the first-discovered scene is unsatisfactory, we tell our patient that this experience explains nothing, but that behind it there must be hidden a more significant, earlier, experience; and we direct his attention by the same technique to the associative thread which connects the two memories... (pp. 195–196)

At the time, instead of hypnosis, Freud was using mostly the technique of putting pressure with his hands on the patient's forehead, as a way of overcoming the patient's resistance to producing the required memories. With Freud (1896c) selecting associative threads and recurrent nodal points in the patient's material, sexual experiences, dating mostly from the time of puberty, were revealed. But these experiences,

> which have been discovered with so much trouble and extracted out of all the mnemic material...are very different from each other both in kind and in importance. In some cases, no doubt, we are concerned with experiences which must be regarded as severe traumas—an attempted rape, perhaps...or the involuntary witnessing of sexual acts between parents...But in other cases the experiences are astonishingly trivial [such as a stroking of the hand or the hearing of a mildly obscene joke]... (p. 200)

Thus, this first stage of the technique fails to find a uniform category of clear traumas from which the origin of the neurosis could be derived.

There must be an earlier sexual trauma whose unconscious memory can account for the pathogenic effect of these often innocuous experiences of later years. So the search must go on toward the more remote past. This search ends with the patient's "reproduction" of a sexual event—a sexual assault or seduction by an older person always involving bodily and genital contact. The trauma had occurred in early childhood, roughly between the ages of 2 and 5, and never later than age 8.

Freud (1896c) does not go on to describe how this trauma was reproduced in the treatment and what kind of material the patient presented. Instead, he is primarily concerned with demonstrating that these reproductions of the past refer to actual events and are not the product of the patients' imagination or of their compliance with his expectations and suggestions. He readily admits that the scenes only emerge "under the strongest compulsion of the treatment" (p. 204) and that he had warned the patients that such scenes were going to emerge. But he argues that the reproductions are genuine because when the patients are undergoing and living through these experiences in the treatment,

> They suffer under the most violent sensations, of which they are ashamed and which they try to conceal; and even after they have gone through them once more in such a convincing manner, they still attempt to withhold belief from them, by emphasizing the fact that, unlike what happens in the case of other forgotten material, they have *no feeling of remembering* the scenes. (p. 204; italics added)

This could, of course, be attributed to defense and resistance, but, whatever the reasons, it is clear that the scenes did not emerge as conscious memories—as recognized experiences of past events. Nor is this an isolated remark of Freud's. The same point is made in the two other presentations of the seduction theory (1896a, 1896b). But it had already been spelled out in 1895, even when referring to material which did not go as far back into the past: "The deeper we go the more difficult it becomes for the emerging memories to be recognized, till near the nucleus we come upon memories which the patient disavows even in reproducing them" (Breuer & Freud, 1895, p. 289). And he raises some unanswered questions:

> Are we to disregard this withholding of recognition on the part of patients, when, now that the work is finished, there is no longer any motive for their doing so? Or are we to suppose that we are really dealing with thoughts which never came about, which merely had a *possibility* [Freud's italics] of existing, so that the treatment would lie in the *accomplishment of a psychical act which did not take place at the time* [italics added]? (p. 300)

And, by 1900, as I shall illustrate further on, Freud had already concluded that the crucial early experiences did not emerge directly as memories but had to be reconstructed from their reproduction in fantasies, dreams, and transference.

It is clear that these "reproductions" were not presented and experienced as memories and thus were not acknowledged and recognized by the patient. It is Freud who concluded that the material refers to a trauma that actually took place in the patient's early childhood. So what did these reproductions consist of? Freud is not very specific or forthcoming on this point, so we shall never have a complete and clear-cut answer. We can only make plausible inferences by piecing together Freud's description of his technique and its immediate results during the 1895–1896 period and the ways in which he used the term "reproduction" in various contexts at the time.

Freud does give some detail about his technique and about what kind of material the patient provided. The patients produced the material in response to Freud's continuing pressure (verbal and physical), and his repeatedly asking, "What did you see?" or "What occurred to you?" They seem to have produced visual scenes, often of hallucinatory intensity, accompanied with strong displays of affect, physical sensations, and motoric gestures. All this material could be seen as the enactment of a seduction scene and the reliving or reproduction of a past experience (or experiences), under the influence and "compulsion" of the immediate treatment situation. Freud describes how this material emerges only in a piecemeal and fragmentary fashion, often with an appearance of "disconnections and irrelevance" (Breuer & Freud, 1895, p. 276; Freud, 1896a, p. 13).

Freud had to push for more details, bring order and connectedness to the material, and make inferences and interpretations which he communicated to the patient as the process unfolded. In 1895 and in the first part of "The Aetiology of Hysteria" (1896c), Freud is referring to the recovery of material from later childhood and early adolescence; it seems safe to assume that this description of the fragmentary and disjointed nature of the evidence and the consequent need for inference would have been even stronger in the case of traumas dating from the earliest years of childhood, when the child at the time would have had a very limited understanding of the traumatic event and little, if any, capacity to encode its memory in verbal terms. In a letter to Fliess, written during the same month as "The Aetiology of Hysteria," Freud (1892–1899) states: "That is, the scenes for hysteria occur in the first period of childhood (up to 4 years), in which the mnemic residues are not translated into verbal images" (p. 230).

There must also have been a good deal of individual variation in the ways in which a particular patient "reproduced" the original trauma, especially in the relative predominance of visual material or affective expression and in the degree of coherence, openness, and completeness of the verbal reproduction of the scene. One cannot rule out the possibility that in some cases the patient "told" a relatively complete and clear story and gave a coherent and self-evident description of a sexual trauma. But it would be precisely these accounts which would have undergone the most transformation and fantasy elaboration and have become what Freud (1899) was soon to refer to as "screen memories."

The reproduction of the seduction scenes may have often been a kind of minor hysterical attack, with both verbal and nonverbal expression, in a somewhat altered state of consciousness. (Freud mentioned the similarities between the pressure technique and hypnosis.) Freud readily admits that the occurrence, if not the main contents, of these episodes was strongly influenced by his insistent suggestions and relentless pressure. But my emphasis is not primarily on the role of suggestion in the contents of the patients' material. My main argument is that the original infantile traumas were not directly reported by the patients but were (re)constructed by Freud on the basis of his interpretation of a variety of more or less disguised and partial manifestations and "reproductions," with the likelihood of a strong transferential element.

Before going further, I have to consider the rest of the arguments, data, and formulations in "The Aetiology of Hysteria" (1896c). Freud continues by giving as evidence for the reality of the scenes "the uniformity which they exhibit in certain details." He then adds, as a major argument, "the relationship of the infantile scenes to the content of the whole of the rest of the case history" (p. 205). The scenes are the last missing piece of a puzzle, whose shape is predetermined by the rest of the picture; the scenes are "indispensable supplements to the associative and logical framework of the neurosis" (p. 205).

Let us note that both these arguments can also be interpreted as highlighting the role of Freud's theoretical assumptions and reconstructions in providing the uniformity and consistency of the original scenes. In fact, in his later writings, Freud was to use the same argument—that specific scenes were demanded by the logical necessity of the neurosis—to justify the use and validity of constructions which could never be directly confirmed by the patient's recall. Here Freud continues his search for proofs by referring briefly to two instances where a childhood seduction seemed confirmed by the report of a relative. But these examples—in one case dating from later childhood and in the other from an unspecified age—are only marginally relevant to Freud's formulation and at best can only indicate that actual childhood seductions do occur.

Freud (1896c) finally gets more specific about the sexual experiences involved: "Lastly the findings of my analysis are in a position to speak for themselves" (p. 207). But are they really? Freud does not indicate in what form the findings were presented by the patients, nor does he specify the actual ages involved. He merely divides the material of his 18 cases into three general groups "according to the origin of the sexual stimulation," without giving numbers for each group (p. 208).

The first group involves an isolated assault by a stranger with no question of the child's consent and a preponderant affect of fright. The second, much larger group involves a sexual relationship with an adult caretaker, "all too often a close relative," which has become a "love relationship...with its mental side developed" and has often lasted for years. The third and probably largest group (7 out of 13, in the two presentations of the theory published 3 months earlier) includes incestuous relations between siblings, generally a girl and her older brother, "often prolonged beyond puberty." It is immediately obvious that these events vary greatly in kind, in importance, and in traumatic force; the only thing they have in common is sexual behavior between the young child and an older person.

Such findings must have involved a good deal of conscious remembering and narrative, with specific details directly "told" by the patients. But do these findings refer to the original traumas, as Freud seems to imply? If so, we are faced with serious inconsistencies in trying to fit them within the etiological theory that Freud is presenting here. The theory assumes that the trauma occurred between the ages of 2 and 5 and never after age 8. In order to produce conflict, repression, and neurotic symptoms by the time of puberty, the memory of the early trauma must have remained unconscious. "The scenes must be present as unconscious memories; only so long as and insofar as they are unconscious are they able to create and maintain hysterical symptoms" (Freud, 1896c, p. 211).

But only the first and smallest group of cases (an isolated sexual assault by a stranger) could readily fit these requirements. For the other two groups, the majority of cases, how could we assume that a love relationship lasting many years, often beyond puberty, remains only as an unconscious memory? And that even when it is finally reproduced under "the strongest compulsion of the treatment" it does not bring about any "feeling of remembering"? A relationship which is still ongoing at puberty, when hysterical symptoms are formed, can hardly be identical with the original trauma whose unconscious memory starts having a "delayed" pathogenic effect at puberty. Was it then only the earliest seduction (by a different individual?)

that remained unconscious and was never directly remembered? And, last but not least, on the basis of these three different types of seduction, how was Freud going to conclude, later in the same year, that the father was always the original seducer?

As a further indication that most of these specific findings do not refer directly to the original trauma, we may note that Freud never relegated them to the level of fantasy, even after he had concluded that the original seduction was based on universal oedipal fantasies (which may or may not have become reinforced by actual events). Throughout his writings, Freud kept stating that actual seductions, typically by an older sibling (the largest of the three groups mentioned in 1896), occur "all too frequently."

How can such inconsistencies be clarified? One may need to distinguish between data from later childhood (typically, lasting incestuous relationships, most frequently with an older sibling), which are mostly derived from the direct memories of the patient, and, on the other hand, a uniform early trauma (soon to be, in Freud's thought, seduction by the father), which was never remembered by the patient but had to be reconstructed from partial, indirect "reproductions" (and whose existence was demanded by the "logical necessity" of the structure of the present neurosis). Yet, Freud did not make such a distinction between what was consciously remembered, unconsciously reproduced, or mostly reconstructed.

A hazy chronology is also evident in Freud's reporting of his findings and was probably also characteristic of the data as presented by the patients. It seems likely that Freud, in reconstructing the original scenes, made use of both the patient's direct reports (dealing mostly with later years of childhood) and the contents of enacted "reproductions" in the treatment situation. However, he did not clearly or consistently distinguish between his various sources of evidence or specify the amount of inference and interpretation involved in reaching his conclusions.

THE POWER OF MEMORY: TRAUMA AS DEFERRED ACTION

The etiologic formulation of 1896 states that the occurrence of passively endured sexual abuse in early childhood is a necessary precondition for the later formation of neurotic symptoms. But it is not the early event itself, nor its immediate consequences, that account for later conflict and neurosis. For Freud (1896b), the event becomes only a psychic trauma through the deferred action of its unconscious memory: "it is not the experiences themselves which act traumatically but their revival as a memory after the subject has entered on sexual maturity" (p. 164). The concept of the deferred traumatic action of a memory is much broader than that of the delayed discharge of a trauma which could not be abreacted at the time.

The psychic trauma occurs when the memory of the original event, which has persisted in an unconscious dissociated state, acquires new meaning and intensity later on, in the context of the maturational changes of puberty. The unconscious memory becomes merged with an experience of the time of puberty and is then revived as if it were a new contemporary experience; it can now generate conflict and anxiety, and thus repression and symptom formation. The "posthumous" effect of the memory is much greater than that of the original event, which had "little or no effect at the time."*

In a letter to Fliess of the same period as the 1896 papers, Freud (1892–1899) wrote that "the scenes for hysteria occur in the first period of childhood (up to 4 years), in which the mnemic residues are not translated into verbal images" (p. 230). This "translation" occurs only later as these unconscious "mnemic residues" express themselves through the content of later experiences to which they have been transferred, somewhat like the infantile wishes to the day residues of the dream. Freud assumes that the original event, while clearly sexual in an objective, adult sense, was "presexual" for the young child because of his sexual immaturity and thus was not experienced as a sexual trauma at the time. This formulation is closely linked to the fact that in 1896 Freud had not yet included infantile sexuality in his theory.

But, as Laplanche and Pontalis (1973) have indicated, it is a major oversimplification to assume, with the editors of the *Standard Edition* (vol. 3, p. 161), that this concept "lost its meaning owing to the discovery of infantile sexuality." The discovery of infantile sexuality did not exhaust the significance and usefulness of the concept of deferred action for Freud; it still played a major role in his later case formulations. Then it involved a different time span, earlier in life, but it still referred to experiences which have a delayed traumatic effect.

Freud did not discard the concept of "deferred action," but used it prominently in his later case formulations of Little Hans (1909b) and the Wolf Man (1918). However, then it referred mostly to things "heard and seen" by the child (primal scene, castration threats and sight of female genitals, etc.), registered and remembered but not understood at the time; they have a deferred traumatic action when combined with later experiences at the oedipal period. The basic assumption is still that memories of the past remain preserved in the unconscious, but can acquire new meaning and

* It may be difficult to reconcile this statement with Freud's (1896b) description of the original traumas as "grave sexual injuries" (p. 164) and as "stamped upon the later development of the individual and of his neurosis, in countless permanent effects which deserve to be traced in the greatest detail" (1896c, p. 215). One could say that Freud assumes that the original trauma was basically traumatic in an objective sense, but not as a subjective experience, whereas the later "trauma" at puberty could be trivial in an objective sense, but was experienced as a psychic trauma. Such a view presupposes, of course, that the original trauma was an actual physical event, something done to the child.

greater pathogenic strength in the context of later events, with the further development of sexual (and, one should add, cognitive) capacities.

The assumption of a deferred action of early memories, whatever its merits and problems, shows that already in 1896, it is an inner psychic experience—namely, the new meaning of a memory—which becomes the major pathological agent, interpolated between the original external event and the later symptoms. When Freud (1896a) makes the assumption that "a memory will operate as though it were a contemporary event" and "display a power which was completely lacking in the event itself" (p. 154), he is moving toward a realm of explanation which gives prominence to inner psychic factors (he even calls the delayed effect a "psychical effect") over physical external ones.

The later fate of the unconscious memory is already becoming equally relevant to if not more relevant than the exact objective features of the events from which it originated. And the necessary role of conflict and repression as autonomous inner factors in symptom formation (not all children who suffer sexual abuse become neurotic) reflects the same, soon to become dominant, trend in Freud's theory. The concept of the deferred action of memories anticipates the later focus on unconscious fantasy and psychic reality.*

THE FATHER AS SEDUCER AND THE TRIUMPH OF FANTASY (1896–1897)

The father does not play a major role (in fact, is not even directly mentioned) in any of the published versions of the seduction theory. At most, he is alluded to indirectly through the statement—"all too often a close relative"—as one kind of seducer among several others. This omission was not likely to be merely political cautiousness on Freud's part. Freud lists several categories of seducers: strangers, hired caretakers, older siblings, and "all too often a close relative." This last category would certainly include fathers as the

* This concept is also linked to a particular view of causality and chronology implicit in most of Freud's formulations. Certain unconscious, dissociated, or repressed memories of the early past act on the present as contemporary experiences, "not indirectly, through a chain of intermediate causal links, but as a directly releasing cause" (Breuer & Freud, 1895, p. 7). In line with what Freud was to call later the timelessness of the unconscious, such memories do not become part of a continuous developmental and chronological sequence in which the early past could only have an effect on the present through a whole series of intermediate steps and stages. Instead, a fragment of the past is directly transferred to the present and acquires a different meaning and effect in this new context. As Freud (1918) was to put it later, "the patient...puts his present ego into the situation which is so long past" (p. 45n), disregarding the time intervals. Such a conception of causality seems quite alien to a causal sequence between material events and already implies a frame of reference based on internal representations and transformations of meaning.

main, if not the only, group of culprits. (Freud admitted in 1924 that in two cases in the *Studies on Hysteria* involving sexual assaults on adolescent girls, he had substituted "uncle" for "father" [pp. 134n and 170n]).

But are all the other categories merely Freud's inventions and disguises for the role of the father? This seems more than unlikely, especially because we find no evidence for this in letters to Fliess of the same period, which contain many references to the seduction theory. In these letters, it is only by December 1896 that Freud expresses his conviction that not just any sexual trauma, but specifically seduction by the father, is the original cause of hysteria; "heredity is seduction by the father" (Freud, 1892–1899, p. 239), in the sense that the perverted father now plays the main etiologic role that was attributed to heredity in the theories of Charcot.

Considering that some recent authors (e.g., Blamary, 1979) speculate that guilt over his father's death may have been the main reason why Freud soon abandoned the seduction theory, it is interesting to note that Freud made the father into the prime seducer at least 2 months after the death of his father, in October of 1896. In May of 1897 Freud speaks of his "wish to catch a father as the originator of neurosis." While it is not unlikely that some of his patients confessed to an incestuous relation with their father, one may wonder, based on what new clinical evidence, personal motives, and theoretical reasons (e.g., the ongoing search for a uniform trauma), Freud made the generalization that the father was the original seducer.

There are only three instances where Freud gives specific clinical material as evidence for the role of the father as seducer in early childhood. All of them are in the Fliess letters (12/6/1896; 4/28/1897; 12/22/1897), and only the second one is included in the *Standard Edition*. The two others have only recently been published (Freud, 1887–1904). The last one is from December 1897, 3 months after the September 1897 letter where Freud repudiated his "neurotica." We thus have further evidence, if any is needed, that this repudiation was hardly final and complete by September 1897. In a letter of December 12, 1897, one finds the following passage:

> My confidence in paternal etiology has risen greatly. Eckstein deliberately treated her patient in such a manner as not to give her the slightest hint of what would emerge from the unconscious and in the process obtained from her, among other things, the identical scenes with the father. (Freud, 1887–1904, p. 286)

We do not really know what these scenes involved and how they were obtained. More importantly, a close examination of this material shows how inconclusive the evidence is. It is hard to tell what was presented by the patients as memories or as dreams and hallucinations; it is also difficult to separate Freud's suggestions and interpretations from the patients' direct and spontaneous statements. Furthermore, two out of the three cases refer to later periods of childhood, and in one instance the father is only indirectly incriminated.

The Fliess letters (Freud, 1892–1899) show that a growing emphasis on the role of fantasy emerges at the same time as the conclusion that the primal trauma always involves the father. In April 1897 (letter 59), Freud wrote:

> The point that escaped me in the solution of hysteria lies in the discovery of a new source from which a new element of unconscious production arises. What I have in mind are hysterical phantasies, which regularly...go back to things heard by children at an early age and only understood later. (p. 244)

And in May 1897 he wrote:

> The aim seems to be to arrive at the primal scenes. In a few cases this is achieved directly, but in others only by a roundabout path, via phantasies. For phantasies are psychical facades constructed in order to bar the way to these memories. Phantasies at the same time serve the trend toward refining the memories, toward sublimating them. They are made up from things that are heard, and made use of subsequently... (p. 248)

In the famous letter of September 1897 repudiating his "neurotica," the father etiology, Freud was to conclude that "in the unconscious...one cannot distinguish between the truth and fiction that is cathected with affect" (p. 260), between unconscious memories and unconscious fantasies. So 1 year after the public presentation of the seduction theory, the delayed effect of unconscious memories is gradually giving way to an emphasis on fantasy as an even greater transformation of these memories. By 1900, we find the following statement in *The Interpretation of Dreams:* "Hysterical symptoms are not attached to actual memories, but to phantasies erected on the basis of memories" (p. 491).

Once Freud's etiological formulation required the necessary occurrence of a specific trauma—namely, seduction by the father in early childhood—this hypothesis became less and less plausible if it had to rest on actual events, on external accidents of individual history. The universal role of the father could only be maintained by switching from accidental real events to inner determined fantasies. And, indeed, in the letter to Fliess of September 1897 mentioned earlier, Freud (1892–1899) gives another reason for doubting his theory: the improbability of "the fact that in every case the father, not excluding my own, had to be blamed as a pervert" (p. 259). In the same letter, Freud gives two additional reasons for doubting his theory. One is the lack of therapeutic success and the other, which is most relevant to one of my main points, is

> that in the most deep-going psychosis the unconscious memory does not break through, so that the secret of the childhood experiences is not betrayed even in the most confused delirium. If in this way we see that the unconscious never overcomes the resistance of the conscious, then, too, we lose our expectation that in treatment the opposite will happen. (p. 260)

If the primal seduction scenes do not emerge as conscious memories even in psychotic states, they are not likely to do so in the treatment of hysterics. This seems clear proof that not only the patients had "no feeling of remembering the scenes" once they had been "reproduced," but also that Freud was well aware that they never emerged as conscious memories.

In the two subsequent letters Freud gives well-known details of his self-analysis, essentially an awareness of his own oedipal wishes, including hostility toward his father (he also gives the role of the actual seducer to the nurse of his earliest years). One may readily infer that these personal factors had contributed to Freud's construction of an etiology which always blamed the father: "my [father] played no active part in my case, but...no doubt I drew an analogy from myself on to him" (p. 261). His awareness of these factors, as the result of the self-analysis of his own "hysteria," was probably a major influence on his modifying his conclusions (Jones, 1953).

But at no point did Freud doubt the method or the core content of his reconstructions, even if they had to refer mostly to fantasies rather than objective events. In fact, he extended them beyond the realm of the etiology of neurosis and immediately viewed his own just discovered childhood feelings and fantasies as manifestations of "a *universal* event of early childhood" exemplified in the mythical figures of Oedipus and Hamlet (Freud, 1892–1899, p. 265; italics added).

During 1893 to 1897, Freud started searching for traumas, then sexual traumas, and then a very specific type of sexual trauma. This required going further and further back into the past to find the expected trauma. Even with the pressure technique, the patients could not provide the necessary memories; there had to be ever greater reliance on interpretation and reconstruction, based on indirect and disguised "reproductions" of the past (transference enactments, fantasies, dreams, etc.). The recovery of repressed memories was not sufficient; it could at best provide somewhat less disguised derivatives of the original trauma.

It did not take long for Freud to acknowledge explicitly that conscious memories of early childhood were scarce and unreliable and that the crucial aspects of the early past had to be reconstructed through the interpretation of dreams, fantasies, and transference behavior. Already, in 1899, in his paper, "Screen Memories," he concluded:

> It may indeed be questioned whether we have any memories at all from our childhood: memories relating to our childhood may be all that we possess. Our childhood memories show us our earliest years not as they were but as they appeared at the later periods when the memories were aroused. (p. 322)

In *The Interpretation of Dreams* (1900), commenting on the words in a patient's dream, Freud makes the following incidental remark: "A few days earlier I had explained to the patient that the earliest experiences of childhood were 'not obtainable any longer as such,' but were replaced in analysis by 'transferences' and dreams" (p. 184). This issue was further elaborated in several later papers (1914b, 1918, 1937). Freud's position can be summarized by one quote: "[A]s far as my experience hitherto goes, these scenes from infancy are not reproduced during the treatment as recollections, they are the products of construction" (1918, pp. 49–50). Freud states repeatedly that, if the treatment is going well, the patient will eventually believe that the content of the reconstruction is required by the logic of the neurosis, and he will no longer use his lack of remembering as a resistance. Freud had made a similar statement much earlier (Breuer & Freud, 1895, p. 300).

In Freud's most extensive case histories (1909b, 1918), the crucial early events (castration threat, primal scene) are never remembered but only reconstructed. The overcoming of resistances and the lifting of repression through the psychoanalytic process do not lead to the emergence of early experiences and conflicts in their original form but, at best, as less distorted derivatives. Most of this has become standard analytic theory, but I have tried here to demonstrate that most of it already was part of the seduction theory in 1896, even though Freud did not explicitly recognize or acknowledge this at the time.

LATER VICISSITUDES OF THE SEDUCTION THEORY (1905–1933)

There is a wide gap between the seduction theory of 1896 and Freud's account of it in 1933. We have to look at some of the intermediate steps (1905b, 1906, 1914b, 1917, 1925c). The revisions were only gradual; the reasons given for them and the references to the original theory are changing, incomplete, and far from consistent. They always reflect Freud's dominant interests at the time each was written—a good example of the constant reworking of the past in the light of the present.

The passages of 1905 and 1906 were written practically at the same time and are, of course, very similar, except that the second one is much more detailed. All of the points had already been mentioned, although sometimes only very cryptically, in the letters to Fliess of 1897. In 1905, we learn that, although actual seductions are not infrequent, they are no longer required "to arouse a child's sexual life"—specifically, his autoerotic activity; this occurs spontaneously as part of the biological maturation of infantile sexuality. The most relevant passage of 1905 is revealingly ambiguous and ambivalent: Referring to actual seductions, Freud (1905b) states:

> I cannot admit that in my paper on the "Aetiology of Hysteria" I exaggerated the frequency or importance of that influence, though I did not then know that persons who remain normal may have had the same experience in their childhood [but he did know it, and said it then! See 1896c, pp. 209–211], and though I consequently overrated the importance of seduction [how does this fit with the beginning of the sentence?] in comparison with the factors of sexual constitution and development. Obviously seduction is not required in order to arouse a child's sexual life; that can also come about spontaneously from internal causes. (pp. 190–191)

This main conclusion is repeated and clarified in 1906: "the 'traumatic' element in the sexual experiences of childhood lost its importance…infantile sexual activity (whether spontaneous or provoked) prescribes the direction that will be taken by later sexual life after maturity" (p. 274). Seductions in childhood occur in people who remain normal as well as in neurotics: "Thus it was no longer a question of what sexual experiences a particular individual had had in his childhood, but rather of his reaction to these experiences—of whether he reacted to them by 'repression' or not" (pp. 276–277).

Freud's stated reasons for correcting his earlier conclusions show the same unclarity and ambiguity as the 1905 statement. He says that he may have overestimated the frequency of actual seduction because of his small and maybe atypical sample of cases, "though in other respects they [the events] were not open to doubt"; this seems to imply that he did not doubt the actual occurrence of seduction in his sample and only questioned the generalization of this finding. But then in the very next sentence, he admits (as he had in the September 1897 letters) that he could not distinguish distortions from traces of real events in the memories of his patients.

He concludes that he was dealing with unconscious fantasies, "mostly produced during the years of puberty" and "built up out and over the childhood memories"; fantasies of seduction are "attempts at fending off memories of the subject's own sexual activity (infantile masturbation)" (p. 274). The basic factual reality of the infantile past was the child's autoerotic activity, not the external seduction (although this could occur as an intensifying factor). The repressed fantasies from puberty are inserted between the activity of childhood and the adult symptoms. This formulation, too, goes back to the 1897 letters; what is more interesting is that Freud kept it in his later accounts until 1925.*

But long before this he had stated, in other contexts, that oedipal fantasies originate in childhood and are not just the retroactive cover-up for the shame of an early objectless masturbation. This may be another example of how Freud never completely discarded his earlier ideas as his thinking evolved. Here, and on many other occasions, Freud compared these later fantasies to the legends and myths of nations which contain remnants of a now unacceptable historical truth, extensively transformed to meet the needs of the present. But how much is it possible or necessary for psychoanalysis to separate out the components of original historical truth from their later transformations? It seems that Freud could never settle this issue to his satisfaction; it remains very alive in psychoanalysis to this day.

In 1914, an important new element is that Freud (1914b) claims to have been misled by "the statements made by patients in which *they ascribed* their symptoms to passive sexual experiences in the first years of childhood—to put it bluntly to seduction" (p. 17; italics added). Here, for the first time, Freud clearly claims that the patients directly provided the evidence for the seductions and connected them with their symptoms; he comes close to blaming his error on his credulity toward his patients. The second new aspect is that Freud uses the concept of psychic reality in reference to the patient's statements:

> If hysterical subjects trace back their symptoms to traumas that are fictitious, then the new fact which emerges is precisely that they create such scenes in phantasy, and this psychical reality requires to be taken into account alongside practical reality. (pp. 17–18)

It is probably not a coincidence that directly attributing the fantasies of seduction to statements of the patients occurs for the first time in the same context as the reference to psychic reality. Here, the immediate psychic

* Yet the concept of retroactive fantasies, once it had been used by Jung to minimize the role of childhood in present pathology, became anathema to Freud, and the case study, "From the History of an Infantile Neurosis" (1918), is an attempt to refute such a concept. Yet, it is in this case that one finds the only explicit clinical illustration, as far as I know, of the idea of unconscious fantasies from a later age covering memories of earlier unacceptable events (pp. 19–28). The Wolf Man's repetitive dreams of forcefully undressing his sister are interpreted by Freud as the disguised expression of adolescent fantasies with similar content, which Freud then connects with the patient's recollection of having been passively seduced by his older sister at around age 3. The later fantasies "were meant to efface the memory of an event which later on seemed offensive to the patient's masculine self-esteem" (p. 20). Here the dreams are interpreted as derived from adolescent fantasies, and it is the memories that refer to the actual seduction in childhood; yet in most instances, Freud uses the interpretation of dreams as the best evidence for the experiences of early childhood (e.g., the Wolf Man dream and the primal scene) and assumes that early memories are screen memories, which also have to be interpreted rather than taken literally.

reality is the fact that the patients have created and directly expressed such fantasies or memories, regardless of their objective truth. But in other contexts, Freud makes clear that the true psychic reality is that of unconscious fantasies, which can only be inferred through the analyst's interpretation of their indirect and disguised manifestations. In 1914, the fantasies are still explained as a later cover-up and embellishment of the autoerotic activity of early childhood. No mention is made of the central role of the father, of the Oedipus complex, and of primal fantasies.

In "The Paths to Symptom-Formation," Freud (1917) gives a detailed discussion of his revised etiologic formulations. With direct reference to the seduction theory, Freud states that "childhood experiences constructed or remembered in analysis are...in most cases compounded of truth and falsehood" (p. 367). He mentions for the first time that girls "fairly regularly" blame the father as a seducer. This is still described as a way of hiding shame about masturbation by "retrospectively fantasying an object into these earliest times" (p. 370). But the main emphasis has shifted to the relevance of psychic reality for the understanding of neurosis and the role of universal primal fantasies.

The summary of 1925 for the first time clearly places the father at the center of the seduction fantasy, which becomes an expression of the universal Oedipus complex. This account is also somewhat more in keeping with the original presentation of 1896; Freud states that the patients "reproduced" scenes of seduction under the pressure of his technical procedure, and wonders whether he may have forced these scenes upon them. But he concludes that "it could not be disputed that I had arrived at these scenes by a technical method which I considered correct, and their subject-matter was unquestionably related to the symptoms from which my investigation has started" (1925c, p. 34). This is the same argument we found in 1896: namely, that the content of the scenes is required for a logical and consistent explanation of the present symptoms.

Finally, the brief and trenchant statement of 1933, already quoted, also centers around the father and the Oedipus complex, and, as in 1914 only, attributes the evidence completely to the patients' statements:

> Almost all my women patients told me that they had been seduced by their father...It was only later that I was able to recognize in this phantasy of being seduced by the father the expression of the typical Oedipus complex in women. (p. 120)

I think the most remarkable aspect of Freud's successive accounts of the seduction theory is that only by 1914 is the evidence for the early seductions clearly attributed to the patients' direct statements, and only by 1925 do we learn that the theory always involved the father. The seduction theory that Freud repudiated in 1925 and 1933 gave a central role to the father; yet such a theory had never actually appeared in print because, as we have seen, the 1896 papers made no specific reference to the father. What Freud repudiated was his private version of the seduction theory, the one he alluded to in his letters to Fliess, from December 1896 to December 1897.

CONCLUSIONS

I have presented detailed evidence to show that Freud's later accounts of the seduction theory (particularly in 1914 and 1933) are widely discrepant from the way he initially presented it. From Freud's writings of 1896, we may assume that many of his patients related stories of incestuous relations in childhood with a member of the household, sometimes the father but more often an older brother. They also "reproduced" and enacted something that Freud interpreted as the original seduction. From this, guided by his hypotheses, Freud concluded (in his letters to Fliess more than 6 months after the public presentation of his theory) that the original trauma had to be seduction by the father.

My main argument has been that the knowledge of this original trauma, whether considered as unconscious memory or fantasy, was based on Freud's interpretation and reconstruction; it was not directly revealed by the patient. Despite Freud's later statements of 1914 and 1933, this view is far more plausible and consistent with the original texts and the bulk of Freud's writings after 1896, particularly about the reconstructed rather than remembered basis of the knowledge of the crucial early past. Of course, the issue cannot be settled with complete certainty because we will never know the exact nature of the original data provided by the patients.

I think that the authors who state that, by changing the seduction theory, Freud neglected or suppressed firm and clear evidence should first take a closer look at the evidence and inference on which the theory was based. If one wishes to speculate on these matters, it may be more relevant to consider first the motives, personal and theoretical, that influenced Freud in his construction of the seduction theory. One may also wonder why, in 1896, Freud presented his data in an ambiguous and inconsistent fashion, and why he saw them as much clearer and stronger ("almost all my women patients told me...") once they had become evidence for universal oedipal fantasies rather than proof of the past misdeeds of some individual fathers.

The clarification attempted here also reveals a far greater continuity than is usually assumed between the major aspects of Freud's thinking before and after the "abandonment" of the seduction theory. Reconstruction and interpretation already played a major part in the original theory, as did the role of internal psychological factors through the concept of the deferred action of unconscious memories leading to later conflict and repression. While the assumption of the occurrence of the initial trauma in early childhood was a necessary part of the etiological formulation of 1896, this trauma by itself did not predetermine or account for the ultimate outcome; the external trauma was only the starting point ("the source of the Nile," to use Freud's metaphor) of a lengthy and complex process which could eventually lead to neurosis. Conflict and repression, too, were indispensable factors from the beginning; in the evolution of Freud's thinking, their role soon became more crucial than that of the material reality of the initial trauma.

From early on, Freud's hypotheses were dominated by a search for uniform types of traumas and conflicts which would apply to all neuroses. The switch to the psychic reality of oedipal fantasies, anchored to the biological aspects of infantile sexuality, allowed Freud to maintain his core conclusion about the central role of the father and disposed of the objection of the improbability of the chance occurrence of the same actual event in all cases (all fathers are perverts). His conclusion could now even be promoted from a necessary etiologic factor in neurosis to a major universal aspect of human development and functioning. But it was no longer the actual father of the individual case but more a "prehistoric, unforgettable other person who is never equaled by any one later" (1892–1899, p. 239).

In the spring of 1896, Freud believed he had discovered a causal theory of neurosis: his "neurotica." It rested on the assumption of a real external trauma, sexual seduction in early childhood, which soon became even more specific—namely, seduction by the father, usually occurring between the ages of 3 and 6. Freud had doubts about his theory from the beginning, and finally these doubts prevailed. Yet he never quite gave up the hope of discovering "the source of the Nile"—the primal event in external reality which would provide a firm material ground for his etiologic formulation.

The same struggle was repeated between 1914 and 1917 (approximately) in the search for the reality of the "primal scene," instead of the primal seduction, in the Wolf Man case. The same issues recur (including the concept of delayed action)—only the chronological time span is different. Freud tries hard to convince the reader and himself of the factual reality of the primal scene, in all its specific details. However, we see him doubting his own arguments in the very process of stating them and finally rather reluctantly settling for the concept of the psychic reality of primal fantasies.

With this switch to psychic reality and universal primal fantasies, new problems arose. Could unconscious fantasies be true etiologic agents? Did psychic reality imply a kind of psychic causality, different from chronological linear causal sequences in material reality? What role did actual events play in determining the content and influence of fantasies? Freud does not seem to have been fully willing to accept and elaborate the implications of his emphasis on psychic reality. As a nineteenth century positivist, he believed that mental processes had only a kind of borrowed reality, which had to be grounded ultimately on material events and processes as the only true reality (bodily stimulation by the mother in infancy, prehistoric events, physiological basis of drives, etc.).

A second set of problems is that universal fantasies and conflicts cannot by themselves provide a specific explanation of a particular type of pathology or an understanding of the individual case. In principle, it is not difficult to assume, as Freud does, that individual differences in constitutional factors as well as external environmental events will account for individual variations, normal and pathological, in the specific manifestations of universal factors. But, at the level of clinical data, how is it possible to assess individual differences in constitutional factors, such as the strength of particular components of the libido or of inherited primal fantasies? In most cases, these factors seem to serve as a kind of *deus ex machina*, invoked when no specific explanation is available.

In evaluating the role of individual life events, it seems essential to distinguish the period of infancy and early childhood from later periods, when continuous recall and narrative have become possible (roughly after the age of 6 to 8). For the earliest period, the analyst has to rely on reconstruction and have some faith in his ability to separate out the role of external events from the way they were perceived and selectively transformed by the individual at the time and later on. This is precisely what Freud (1918) reluctantly concluded he could not do. For later periods and for the patient's present life, we do not usually question the basic factual nature, the material reality of the events a patient is reporting—even while assuming that his narrative is incomplete and distorted (especially when it comes to the causes, motives, and consequences he attributes to these events). These two different levels of data and of interpretation are already evident in Freud's seduction theory of 1896 and persist in his later formulations (1917, as the most comprehensive example).

The seduction theory assumed two stages: a predisposition created by a specific sexual trauma in early childhood and a later event, highly variable in content and traumatic force, occurring after puberty and leading to conflict, repression, and symptom formation. As I tried to show, the data of this second stage may be retrieved as specific recollections and memories, but the original infantile trauma is only reconstructed. It manifests itself through various "reproductions" induced in the treatment situation. This two-stage process is also found in Freud's later formulation of 1917: Here, too, we have a "disposition (fixation of the libido)," acquired in early childhood, and then the later adult or postpubertal experiences, which trigger the neurosis. The main difference is that in the first theory the "reproduction" and reconstruction refer to a veridical actual event, whereas in the second theory they have become an inner-determined fantasy, schema, or scenario, to which external events have contributed to a variable and essentially unspecifiable degree. Despite these differences, there seems to be a clear continuity between the early and later theories: In both cases the crucial early past is not recollected, but rather inferred and reconstructed as individual variations on a small number of universal themes or scenarios. By contrast, the data from later years are much more variable, detailed, and individualized, and they are based largely on the narrative and retrieved memories of the patient.

What specific role was left for external environmental factors in development and etiology? To what extent can and must psychoanalysis be able to recover the external facts of the early past as they once occurred? These seem to be the basic, lasting questions raised by the seduction theory. Such issues are still unsettled and remain relevant for many trends in contemporary psychoanalysis, particularly those that put heavy emphasis on the etiologic role of cumulative external traumas and acquired deficits, presumably dating from a very early preverbal period, which are reconstructed through the interpretation of the transference. A critical review of Freud's concepts of unconscious fantasy, psychic and material reality, and their developments in contemporary psychoanalysis is a necessary task—one quite beyond the scope of this chapter. My reexamination of the seduction theory only attempts to provide a needed introduction to such a larger goal.

Chapter 8

The interpretations of the past

Childhood trauma, psychical reality, and historical truth*

A well-known milestone in the development of Freud's thought is his relinquishing the belief in the factual reality of the sexual traumas which he had previously come to view as the universal cause of later neurotic symptoms. What had been unconscious memories of actual past events became fantasies expressing unconscious infantile wishes.

My main intent in this chapter is to take a closer look at this fundamental change in the evolution of Freud's thinking. I will try to show that one is not dealing with clear and settled issues of only historical interest. Freud did not resolve these issues when he first announced this change in 1906: They went through many reformulations and continued to preoccupy him until his very last writings.

After dealing with Freud's initial theory and the shift from actual childhood trauma to childhood fantasies (essentially 1896b, 1896c, 1898a, 1899, 1900, 1905a, 1906), I will consider later developments, particularly the concepts of "psychical reality" and "historical truth." Finally, I discuss some of the relevance of these issues for contemporary thought, particularly in regard to the nature of psychoanalytic interpretations and the kind of reality that they unearth or construct.

Two sets of factors seemed, in combination, to have played a determining role in Freud's changing approaches to these problems: first, a personal and clinical orientation, which may be called "the great father theme," to use Erikson's (1956) expression; second, Freud's commitment to a certain model of science and causal explanation that forced him to struggle to reduce the results of a method of interpretation—one that dealt essentially with relationships of meaning mediated by symbolic and linguistic processes—to causal mechanistic links between factual events and forces associated with them.

* This chapter originally appeared in the *Journal of the American Psychoanalytic Association*, 23(4), 1975, pp. 845–865. Reprinted with permission.

HISTORICAL TRUTH AND FREUD'S PATRIARCHAL FATHER

Freud gave five successive accounts of the change in his views about the reality of infantile sexual traumas (the first in 1897, in a letter to Fliess, and four published ones in 1906, 1914, 1925, and 1933). Let us take the last and shortest account as a starting point for our examination:

> In the period in which the main interest was directed to discovering infantile sexual traumas, almost all my women patients told me that they had been seduced by their father. I was driven to recognize in the end that these reports were untrue and so came to understand that hysterical symptoms are derived from phantasies and not from real occurrences. It was only later that I was able to recognize in this phantasy of being seduced by the father the expression of the typical Oedipus complex in women. (1933, p. 120)

Freud's first sentence clearly states that the earlier theory was based on direct empirical evidence—namely, almost all female patients "told" him that they had been seduced by their fathers. Most of his other published accounts of the change carry the same implication. But a close look at Freud's presentation of the original theory (1896b, 1896c) shows clearly that this is not the case. The majority of his female patients did not report conscious memories of seduction, but merely memories, thoughts, and symptoms that Freud interpreted as the disguised and indirect manifestation of an infantile sexual trauma. In other words, we are dealing with inferred, unconscious repressed memories of seduction that are related to the patient's conscious production, much as the latent is to the manifest content of a dream. Referring to such childhood traumas, Freud (1896b) writes that "their traces are never present in conscious memory, only in the symptoms of the illness" (p. 166).

Freud's description of the method by which these unconscious memories were constructed is very similar to that of dream interpretation, which he was beginning to formulate at the time and described 3 years later—a similarity so striking that it was noted by Strachey (1896c, p. 199n). In the 1896 paper on the etiology of hysteria, as part of a lengthy and somewhat labored attempt to prove the genuineness and freedom from suggestion of the experiences from which he inferred the infantile trauma, Freud (1896c) even stated:

> While they [his patients] are recalling these infantile experiences to consciousness, they suffer under the most violent sensations, of which they are ashamed and which they try to conceal; and, even after they have gone through them once more in such a convincing manner, they

> still attempt to withhold belief from them, by emphasizing the fact that, unlike what happens in the case of other forgotten material, they have no feeling of remembering the scenes. (p. 204)

So even then, the supposed seduction was reenacted, rather than remembered, in a way that suggests a transference phenomenon: the readiness of Freud's female patients to experience his unrelenting and penetrating pressure to reveal their hidden memories as a seduction, or at least an encouragement to enact in thinly disguised form their wish to be seduced by a parental figure. Freud's attitude certainly did not create this seduction wish, but his method was hardly a neutral and unbiased one; with a strong need to justify and find evidence for his growing intuitive conviction of the crucial role of early childhood events and infantile sexuality (Sadow et al., 1968), he actively searched out and selectively interpreted his data. The basic proof of his reconstructions was in the fact that they were able to make sense out of neurotic symptoms and give them a consistent meaning.

The point I want to stress is that Freud's doubts about his "neurotica" and the later changes he made in his formulations do not involve the question of the accuracy or objectivity of the patient's conscious memories, but rather that of the factual basis of Freud's interpretations and explanations. Nowhere does he question his conclusions about unconscious infantile experiences as the universal basis of neurotic symptoms or the technique by which he reached these conclusions. The question for him was whether these inferred unconscious contents were the direct reflection of actual external trauma, or, if not, what their origin was and what kind of a reality they did have.

His initial answer, the attempt to explain neurotic symptoms as the delayed causal effects of real external trauma, is very much in keeping with the intellectual and conceptual framework in which his scientific thinking was grounded. Freud (1914b) states that he was influenced by "Charcot's view of the traumatic origin of hysteria" (p. 17). More broadly speaking, he seems to have been influenced by his neurological training, which would predispose him to seek a causal explanation of present impairment and symptoms in terms of earlier lesions or traumas. Furthermore, it is likely that his implicit cognitive psychology—which essentially reflects the association psychology dominant in his time—also favored his initial belief that memories were simply a registration or copy of actual past events. It led, as well, to an implicit dichotomy between what is external, factual, and objective and what is internal, psychical, and subjective.

It is time to consider some of the reasons why Freud found it difficult to hold on to his initial solution. As I have implied, his early theory of neurosis was not an empirical finding of the relatively high frequency of childhood seductions and their pathological effect on development, but an assertion that such traumas were the universal basis of later neurosis. It is precisely the difficulty of maintaining that all hysterics had actually been seduced by their fathers that Freud gave as one of the main reasons for abandoning the initial formulation. Even if actual seductions are not infrequent, how could a universal factor be based on accidental, contingent events of an individual's history? Thus, Freud did not give up the belief in the universality of childhood sexual experiences and their causal role in neurosis; on the contrary, he saw the need to base this universal factor on a firmer foundation than variable accidental events. How he dealt with the question of the origin of such universal fantasies will be considered later.

Neither Freud's neurotica of 1896 nor its abandonment can be fully accounted for on purely conceptual grounds or by changes in his clinical material. Deep aspects of his own conflicts and the development of his self-analysis, following shortly upon the death of his father, were involved. The details remain in darkness or shaky speculation, but we have enough clues—particularly through the Fliess correspondence—to get a sense of the dominant issues (Erikson, 1956; Jones, 1953). In the famous letter to Fliess of September 21, 1897 (Freud, 1892–1899, p. 259), he first rejected his neurotica; other letters of the same period prove that this coincides with the height of his self-analysis, including the understanding of his own "hysterical" symptoms and the discovery of his Oedipus complex.

In his later published accounts (particularly the already quoted statement of 1933), Freud implies that it is the recognition of the fantasy basis of infantile seduction that opened the way for the discovery of the Oedipus complex. But this sounds somewhat like a rationalized explanation, a reversal of the actual sequence. It seems more likely that it is Freud's discovery of his own Oedipus complex (as well as a growing awareness of the primarily transference aspects of the seduction scenes his patients were enacting) that led him to believe he was dealing with universal fantasies rather than actual seductions.

I shall take this main point for granted and concentrate on some aspects only. Freud himself alludes to at least one personal oedipal motive behind his seduction theory. In a letter to Fliess in May 1897, he interprets one of his own dreams as an expression of "over-affectionate feelings" toward his daughter, and he rejoices in the fact that the dream shows "the fulfillment of my wish to catch a father as the originator of neurosis" (pp. 253–254) and thus seems to confirm his seduction theory.

Insofar as Freud's first rejection of his theory coincides with the discovery of his own Oedipus complex, it is likely that his awareness of the hostile wish to blame the father may have contributed to his rejection of the seduction theory. In a revealing passage of the crucial letter of September 1897, he lists some of the reasons for his doubts about the seduction theory and writes, "Then came surprise at the fact that in every case the father, not excluding my own [words omitted in the first published edition of the letters] had to be blamed as a pervert" (p. 259).

From its beginnings, the issue of the kind of reality and universality that could be attributed to the unconscious past was for Freud closely tied up with the central role of the patriarchal father. His continued attempts to deal with this question by introducing the concept of "historical truth" and inherited memories of prehistoric events (to be considered in more detail later) also contain as their main theme the dominance and eventual murder of the primeval father as the basis of religion and civilization. Furthermore, even in the clinical theory, the father continued in many ways to be "the originator of neurosis"—no longer by inducing childhood sexual traumas, but by being the ultimate originator of many of the pathological defenses that force normal childhood sexuality into symptomatic outlets. Defenses are necessary because of the demands of reality and the prohibitions of the superego; however, behind these, we see primarily the shadow of the patriarchal father. In all of this, the child's needy and affectionate relation to the father, especially in its pre-oedipal aspects, is underplayed, if not ignored.*

One of the final revisions of the seduction theory, late in Freud's life, gives us another facet of the issue. In the context of his extended presentation of female psychosexual development (1933), he concludes that the seduction fantasy of the little girl "touches the ground of reality" by referring to the real libidinal stimulation provided by the mother's bodily care of the child. Interestingly, this new clinical formulation is already implied and illustrated in Freud's report of his self-analysis, 36 years earlier! In a letter to Fliess in October 1897, following by 2 weeks the letter in which Freud announced the rejection of his neurotica, he reports, referring to his childhood nurse, "the 'prime originator' was a woman, ugly, elderly, but clever, who told me a great deal about God Almighty and Hell and who gave me a high opinion of my own capacities" (Freud, 1892–1899, p. 261).

In the same letter, he adds, "[T]he old woman provided me at such an early age with the means for living and going on living" (p. 262). But she was also a thief and used Freud as an innocent accomplice. Freud goes on to relate a dream about her in which "[s]he was my teacher in sexual matters and scolded me for being clumsy and not being able to do anything... Besides this, she washed me in reddish water in which she had previously washed herself" (Freud, 1892–1899, pp. 262–263). Here we have an actual seduction, but by a woman, an essentially pre-oedipal mother who gives basic nurturance and support, but is also a dangerous seductress who deceives, humiliates, dirties, and fosters false beliefs.

It is not necessary to document Freud's general tendency to give greater emphasis and value to activity, masculinity, father, and the oedipal

* The analytic literature of the last 20 years, stressing the prime importance of the early pre-oedipal relation to the mother, has more than corrected this one-sided emphasis. But the pre-oedipal father does not seem to have yet clearly emerged in psychoanalytic theory, despite the fact that in our contemporary middle-class culture, he assumes a much greater share of child care than in the Victorian family of Freud's days.

constellation—in contrast to passivity, femininity, mother, and pre-oedipal stages, viewed more as precursors or deviations from what is essential and prototypical. But we can also sense the extent to which this emphasis may have had a defensive and adaptive aspect for Freud personally and also highlighted the growth-furthering aspects of the oedipal stage in human development generally. For the image of the oedipal father also stands for objectivity, autonomy, and individuation, the source of sublimation and "higher" cultural aims. He is the powerful protector against the regressive seduction of a passive and merged relationship to the pre-oedipal mother and all the dangerous illusions of omnipotence and security that such a relationship seems to symbolize in much of Freud's thought (Jones, 1953; Loewald, 1951).

THE SOURCE AND ORIGIN OF UNCONSCIOUS FANTASIES

When Freud first announced to Fliess in September 1897 that he no longer believed in his neurotica, he added that he was in no hurry to proclaim the news in the land of the Philistines. It was indeed to be 9 years before he did.* Even more significant than this long delay is that the issue remained very much alive and unresolved for Freud and continued to preoccupy him until the end of his life. It is these further developments that I wish to consider now.

To account for how memories become distorted and provide the content of later conscious fantasies or screen memories was not a problem, of course. The mechanisms of the primary process and the censorship provided a specific explanation, already spelled out in *The Interpretation of Dreams* and the paper on screen memories (1899). The main questions for Freud remained the source and origin of unconscious fantasies, the kind of reality that could be attributed to them, and the justification of the universality of their basic contents. Starting in 1913, Freud seems to have coined the concept of "psychical reality" specifically to deal with this problem. The factual reality of unconscious memories was replaced by the psychical reality of unconscious fantasies. This is the way Freud summed up the change in his formulation of 1914 and in several later presentations (1917, 1925c). "The phantasies possess psychical as contrasted with material reality, and we gradually learn to understand that in the world of the neuroses it is psychical reality which is the decisive kind" (1917, p. 368).

* In the meantime, we find an article (1898a) that still includes the old formulations, unchanged; a footnote in the first edition of *The Interpretation of Dreams* (1900), where the change is incidentally mentioned for the first time in print (interestingly, in the context of Freud's interpretation of the Count Thun dream, dealing primarily with rebellion and defiance of fathers' authority); and a brief ambiguous sentence in the *Three Essays* (1905a, p. 140).

This basic distinction between factual and psychical reality implies more than the tautology that fantasies refer to the world of personal and subjective experience rather than to an objective and veridical picture of the external world. For Freud, unlike current usage, the construct of psychical reality is not simply synonymous with immediate subjective experience, in a phenomenological sense. One of the most explicit definitions of psychical reality was given by Freud in 1914: "If we look at unconscious wishes brought to their ultimate and truest expression, we shall have to conclude, no doubt, that psychical reality is a particular form of existence not to be confused with material reality" (p. 620, third edition of *The Interpretation of Dreams,* translation mine). Freud adds in the same passage that such a reality "must of course be denied to any transitional or intermediate thoughts." Psychical reality is the reality of basic unconscious wishes and fantasies "brought to their ultimate and truest expression" through the interpretive and reconstructive activity of the analyst. The individual's conscious thoughts and fantasies have only a borrowed reality, insofar as they are the incomplete, distorted, and transient derivative of the basic unconscious wishes that constitute psychical reality.

But from where do unconscious fantasies acquire their reality, if not from external events? How can the assumed universality of their basic contents be accounted for? In the *Introductory Lectures,* Freud (1917) asks:

> Whence comes the need for these phantasies and the material for them? There can be no doubt that their sources lie in the instincts; but it has still to be explained why the same phantasies with the same content are created on every occasion. I am prepared with an answer which I know will seem daring to you. I believe those primal phantasies, as I should like to call them, and no doubt a few others as well, are a phylogenetic endowment. (pp. 370–371)

Freud repeated and elaborated this answer in the clinical discussion of the Wolf Man, written at about the same time, and in several other writings ranging from *Totem and Taboo* (1913) to *Moses and Monotheism* (1939). We are not dealing with the kind of incidental speculation that Freud occasionally indulged in (for instance, that women may have invented weaving to hide their lack of a penis), but rather with a central aspect of the conceptual structure of his theory.*

* The significance for Freud of the idea of inherited cognitive contents and schemata cannot be reduced to the need both to assimilate and to repudiate some of Jung's views—even though these clearly influenced the timing and the content of Freud's first writings on the subject. It is also true that Freud, in response to Jung's emphasis on the collective unconscious at the expense of individual childhood experience, stressed that the analyst, in his clinical work, must concern himself first and foremost with the specific individualized aspects of a patient's fantasies, rather than with their core of universality.

First we note that the problem has been extended from the issues of seduction to include "all these events of childhood [that] are somehow demanded as a necessity" as "among the essential elements of a neurosis" (1917, p. 370), as well as universal aspects of psychosexual development (seduction, primal scene, castration threat, Oedipus complex—with even the earliest relation to the mother as a belated addition to the list).

This does not justify, however, the way the implications of Freud's formulations about primal fantasies have been minimized or ignored in most of the psychoanalytic literature (the Kleinians being a conspicuous exception).

We may well ask ourselves why Freud chose such a solution, why he had to hold fast to the belief in real events, even if they had to be pushed back to some nebulous prehistoric past. Why did he not rest content with the first part of his answer—the one that most psychoanalytic writers seem to have taken for granted, somewhat uncritically—that the sources of unconscious fantasy "no doubt lie in the instincts." After all, instincts have by definition a biological reality and universality; if they can be the source of fantasies, they can also account for the universality of their basic contents. I would like to show briefly that such an answer is unsatisfactory, as Freud seems to have been implicitly aware; it merely takes the problem back to the nature and origin of instinctual drives and the ambiguity of Freud's definition of them.

The question is how a drive can create the original contents of a fantasy? The answer obviously depends on the definition of drive. Instinctual drive is a "borderland" concept—"the psychical representative of the stimuli originating from within the organism and reaching the mind" (1915b, p. 122). Depending on the context, Freud stresses either the psychical or the organic aspects of this dual definition (pp. 111–113). If an instinct is already a "psychical representative," it is in effect equated with the contents of an unconscious wish or fantasy; this merely rephrases the question of how organic stimuli create mental contents or become represented by them.

But the view that Freud started out with (e.g., in the 1895 *Project*), even before his major clinical discoveries and which remained dominant in most of his theoretical formulations, is that of drive as a quantity of displaceable energy seeking discharge by the quickest path available and cathecting the memory images of the external objects that had provided discharge as an experience of satisfaction. A drive energy does not, by itself, create a mental or cognitive content. This content is provided by the perception of the object that made possible the experience of satisfaction, the memory of which becomes the cathected psychical representative of the drive—a wish for the reappearance of the object or situation associated with the experience of satisfaction.

This formulation of drives acquiring psychical representation as wishes rests on the assumption of an actual experience of satisfaction, a real event; if we can no longer postulate such an event, the whole theory is left in the lurch. Freud's concept of instinctual drive cannot account for the original mental contents of the unconscious (Wolff, 1967), unless drives are already defined as synonymous with such contents as object-seeking wishes rather than displaceable quantities of energy or somatic needs. Within Freud's conceptual structure, the contents of psychical reality had to remain grounded on some factual events, just as psychic energy had to have its causal origin in somatic neurological processes. The hypothesis of inherited memories was a way of grounding the contents of universal fantasies on actual events—in the history of the race, if no longer that of a specific individual.

It is worth taking a further look at Freud's elaboration of how these inherited memories combine with memories of actual events to produce the contents of unconscious fantasies. In a remarkable passage at the end of the Wolf Man case, Freud (1918) described these inherited elements as

> phylogenetically inherited schemata, which, like the categories of philosophy, are concerned with the business of "placing" the impressions derived from actual experience. I am inclined to take the view that they are precipitates from the history of human civilization. The Oedipus complex, which comprises a child's relation to his parents, is one of them—is, in fact, the best known member of the class. Wherever experiences fail to fit in with the hereditary schema, they become remodeled in the imagination. (p. 119)

On the following page, Freud goes on to speculate that even the youngest child may have "a hardly definable knowledge, something, as it were, preparatory to an understanding," maybe analogous to "the far-reaching instinctive knowledge of animals." Here we have at least the suggestion of a formulation rather different from Freud's usual conception of drives and their relation to cognition and behavior. What is inherited is not so much specific memory contents but schemata, which, like Kantian categories, have no fixed contents, but act as selective organizers of the data of immediate experience to give them some predetermined configuration and overall meaning.

The nucleus of the unconscious includes an instinctual knowledge as a way of relating to selective aspects of the environment (e.g., the Oedipus complex as "a child's relation to his parents"), a predisposition to acquire certain patterns of acting and reacting to specific classes of objects and situations. In its core content, psychical reality is created by such schemata, which make use of whatever material accidental individual experience provides (for instance, the observation of animal copulation can provide material for the primal scene fantasy [1918] or, as mentioned earlier, the reality of a mother's bodily care of the infant can play the same role in relation to the primal fantasy of seduction by the father). Unlike unconscious wishes, which acquire their contents from memories of actual events and their cathexes from actual experiences of satisfaction, these inherited schemata are not derived from individual experience, nor is their determining influence in shaping basic wishes and motive accounted for by the process of drive discharge. The "remodeling" of experience to fit certain schemata does not readily fit a causal mechanistic model and seems a different process from the subjective distortion of memories through the primary-process displacements of drive energy.

In Freud's dominant metapsychology, drives as blind energy seeking discharge can acquire content, structure, and consistency only through being shaped by the environment's providing experiences of satisfaction or unpleasure—by reinforcement contingencies, as a behaviorist would say. Whatever in Freud's genetic principles cannot be reduced to associationism, conditioning, and biology rests ultimately on some idea of an epigenetic unfolding of inherited schemata. The idea of inherited schemata shaping from the start the data of experience is very close to much of contemporary structuralist thought. However, we would add that these schemata are not fixed and rigid, but are themselves remodeled by experience (e.g., Erikson's concept of modes and social modalities and Piaget's principle of a constant interplay between assimilation and accommodation).

But let us go on with our main story as reflected in Freud's last writings. In *Moses and Monotheism* (1939), Freud again argues that, while the idea of a single god and the stories of religion lack "material truth," they do have "historical truth" in the unconscious universal memory of a primeval father. In the last pages of this essay, he concludes with the general statement:

> We must finally make up our minds to adopt the hypothesis that the psychical precipitates of the primaeval period became inherited property which, in each fresh generation, called not for acquisition but only for awakening. In this we have in mind the example of what is certainly the "innate" symbolism which derives from the period of the development of speech, which is familiar to all children without their being instructed, and which is the same among all peoples despite their different languages. (p. 132)*

In a more clinical paper of the same period, "Constructions in Analysis" (1937), Freud seems to be pulled back to some of his earliest formulations. He states that the quasihallucinatory vividness of certain memories as well as the compulsive belief in delusions is due to the core of historical truth

* This passage shows that the same issues discussed here in relation to the origin of unconscious fantasy also apply to the origins of symbolism as a basic primitive language because, in both cases, the economic concepts of drive and primary process could not satisfactorily account for them.

they contain; however, here, this historical truth refers primarily to something actually "experienced in infancy and then forgotten." He suggests that the turning away from present reality in psychosis and in sleep allows the emergence of these original memories, presumably factual in their core, while wish fulfillment and defenses are only responsible for the distortion rather than the creation of their contents. This formulation is then extended to neurotics:

> Often enough, when a neurotic is led by an anxiety-state to expect the occurrence of some terrible event, he is in fact merely under the influence of a repressed memory (which is seeking to enter consciousness but cannot become conscious) that something which was at that time terrifying did really happen. (p. 268)

Freud adds that "our construction is only effective because it recovers a fragment of lost experience," and he then concludes with an explicit reference to his earliest statement of 1893 that hysterics are "suffering from their own reminiscences."

So the story seems to end. Freud started with the assumption that the analyst was unearthing unconscious memories of actual events, then only fantasies, then a psychical reality inherited from prehistoric events, and, finally, back to individual experiences that "did really happen."

FREUD'S PERSISTENT HOPE

It remains for us to take a critical look at some of the basic conceptual issues underlying Freud's persistent hope that analytic constructions can provide a picture of the past rooted in factual reality and his belief that the therapeutic effectiveness of interpretations rests on this core of recovered objective truth. "What we are in search of is a picture of the patient's forgotten years that shall be alike trustworthy and in all essential respects complete" (1937, p. 258).

The central paradox is a familiar one. The empirical foundation of the psychoanalytic approach is a method of interpretation, essentially of the verbal productions of an individual patient in a special interpersonal situation; this method reveals hidden meaning, consistency, and purpose in what seemed meaningless, accidental, and aimless. Yet, from the beginning to the end of his writings, Freud held to the aim of making psychoanalysis a natural science, on the model of the neurology and physiology of the nineteenth century. He wanted to equate the process of interpretation with a causal explanation based on the same method of inference about causal sequences that are fundamental to the natural sciences. The belief in the factual reality of the past was essential to such an undertaking; without it, the ground of reality was lost because fantasies are not suited to be etiological agents.

More generally, Freud's attempt to reduce interpretation to an objectified causal process rests ultimately on an implicit postulate about the relation of thoughts to external reality. Freud assumed that the contents of perceptions and thoughts, in their original form, are a direct reflection or copy of external objects and events, so the relation between one thought and another is, in principle, the same as the causal relation between one material event and another. This postulate is, of course, part of a very old epistemological tradition and is at the core of nineteenth century associationism and modern behaviorism.

The contents of the unconscious are grounded in the passive registration of external events, just as drive cathexes are grounded in biological processes and somatic needs. The later distortion of memory is explained by the displacement of energies and the inhibition of this distorting process by the demands of external reality. In such a scheme there is no need—indeed, no place—for psychical reality as a separate form of existence. The basic difficulty with such an approach is that it essentially ignores—by simply taking it for granted—the problem of how external events get represented, internalized, and symbolically mediated as memories and thoughts and how somatic needs or energies become psychological motives and reasons (see Chapter 10).

We may also ask—as a number of contemporary psychoanalysts have done—if it is possible or even necessary to reduce relations of meaning and logical implication within the realm of psychic reality to causal links between objectified external events. Can we have material causality directly applied to psychic reality, to the relation between one thought and another? Can we say that the meaning of the word, a symbol, a dream, is its cause? Does an object cause its mental representation, as image or concept?

Whatever our definition of causality, these relations are mediated by language and more generally by symbolic or semiotic processes; these imply rules and systems of transformation involving both universal structural aspects and individualized context-bound manifestations. Particularly relevant here is the study of the early and basic levels of language as symbolic representation in its connotative, metaphorical, and evocative aspects—rather than its later specialized level as a system of fixed, impersonal, and unambiguous denotations.

Once freed from the straightjacket of associationism and a certain model of causal explanation, one has no special difficulty in dealing with the fact that psychic reality—in the broad sense of individual experience in the nonreflective immediacy of concrete interactions—is the primary common matrix out of which both subjective and objective worlds get constructed and contrasted. Not only memories, as Freud assumed, but also the perception of immediate experience, far from being a passive camera-like registration, is selectively organized and given meaning by schemata, motives, and past experience. It is the factual, objective, impersonal description of reality that is the product of a lengthy construction, one that involves an interpersonal abstracting and conceptualizing process and is not merely the result of the inhibition of the distorting effect of drive discharge.

The dichotomy between factual reality and fantasy, despite its reassuring simplicity, may lead us into hopeless dead ends. It loses much of its relevance when childhood events are considered, not in terms of some adult "objective" construction of reality but in terms of the "actuality" (Erikson, 1962) of the child's world. For instance, the original reality of a childhood seduction can be an actual interaction with a parental figure, which the child, and sometimes the adult, perceived, experienced, and reacted to as a seduction—even if it did not meet some objective adult criteria of a deliberate sexual act. This is what is usually meant by psychic reality in contemporary psychoanalytic literature; however, as I tried to indicate, such a meaning cannot readily be fitted into Freud's conceptual structure, even if it expresses much of the spirit of his clinical approach.

In addition to a specific view of causality, the role that Freud gives to the past implies a second, more specifically psychoanalytic postulate. It is that even the remote past—whether factual or psychical in origin—remains preserved essentially intact in the present and therefore can act as an immediate causal agent of present behavior. Infantile experiences have been preserved by repression and thus function as a direct cause of present symptoms. This implies a kind of short-circuiting of what would otherwise be a lengthy time sequence where all the causal links would have to be filled in. Unconscious wishes and cathected memories of past events are synonymous for Freud. Clinically, this means that the reconstruction of the past and the search for the underlying unconscious motives of present behavior are essentially the same process.

Psychoanalytic interpretations and constructions do not aim at creating something new but try to bring out the past living in the buried depths of the present, as a kind of archeology. Interpretation becomes the undoing of the defensive distortions that have occurred from the depths to the surface manifestations. It is, to use Freud's familiar analogy, the deciphering of a rebus, merely the breaking of a code which hides an already stated and articulated message. By assuming that interpretation travels in the reverse of an already established path from latent to manifest, from past to present, Freud is trying to give it scientific justification as a causal procedure. But it is only the process of interpretation itself, from surface to depth, that provides the empirical basis for any inferred transformation process (e.g., the dream work) from depth to surface and the reconstruction of the unconscious past.

Maybe we have here what I would like to call the genetic fallacy (which, of course, is not limited to psychoanalysis, but is a danger in all developmental approaches, including that of transformational linguistics). Interpretation establishes similarities and common meanings between such seemingly disparate phenomena as symptoms, dreams, memories, and fantasies; it then constructs an explanatory model in terms of transformation processes (i.e., the dream work) of an inferred common kernel (i.e., the unconscious infantile wish) into manifold surface manifestations.

By genetic fallacy, I refer to the claim that such transformations actually describe a prior psychological reality in the mind of the patient or empirically retrace a genetic formative process in time, starting with an actual past event or original state as the ultimate cause of present conditions. Empirically, such reconstructions and models of formative processes refer to relations and regularities between present phenomena and can alter the meaning and influence of the present on future behavior; their validity need not rest on the claim that the past and its transformations once occurred as now conceptualized.

To be sure, Freud had the insight early on that psychoanalysis deals with the past only as psychical reality; consequently, the only directly relevant criterion for the validity of an interpretation is also a psychical one—namely, the patient's reaction to the interpretation and the degree to which it changes his psychical reality. Freud even occasionally questioned whether the repressed past still exists unchanged in the present: "[D]o the old wishes, about whose former existence analysis tells us, still exist?" He answers that maybe "the old wish is now operating only through its derivatives, having transferred the whole of its cathectic energy to them" with the possibility that "in the course of the neurosis it may have become reanimated by regression, anachronistic though it may now be. These are no idle speculations" (1926b, p. 142n).

Can analytic interpretations reconstruct the past as it once was? Freud's view could be contrasted with a concept of interpretation as the selective construction of new meanings, of broader and more abstract symbolic relationships between what previously existed only as patterns of actions or concrete imagery. Maybe the past exists only insofar as it has once helped shape the present and is in turn still constantly being reshaped and recreated by it, in ways that can be both repetitive and innovative (Viderman, 1970). What Freud (1899) said about conscious childhood memories—namely, that they are only memories "relating to our childhood," which do not simply reemerge in the present, but are "formed at that time"—should apply as well to the reconstruction of the past through the psychoanalytic process.

In our clinical work, we hope that the patient–analyst interaction will help the patient construct a new representation of his past, a more complete and integrated personal history, with a sense of continuity of the motives that make him an active agent in his present life, neither helpless nor omnipotent. And precisely to the extent that this new construction of the past is more objective and realistic, it cannot be a faithful duplicate of the past as it was originally lived or experienced. If we accept such a point of view, and I think most of us do (at least implicitly), we must face the fact that Freud's explanation and rationale for the process of interpretation are no longer adequate.

I cannot do justice to these questions here. But I believe that any reformulation will need to get away from the idea of a basic dichotomy between factual and psychical reality, with psychical reality located from the start in some unconscious inner space, a storage container of encapsulated memories energized by blind forces. Alternate approaches may begin by considering the unconscious level of behavior, not as mental contents, but as patterns of action, as preorganized ways of acting and reacting to specific classes of objects, without any mental representation beyond the level of immediate action. Such patterns could then acquire different levels of symbolic representation, from private imagery to conceptual thought, and thereby be modified in their effects and functioning. Although there is continuity and consistency between the earliest patterns of action and later patterns of fantasy and thought, this does not justify the assumption that the higher levels are already contained ready-made in the earlier ones, in an unconscious state.

One of Freud's seemingly most far-fetched ideas—that of inherited "schemata" remodeling the data of experience—may turn out to be a lasting and promising contribution. If modified to include the role of later experience in altering previous schemata, it may even provide the beginnings of a better model for the process of interpretation and insight—as the creation of new schemata, through the analytic interaction, which then remodel the data of experience, including the experience of the past. Before such an approach can be made directly relevant to our clinical data, there is a great need for a study of the process of interpretation itself, of the kinds of rules, logic, and transformation processes that the analyst uses in finding hidden meanings and constructing new connections—a topic singularly neglected in the psychoanalytic literature.

My aim in this chapter has not been an attempted reformulation of these problems. I have merely tried to demonstrate that an examination of some of their neglected historical roots in Freud's thought may provide a better understanding of the underlying issues and help us construct new solutions grounded in the past but not merely repeating it. Perhaps we only need to give a new interpretation to Freud's unshakable belief that "in the beginning was the Deed," and keep the hope that the psychoanalytic endeavor has something to do with transforming causes into meaning and reasons.

Even Freud's initial "seduction" theory deals with the past as reconstructed by the analyst, not as remembered by the patient. The changes in the belief in the factual reality of infantile traumas reflect the vicissitudes of "the great father theme" in Freud's self-analysis and clinical thought, as well as his lasting commitment to a certain model of causal explanation. The concept of a psychical reality created by instinctual drives was never a sufficient substitute for actual events. Aspects of human development that Freud considered basic and universal, such as the Oedipus complex, had to be grounded on prehistoric deeds, transmitted as universal inherited memories and phylogenetic "schemata."

Is it still possible or even necessary to assume that interpretations, like archaeology, aim at the recreation of the past as it once existed? Or that the creation of new meanings and relationships, mediated by different levels of symbolic and linguistic processes, can be reduced to a causal explanation on the model of natural science? Such questions point to the need for a new look at the actual process of interpretation and its underlying rationale and function. Freud's ideas about universal schemata and the search for actual deeds or action patterns—as the source of later ideational structures—can be related to some aspects of modern developmental psychology (e.g., Piaget) and structuralist approaches.

Part 3

On unconscious fantasy

Deborah L. Browning

> Putting Freud to work means demonstrating in him what I call a *demand*, the demand for a discovery which impels him without always showing him the way, and which may therefore lead him into dead ends or wrong turnings. It means following in his footsteps, accompanying him but also criticizing him, seeking other ways—but impelled by a demand similar to his.
>
> Laplanche (1992a, p. 434)

Laplanche's words describe well Schimek's approach to Freudian scholarship. Where does Freud seem to bump into himself in the dark? And what can we learn as we try to figure out how and why this may be happening? Schimek's writing reflects a particular interest in Freud's hypothetical constructs of unconscious fantasy and primary psychical processes. Indeed, could there be a Freudian psychoanalytic theory without the concepts of unconscious fantasy and primary process? Yet these two essential ideas together create a kind of paradox. The primary process implies a fluidity of thought, an ever changingness, as a purposive idea guides associations and finds expression by whatever route possible, following the path of least resistance, randomly contingent on external and superficial associations. At the same time, the idea of unconscious fantasy assumes a structured unconscious that, in being timeless, represents the past again and again in the present, seemingly rigid and impervious to change.

How are these two conceptions of the backstory of the individual mind to be reconciled? This is, in fact, the problem that the analytic couple, working out the many manifestations and variations of the same (self-defeating) patterns, implicitly seeks to reconcile, thereby offering the patient the opportunity for a higher level of organization of experience and self-knowledge.

Recognizing this paradox, in these chapters Schimek seeks to elaborate each concept separately and then to examine the difficulties that ensue when they are brought into juxtaposition. Brief definitions, alone, will suffice to illustrate the problems with which Schimek works in depth. Following

Freud, Schimek defines unconscious fantasy as an organizing structure, a kind of repetitive scenario, involving a limited number of imaginary action scenes representing, implicitly or explicitly, interaction with other people. There may be manifold expressions of an unconscious fantasy, with the patient identifying, in any given permutation of the fantasy, with any individual and any action.

With respect to defining primary process, Schimek points out that Freud worked with two different and somewhat contradictory definitions. In the earlier and narrower view, primary process was a process of distortion or transformation of realistic, objective perception in the service of drive disguise, expression, and defense. In a second view, introduced somewhat later, primary process was "primary," the earliest, most basic, elementary pattern or mode of organized thought and action. It is here that Freud's notion of symbolism as primary process fits best. Primary process in this second definition, then, is not fluid, defensively driven distortion, but rather a primitive, organized pattern, and as such, it is close to Freud's definition of unconscious fantasy.

In his first thinking about unconscious fantasy (Chapter 10), Schimek focused broadly on unconscious representation and the problems inherent in Freud's (outdated) assumption that veridical perception provided representations that were exact replicas of reality experience and yielded memories to be stored in a container-like unconscious. Updating knowledge of the mind's capacities as they related to perception and memory required, then, revisions in thinking about unconscious fantasy and the place and purpose of primary process thought. Schimek suggests, instead, that the earliest foundation for unconscious fantasy could be seen in affectively charged action patterns constructed over time through interactions with important people in early life.

Elaborating these ideas in line with Piaget's researches (see in particular, Chapter 11) Schimek posits that the first forms of knowing and remembering might be better understood as sensorimotor schemas—as organizers of action and affect operating at a preverbal and preideational level. These schemas, ways of going at things, would become represented over time, with each stage of cognitive development involving revisions of these original modes, each layered upon the other, intermixed with the other and never fully replacing one with the other. In reversing Freud's (1911) proposition that ideation must precede organized action—an assumption that underpins classical considerations of acting out and more recent Freudian notions of enactment—Schimek posits that organized action might better be seen as preceding and forming the foundation for fantasy and thought. In this way, then, Schimek suggests that, perhaps in the analytic situation, change precipitated by the analytic interaction may well precede insight.

This position might be seen as congruent with the more interpersonal/relational views of enactment first set forth, without use of the word, by Levenson (1972), which leads us back through Sullivan to the social behaviorist G. H. Mead's (1934) "conversation of gestures"—an idea being brought back into the present discussion of early patterning of attachment. And, most recently, we see ideas about the patterning of interaction finding expression in the work of the Boston Change Process Study Group (BCPSG), with their work on "implicit relational knowing" (BCPSG, 2007; Stern et al., 1998). As one of their members, Dan Stern (2004) defines implicit relational knowing as referring to "the domain of knowledge and representation that is nonverbal, nonsymbolized, un-narrated and nonconscious. It consists of motor procedures, affect patterns, expectations and even patterns of thinking" (p. 242).

Schimek differs from the Boston Group in his assumption that an elaborated unconscious fantasy can come to be built upon and around an early nonconscious, sensorimotor-affective schema as that sensorimotor-affective mode draws material toward it, becoming interwoven with and organized around fantasy, which also becomes (or remains) repressed. In contrast, the Boston Group, as I understand them, is setting out a developmental line that is and will remain separate from, although able to affect, fantasy. Emde (2007), who like Schimek invokes Erikson's (1950) conception of social modalities as part of this nonverbal pattern of interpersonal approach, suggests that it is crucial in discussions of unconscious knowing that one separate theoretically and conceptually the dynamic, the procedural, and the implicit, even though it seems clear that any act will reflect a convergence of motivations.

In his later writing on unconscious fantasy (Chapter 9), Schimek was less concerned with how such fantasy develops (see Erreich, 2003, and Litowitz, 2007, for their views on the development) and more interested in calling attention to the tension between the patient's apparent repeated enactments of unconscious fantasies and the analyst's own preferred interpretive category. Here we also see a shift in Schimek's focus to the second, structured conception of primary process. While continuing to see unconscious fantasy as *the* crucial and central construct in psychoanalysis through to the end of his published and unpublished writings, Schimek appears progressively to question the utility of the concept of primary process, titling an unpublished set of notes, "Should the primary process be buried?"

His problem lay partly with the two contradictory definitions of primary process that I have already pointed out, but also with Freud's claims that with the identification of the dream work (which uses primary process mechanism of displacement and condensation), we will have indications of the lawful, predictable workings of the unconscious. Freud (1938) writes, "In this way...we learn the laws which govern the passage of events in the unconscious" (p. 166). But do we really? Schimek asks. Regarding Freud's motivated forgetting of the name of the Italian painter Signorelli (Chapter 13) and again in "*The Interpretation of Dreams* Revisited: Interpretation,

Primary Process, and Language" (Chapter 14), Schimek points to the various ways that Freud tries to tells us that the dream work or primary process functions like a different language which follows predictable rules and can, following the model of the Rosetta stone and hieroglyphics, be "simply" decoded.

Yet the Rosetta stone provides us with three versions of the same text, whereas in symptoms or a dream we have only the actual manifest symptom or dream and the patient's associations. Those are the data. Everything else is an inference. There is no "solid" other text, the comparison of which will show us the laws of the distortion or transformation of the dream work, from latent to manifest. Schimek's dissatisfaction is perhaps as much with Freud's seeming to promise more than he can provide (e.g., predictable laws) as with the concept of primary process itself. Focusing on the impossibility of defining any "rules" of the dream work or any predictability, as Freud claims to be able to provide, Schimek suggests at the end of Chapter 14, in his closing sentence, that perhaps "the only valid law of the primary process is the law of anarchy."

What is one to make of this typically Schimekian, maddeningly cryptic comment? The law of lawlessness. I will take the risk of going in two directions with it. On the one hand, as a scholar of French psychoanalysis, Schimek may well have been alluding to Laplanche's (1970, 1987, 1993) writing on the primary process in its relationship to the death instinct. Certainly he was familiar with it. Following Freud's economic (drive energy) model, primary process activity seeks the immediate discharge of tension. Energy is "unbound." Laplanche shows that, in Freud's (1895) *Project,* we encounter his principle of constancy (a kind of homeostasis) and also his principle of (neuronal) inertia, which seeks pleasure (avoids un-pleasure) in the reduction of tension to a zero point—an idea that reappears in *Beyond the Pleasure Principle* (1920) in Freud's invocation of the Nirvana principle.

It is here, in fact, where Laplanche locates the primary process: the pleasure principle (related to inertia, not constancy), unbound discharge, tension reduced to a zero point, Nirvana, and the death instinct on one side; secondary process, the reality principle (constancy), bound energy, and Eros "the preserver of all things" (p. 52) on the other. And so Schimek may well be reminding us that, as an expression of the principle of inertia, the primary process moves toward anarchy, dedifferentiation, entropy, and death.

Or is it possible that Schimek was alluding instead to the recent interest psychoanalysts have in linking Freudian concepts with chaos theory? Again, some background is required. In a heroic attempt to present nonlinear dynamic systems theory to a "perplexed" psychoanalytic audience, Galatzer-Levy (2009) reminds us of the extent to which the mechanistic world view that influenced Freud so profoundly was expressed in the methods of observation made available by the mathematics of (linear) differential equations. Today, a newer math—nonlinear dynamic systems theory, providing formulae for understanding a different set of events in nature—provides us with a new set of organizing observations, which may prove useful in our understanding of the activities of humans, where it is difficult, if not impossible, to reliably predict many specific aspects of behavior.

An essential aspect of nonlinear dynamics concerns the very nature of prediction—what can and cannot be predicted—the issue so central to Schimek's dissatisfaction with Freud's exposition on primary process transformation. Nonlinear dynamics helps us with charting and understanding pattern formation, which can emerge over time, but the specifics, details, and timing of which cannot be predicted. A brief example from the developmentalist Esther Thelen (2005) on infant crawling vividly illustrates and concretizes the benefit of this newer way of thinking:

> In a dynamic view, crawling is an online solution that babies discover when they lack the balance, control and strength needed for upright walking, but want to get to something that they cannot reach. It is an opportunistic assembly of the components that results in a temporarily stable and useful pattern. For many months, it becomes infants' preferred mode of self-transport. Infants often begin crawling by using a variety of patterns of limb coordination, but each soon settles on his or her own mode, which is usually an alternating pattern among the four limbs. Some infants, however, find and implement a combat crawl, using hands, feet and the belly, or they scoot on their bottoms, whereas others maintain an idiosyncratic asymmetric gait. Each infant, through trial and error, discovers his or her own pattern, depending on the environment (carpet? smooth floor?), body size, and to some degree by chance solutions. (p. 264)

We assume that eventually these infants will all walk, but their way of getting there, the crawl, is contextually driven, based on such a number of variables as to be unpredictable.

Schimek, in Chapters 13 and 14, shows us how Freud's conception of the unconscious purposive idea provides a link between the seeming randomness of primary process thought and the structure of an unconscious fantasy. Laplanche and Pontalis (1967) explain this notion as

> What directs the flow of thoughts, as much conscious as preconscious and unconscious ones...There is a purpose at work ordering thoughts in a way that is not merely mechanical, but that is determined by certain special ideas which wield a veritable force of attraction over the others. (p. 373)

In dynamic systems theory, where behavior is seen as simultaneously unpredictable *and* self-organizing, the concepts of attractor and strange attractors are essential. Very simply put, an attractor is the pattern that emerges from what had appeared as, and perhaps was, chaotic behavior. Although presented as something that pulls the activity toward it, it actually describes the pattern which emerges. It is a pattern that a system seems to move toward, to end up with. And what makes an attractor "strange" is that one can see a pattern emerge, and then suddenly there is seeming chaos again and the pattern switches to another pattern. Later, more chaos, and the former pattern reemerges. And that oscillation between these two patterns *is* the pattern.

Perhaps we could see the purposive idea, the unconscious fantasy, driving and guiding primary process manifestations, distortions, and transformations as a kind of strange attractor, the oscillations reflecting the way that an individual can switch roles within the fantasy—as Schimek has extensively discussed—from predator to victim, from the one beaten to the one beating, or in the language of Benjamin (1990), from the "doer" to the "done to."

So what does Schimek imply in his reference to anarchy? I suggest that Schimek, who did not really want to give up on the idea of primary process, was showing us, in his ambiguous use of the word, just how ever present primary processes are in our thought—punning being a perfect example. His use of the term "anarchy" condenses both ideas—of death and of patterning in life—and it contains, as well, a potential displacement and condensation of the affects of despair in the recognition of approaching death and of hope for renewal through transformation. The primary process, expressing an unconscious fantasy, can result in distortion and pathology, but by the unpredictable concatenation of psychic and external events, it may also lead to profound transformations, which will instead produce acts of adaptation and creativity. This posthumous publication of his collected works attests to that.

CHAPTER SUMMARIES

In Chapter 9, "Unconscious Fantasy: Developmental Phenomenon and Interpretative Construct," Schimek offers a broad perspective on the place that the concept of unconscious fantasy holds in clinical and theoretical psychoanalysis. He first provides a brief historical overview of Freud's several different meanings of unconscious fantasy from *The Interpretation of Dreams* (1900) through to the *Introductory Lectures* (1916), showing how Freud's affinity for "primal fantasies," which he invoked to account for recurring themes and actions in a patient's life and material, can better be understood as something akin to Kantian categories or organizing schemes, which give structure and meaning to experience.

Schimek distinguishes between what he refers to as the "two realities" of unconscious fantasy. The first is the conception of something, ultimately unknowable, that we nevertheless assume exists in the mind of an individual. The second "reality" is the interpretive category, employed by the analyst, who listens and tries to make sense of the patient's material. He reminds the reader that the actual data that the analyst has to work with are the patient's behavior, speech, and symptomatology, discerned in the patient's reports of life outside and also from the interaction with the analytic situation—but the patient's unconscious fantasy is an inference and a construction.

Chapter 10, "A Critical Reexamination of Freud's Concept of Unconscious Mental Representation," is a dense and difficult chapter on unconscious representation and provides the foundation for Schimek's own life-long Freudian "project." Here, he examines a concept more broadly defined than unconscious fantasy, in that "representation" refers to the reappearance in consciousness of something that has been perceived (either within or in the outside world), and which is then remembered and thus becomes conscious in some form.

Schimek shows how Freud's assumptions about perception and the relationship between perception and memory reflect a view of mental processes that, consistent with the association psychology of his time, is both nonmotivational and nondevelopmental and now largely demonstrated to be incorrect. Yet the psychoanalytic concepts upon which these assumptions are built continue to influence analytic thought and clinical interpretation. Hence, this chapter explores the complex relationship between memory and fantasy, between external and psychical reality, and Freud's distinction between consciousness and unconscious processes, including his conception of primary process.

Within the context of considering Piaget's relevance to psychoanalysis, in Chapter 11, "Affective Schemas: Toward a Structural View of Cognition and Affect," Schimek points out that whereas Freud was concerned with how our wishes, needs, and fears distort our presumably objective perceptions and memories, Piaget's central question asks how the human mind constructs, over time, an objective representation of external reality. The difference between these questions influences how each of them understood the past as reflected in the present and how that continuity comes about and is maintained. Schimek also calls attention to the utility of Piaget's little known conception of affective schemas, which are ways of acting, feeling, and thinking derived from a child's interactions with the important people of infancy and early childhood and which become organized and self-maintaining structures. He compares this notion with Freud's ideas about unconscious fantasy and links the two in their respective explanations for how unconscious fantasy schemata appear to be so impervious to change.

In Chapter 12, "Notes on the Psychoanalytic Theory of Consciousness and Reflective Awareness," Schimek provides a succinct overview of Freud's assumptions about consciousness, the three different models from which he worked, and the difficulty he had in reconciling one with another. For Freud, consciousness came down to consciousness of something, including of the mind, which leads to the view of consciousness as a reflective process. Schimek offers his own psychoanalytic definition of consciousness as the relationship between any two levels of mental functioning, with the more organized or differentiated level taking as its object a less complex level. He indicates the importance of recognizing conscious self-reflection as a developmental line in and of itself.

Chapter 13, "Signorelli: The Parapraxis Specimen of Psychoanalysis," concerns Freud's motivated forgetting of the name of the Italian painter Signorelli, which he wrote about a few weeks after its occurrence in "The Psychical Mechanisms of Forgetfulness" (1898b), and also in the first chapter of *The Psychopathology of Everyday Life* (1901b). Schimek shows how Freud's own detailed analysis leaves much room for reinterpretation and reconsideration of the original material and circumstances of the incident, and he suggests that Freud may have selectively repressed potentially important associative links.

Schimek uses Freud's unconvincing explanation of his forgetting to evaluate critically the concept of primary process and Freud's method of interpretation to which it is linked. He shows here how Freud appears to be working with two different implicit definitions of primary process and that, in his reliance on the explanatory value of what he calls "external and superficial" associations, Freud falls back on outdated nineteenth century association psychology, discussed extensively by Schimek in Chapter 10.

In Chapter 14, Schimek walks the reader through *The Interpretation of Dreams,* pausing at those points where he feels misunderstandings have frequently occurred in later scholarship or where he thinks Freud seems to have become tangled in his own chain of logic. He spends the greatest time on the dream book's Chapters 6 ("The Dream Work") and 7 ("The Psychology of the Dream Process"). This chapter reflects the intersection of two of Schimek's enduring interests: the interpretive process of the analyst and Freud's concept of the primary process. He shows how Freud's attempt to maintain a scientific position with respect to dream interpretation led to internal contradictions in his understanding of the dream work and the functioning of primary process.

Central to Schimek's discussion and critique is Freud's assumption that the process of dream interpretation can follow in reverse order, the hypothesized construction of the dream itself through the primary process mechanisms of condensation and displacement. This chapter provides an important discussion of the theoretical problems with Freud's concept of primary process and elaborates a line of thought introduced in Chapter 10 and extended substantially in Chapter 12.

Chapter 9

Unconscious fantasy

Interpretive construct and developmental phenomenon

The concept of unconscious fantasy is central to both the clinical and theoretical aspects of psychoanalysis. It is the main bridge between the abstract, contentless, drive energy of metapsychology and the hidden motives or wishes at the core of the clinical process of interpretation. Yet, with a few exceptions, the concept of unconscious fantasy has been relatively neglected in the literature in favor of either a focus, in clinical contexts, on the specific content of various fantasies (e.g., oedipal, pre-oedipal, etc.) or, in the context of theoretical discussion, the concept of instinctual drive.

Some of the issues I would like to examine here deal with the relationship between conscious and unconscious fantasy and the relationship between unconscious fantasy, drive, and external reality. My main point will be that unconscious fantasy has two kinds of "reality." The first is as an organizing structure, a fixed scenario, presumably established in early childhood, which tends to repeat itself in manifold changed and disguised ways. Second, unconscious fantasy has a "reality" as the main interpretive category used by the analyst (and ideally in some modified form by the patient) to give some order, consistency, and meaning to various aspects of the patient's symptomatology and behavior. Yet the unconscious fantasy reconstructed in the analytic process cannot simply be assumed to be the recovery, the unearthing from repression, of a set of experiences or patterns from early childhood. One of my main points will be that the two aspects of unconscious fantasy, as organizing structure and as interpretative category, have a complex and problematic relationship with each other and cannot be simply equated.

UNCONSCIOUS FANTASY AS REPRESSED CONSCIOUS FANTASY

For Freud, the descriptive model for an unconscious fantasy is a conscious fantasy or daydream. The fantasy is an imagined situation, a representation of a brief or lengthy plot with one or more actors, with a wished-for or dreaded action being carried out. When the fantasy generates unpleasure (to the extent that it is experienced as real and as somehow equivalent to the deed), it becomes repressed but continues to manifest itself through disguised expressions in thoughts and symptomatic acts. A daydream, as Freud points out in *The Interpretation of Dreams* (1900) and in his paper on hysterical fantasies (1908), is like the dream, the expression of a wish, and its formation involves similar processes. In its role in the etiology of symptoms, the fantasy is really the heir to the repressed memory.

As is well known, after the partial abandonment of the seduction etiology of neurosis, the childhood fantasy had to take the role of the repressed memory of a traumatic event. Thus, for Freud, the fantasy lost its grounding in reality, or, rather, it became based on the biological reality of infantile sexuality. In the formulations of *Three Essays* (1905b), the childhood fantasy becomes the creation or the necessary accompaniment of the biological unfolding of infantile sexuality. But this created new problems to which we have to turn briefly in examining the relationship of unconscious fantasy to drive and unconscious wishes.

These issues will only be briefly summarized here, having been dealt with extensively by Laplanche and Pontalis (1964, 1967) as well as myself in previous chapters (see Chapters 7, 8, and 10). The main question, then, is how a drive can create a fantasy. The answer is complex, partly because of the ambiguity of Freud's concept of drive. We have to keep in mind the following points: First, in the theoretical model of 1900 and 1915(b)—one dear to Rapaport and ego psychology—the drive can cathect or invest only the object of a previous experience of satisfaction, bring it into consciousness, and make it seem real. Second, in Freud's formulation of 1905b and repeated in many other contexts, the primary manifestations of infantile sexuality are autoerotic activities which do have a concrete motor reality. The fantasies are seen as somehow accompanying them and becoming permanently linked with them (1909a). Therefore, the repressed fantasy provides a bridge between the suppressed autoerotic activity and the symptoms, these latter being the disguised enactment of childhood autoeroticism mediated through the fantasy.

Third, much of the difficulty that Freud ran into with his theorizing stems from his implicit assumption of an absolute dichotomy between external objective reality (possibly registered, in camera-like fashion, by the perceptual and memory apparatus of the organism and only thence subject to drive distortions) and subjective reality or fantasy. From a clinical psychological point of view, the difference between a memory and a fantasy is only a relative one, as Freud was well aware in his more clinical formulations. He believed that memories are always distorted screen memories, not *of* our childhood but merely *about* it, and that the content of fantasies has to have some origin in actual experience, however much these contents are transformed, rearranged, and symbolized.

Thus, the difference between reality and fantasy is a relative one in terms of the amount of transformation or assimilation that the presumed original material has undergone and also in the individual's belief in his experience as reflecting a real past event as memory or in his assumption that he is dealing with an idea of his imagination. This can explain Freud's puzzling statement in the *Introductory Lectures* (1917) that, in the context of a psychoanalytic situation, it is only psychical reality that matters, "and we gradually learn to understand that in the world of the neuroses it is psychical reality which is the decisive kind" (p. 368). This does not mean that an actual event, for instance, seduction, does not have an important influence on later development. Rather, it means that the statements of the analysand, whether brought forth as memories, fantasies, or dreams, are never purely factual or purely imaginary and in all cases reflect his own selective organizing tendencies (wishes, motives, defenses) as well as his actual experience and interaction with external reality (particularly what has since been called his object relations).

Fourth, it is pretty clear that the general concept of drive as a somatically rooted quantity of energy seeking discharge cannot account for the content and role of fantasies, unless the drive is viewed as Freud often but not consistently did as already a "psychical representative"—a stable psychological manifestation of biological drives (that is, an unconscious wish or unconscious fantasy). Thus, in its broadest sense, an unconscious fantasy is synonymous with an unconscious wish. It is a wish for an experience of satisfaction, in other words, for a certain situation or, more specifically, for a specific action in relation to an object, including all the sensations and affects connected with that situation. With all the emphasis on the mobile, displaceable, primary process character of most of the manifestations of the unconscious, it has not been stressed enough that Freud's theory rests just as much on the assumption of organized, early, unconscious wishes or fantasies whose organization, structure, and patterning activity remains basically unchanged throughout their later surface manifestations.

Here we get to a definition of unconscious fantasy as an early established organizing structure, a kind of repetitive scenario which can manifest itself in action and thought, in symptoms, and in dreams so that conscious fantasy is only one of many partial manifestations of a basic unconscious fantasy or unconscious wish. Furthermore, Freud's (as well as later psychoanalysts') use of the concept of unconscious fantasy is based on the assumption of a limited number of universal organized and persistent structures. These basic characteristics of what Freud came to call primal fantasies could not easily be accounted for by the accidental events of individual history or even the universality of biological needs, sensations of pleasure and pain, as they became associated with aspects of early experience. It is largely because of this problem that Freud had recourse to the concept of primal fantasies and an inherited, archaic heritage.

UNCONSCIOUS FANTASY AS AN INTERPRETIVE CATEGORY

From a brief historical survey of the different meanings of unconscious fantasy in Freud's thought, we can reach the following conclusions. First, unconscious fantasy is a much broader concept than conscious fantasy. While unconscious fantasy is described in terms of a conscious fantasy, it cannot owe its origins to a specific conscious fantasy that has become repressed. Freud himself states (1909a) that the fantasies may have been unconscious from the beginning and need not have been conscious at any time. Second, unconscious fantasy is synonymous with unconscious wish. It is the basic stable psychological organization of the drive. Third, unconscious fantasies consist of a limited number of typical imaginary action scenes or scenarios, representing explicitly or implicitly interaction with other people and not just an isolated image or scene.

Last, but certainly not least, we come to the conclusion, implicit in Freud, that neither the drive as a biological force nor the accidental contents of individual experience and their memories can account for the recurrent organization and typical contents of unconscious fantasies. Therefore, Freud's concept of primal fantasies as organizing schemes or Kantian categories, which give a structure to the data of experience, is a very central one and need not be tied to the pseudohistorical (primal horde, etc.) and Lamarckian aspects of Freud's formulation.

It is time, then, to take a closer look at the nature and empirical basis of the kind of unconscious fantasies with which psychoanalysis deals. What I would like to consider here are the various fantasies that Freud deals with, all centered around the oedipal constellation. The Oedipus complex as a set of unconscious fantasies can be seen essentially as an organized and organizing structure—in the strict sense of Piaget's (1964) definition of structure:

> We shall define structure in the broadest possible sense as a system which presents the laws or properties of a totality seen as a system. These laws of totality are different from the laws or properties of the elements which comprise the system. (p. 143)

They make essentially a self-regulating system of the relationships among various elements, wherein each element is defined by its role within the total system—a system capable of transformation of various permutations and displacements within the element while maintaining an essential stability of the organization and relationships.

Thus, one can see that the Oedipus complex is a triadic structure (child, father, mother) organized around the elements: child versus adult (powerful versus weak and needy), male versus female (which for Freud becomes essentially the polarity of with or without penis), and love versus hate (primarily wished-for physical, sensual closeness, satisfaction of needs versus the wish to exclude, hurt, castrate, destroy). Now, clearly, in Freud's most inclusive descriptions of the Oedipus constellation—for example, in "The Ego and the Id" (1923b)—it is not reduced to the child's positive libidinal relationship to the mother versus the negative, angry, and fearful (castration anxiety) relationship to the father. It includes not only the conflict between these two tendencies but also the ambivalence between love and hate in relation to each one of the parents. It also includes the child's fantasy of the relationship between the two parents (in terms of dominance–submission, being hurt or gratified). And maybe most important of all, is the assumption that the child can in fantasy identify with any one of the three roles and positions in the triangle, with mother or father—not only in terms of their relation to him but also in terms of their relation to each other.

Furthermore, many other people in childhood or later can be substituted for the original objects and fantasy figures in this pattern or structure. Castration, abandonment, seduction, and primal scene (as well as what Freud calls the sexual theories of children) are an intrinsic part of this fantasy scenario. It should be mentioned that conflict and tension, and therefore the various compromises and defensive operations necessary, are intrinsic to the nature of the unconscious fantasy or, better said, to any specific expression of it.

The idea of unconscious fantasy as a stable structure with many possible permutations and displacements between the elements is well illustrated in Freud's paper, "A Child Is Being Beaten" (1919), referring to a specific regressive, sadomasochistic variant of an oedipal fantasy. In the different stages of this fantasy that Freud describes or reconstructs, the relationship "a child is being beaten by a parental figure" remains constant, but many different people can be put in either role (the self, a sibling, a boy, a girl, and, in the case of the parental figure, the father, the mother, a teacher, a group of people, etc.).

In its simplest form, an unconscious fantasy is the structure of an action as defined by a verb, a certain "mode," and the interaction between a subject and an object in a limited range of roles suitable and defined by the nature of the action. This can be seen, for instance, in the underlying structure of the Irma dream (1900), the basic action being examining-with-helpful-intent, the examiner, and various reluctant or willing women in the role of the examinee. One may also see that many post-Freudian approaches also include a specific set of constructed unconscious fantasies, but with an emphasis on the pre-oedipal, that is, dyadic, relationship organized around the categories of good and bad, self and other (closeness and merging versus individuation and abandonment), cohesive versus fragmented self, and power and grandiosity versus worthlessness and helplessness.

INTERPRETIVE CONSTRUCTION AND DEVELOPMENTAL REALITY

The underlying assumption of psychoanalytic theory is that the unconscious fantasy refers to and describes an actual organizing structure in the mind of a person, which has been formed during the critical period of childhood and which continues to exert its effects on the organization of certain aspects of present adult behavior—most specifically, symptoms and their manifestation in the transference neurosis.

This assumption deserves some critical examination. Considered in its immediate empirical reality, the unconscious fantasy is a creation of the interpretive activity of the analyst. It is first and foremost a construction of the analyst as he tries to find consistent patterns in the patient's symptomatology and behavior, primarily in the behavior expressed in the context of a psychoanalytic situation—that is, the patient's behavior in relation to the analyst. This includes not only the transference in a limited sense but also the patient's accounts of his present and past life.

Here it is important to remind ourselves of a point that is clinically obvious but often forgotten in the more abstract realms of theory: The analyst brings to the analytic situation various concepts and a limited number of general unconscious fantasies which are used as basic interpretive categories; this process by the analyst is unavoidable, if not indispensable, for any interpretive activity. Interpretation, unlike the theoretical model propounded at times by Freud in *The Interpretation of Dreams* (1900), is not a mere work of translation or decoding. This assumption implies that there is a preexisting, organized message (on the model of a latent content of a dream or a conscious fantasy or memory which has then been repressed) and has been disguised in a new language. If we have the code—the syntax and vocabulary of this new language—the root of transformation between the two languages can easily get back to the original meaning without any preconceived idea of what this meaning might be.

But there is no such adequate transformation code; the principles of condensation, displacement, symbolization and the use of specific contexts, while indispensable working tools, do not, by themselves, allow us to go directly and unambiguously from the manifest to the latent. Furthermore, how do we select what is the most relevant context? Rather, our interpretation is always based on the use of some preconceived categories of interpretation, a general range of possible meanings, which our specific interpretive activity based on the prior knowledge of a patient and the specific immediate context will ideally clarify and specify. To stay with the translation analogy despite its limitations, one could say that if we listen to somebody in a foreign language which we have mastered only to a limited degree, we can only understand him if we have some prior knowledge of the general topic and point of view that he is expressing.

My main point is that the unconscious fantasy is not inferred ad hoc from information about the patient's early past but that this past is constructed in terms of the unconscious fantasy as an interpretive category supplied by psychoanalytic theory, individualized and specified by the data of the present in the psychoanalytic situation. In its broadest sense, the limited repertoire of basic unconscious fantasies functions for the analyst, and ideally for the patient as well, as a language or, perhaps more specifically, as a semantic classification which can give some consistency, meaning, and continuity to those aspects of a patient's present behavior (primarily his symptoms and their transference manifestations) which seem to him alien, irrational, and not accounted for by his conscious judgment, goals, or common-sense standards.

The psychoanalyst is not a biographer collecting data outside the psychoanalytic situation from as many sources as possible. How much can he actually know about the patient's early childhood? He usually has only a few memories of the patient to go by, memories which, as Freud said, are at best only "about childhood" and whose relationship to the original experiences is, in principle, no different from that of a dream or conscious fantasy; that is, it is distorted, ambiguous, and subject to interpretation. The basic prototypes of unconscious fantasies, unconscious scenarios with their typical conflicts that the analyst uses, all have a time tag attached to them. They are supposed to represent typical developmental stages. Therefore, insofar as interpretations are guided by these categories, they are bound to be interpretations ultimately in terms of the past. Yet this past I mention is introduced more by the categories than by the immediate data themselves.

Furthermore, the more a reconstruction deals with the earliest years of childhood, the more it is likely to be dominated by the interpretive schemata of the analyst and to be stated in very general form because, in contrast to more recent periods of a patient's life, relatively little specific information is available. So the most ultimate explanations or genetic interpretations are also likely to be the most general and universalized, if not stereotyped, ones. One could answer that the details of a reconstruction of the early years and of dominant unconscious fantasies could be quite specific because they are primarily derived from the analysis of a transference in the here and now; this may indeed be clinically true, but it is somewhat circular reasoning in terms of assumptions about reconstruction and the role of the past.

For purposes of clarification, it may be worth stating here that I am not questioning the general assumption that early development (which means primarily interactions with parental figures as mediated through body needs, zones, and sensations and the internalization of these interactions) has a crucial and lasting effect on later development and is never completely superseded. Nor am I questioning that, as a clinical procedure, psychoanalysis strives for a greater capacity of a patient to "appropriate, to own up to one's own history" (Loewald, 1978b, p. 20) as part of changing id into ego and specifically increasing his understanding and acknowledgment of his present motives and conflicts and his relation to his future. The temporal dimension is intrinsic to psychoanalytic work, not only because of the nature of our interpretive contribution as analysts but also because the patient brings it with him in his immediate experience.

What I am questioning is the uncritical equation of interpretive categories, such as an unconscious fantasy, with specific developmental stages—either in providing an explanation of present behavior in the clinical situation or in translating them directly into developmental facts. The possibility of reconstructing the individual past as it was once experienced by the child is remote at best and impossible to validate, a fact for which psychoanalysis, despite some of its theoretical predilections, has probably provided the best demonstration (aside from contemporary research on the development of perception, memory, and language). I would add that such a view is also quite superfluous except where one holds to the conception of psychoanalysis as the abreaction of actual traumas. Certain aspects of present behavior may justifiably be seen as a partial reenactment of an infantile pattern in terms of a certain similarity of the organization of its behavior and in the scenario that is being enacted; however, the specific content, purpose, and consequences of the behavior cannot possibly be identical with those of the original.

When asking ourselves what kind of reality and validity we can attribute to various formulations of unconscious fantasies and unconscious wishes, it is important to distinguish different levels of abstraction and generality. We can speak of unconscious fantasies as universal organizing structures of the human mind, as kinds of Kantian categories of affective and interpersonal life. But insofar as we give them any reality at all, beyond that of a pragmatic, hypothetical construct or model useful for ordering various kinds of data, it can only be that of a potential pattern, a general contentless framework which could have a reality only at a biological or neurological level in terms of a hereditary element common to the human species.

These would include not only somatic needs, and the biological facts of a slow maturation of a human being, his long period of dependency, sexual differentiation, birth, death, and so on, but also the human potentiality for the development of speech and symbolic functions. Even then, it does not mean that the existence of something like the oedipal structure could be found at a neurological level, but merely that the general principles of organization involved in the construction of his organizers of unconscious fantasy can also be found in human functioning at a bioneurological level. This really means that the same organizational categories can be used for ordering and making sense of these kinds of nonpsychological data.

To move to a further level, we then have to consider the specification of these general categories within the framework of a specific culture and society, including their economic, social, and mythical organization. And, finally, at the individual level, which is the only psychological one, we can deal only with specific manifestations of the culturally shaped versions of these unconscious fantasies within the framework of a life setting and experience of a specific individual. Universal patterns lead back to the presumed reality of a biological-neurological substrate, the more concrete yet general expressions of these patterns, to the relativity of social-cultural systems and their change in time, and any specific individual manifestations to the contingencies of life history.

Obviously, any individual manifestation of the unconscious fantasy is supposed to reflect a general category but cannot be reduced to it because many other coordinates have been added. The question of how unconscious fantasies as constructs of analytic theory or of a specific analytic process in therapy are constructed is another question that I will not address here, except to indicate that it involves just as much the reverse process of induction from the particular to the general, from individual experience and a particular cultural setting to a universalizing tendency.

In closing, let me point out that if we do not reify unconscious fantasies and instead take the most parsimonious view of seeing them as constructs to account for certain patterns and regularities in observed behavior, there is still the complex question as to the origin and history of these patterns. We need not and should not, as has been my main argument, assume that the unconscious fantasy, as constructed in the context of adult analysis, refers back to an identical structure in the mind of a child.

Neither can we assume the existence of conscious fantasies before sometime in the second year of life, before the development of the capacity for evocative memory, for representation of what is absent or missing. Early fantasies in the child are not likely to be experienced clearly as fantasies—namely, to be differentiated from more realistic objective thought. The capacity for pretend and make-believe develops only slowly, probably sometime in the third year, and it is not consolidated until quite a few years later. Therefore, although fantasy necessarily takes some of its main contents from previous experience, including patterns of bodily sensory experience from the earliest months, it is not a replica of a previous experience of satisfaction. Rather, it is always a selective reconstruction of what is absent or missing.

To conclude, unconscious fantasy is certainly more than a daydream that has been repressed. It can be better seen as an organizing structure than as a specific content. But it can also be seen as a construct, the product of an interpretation and an inference. It refers to something which presumably exists and has an actual reality, although the form it has is, as such, unknowable. The unconscious fantasy is a partial explanation for various observable behaviors and conscious beliefs. We cannot know the way in which an unconscious fantasy exists or its original expression or level of experience. We can describe it only in terms of its effects and its manifest consequences, reconstructed in such a way that it can account for them.

Chapter 10

A critical reexamination of Freud's concept of unconscious mental representation*

One of the fundamental concepts of psychoanalytic theory is that of unconscious mental representations, or specific mental contents (images, fantasies, etc.) permanently stored in the unconscious from where they keep manifesting themselves to consciousness in various transformed and disguised ways. Freud's concept of drive is intrinsically linked to that of mental representation. Psychoanalysis, as a psychological theory of motivation, does not deal with drives in biological terms but with their expression as mental representations. It is only through becoming associated with a mental representation that a drive—as a somatic need or quantity of energy—acquires a specific content and becomes a psychological directional force, the wish for a specific object.

In the contemporary reexaminations of Freud's theory of motivation, the main emphasis has understandably been on the concepts of drive and psychic energy and their relation to Freud's scientific and cultural background (Holt, 1967a). The concept of mental representation, its underlying assumptions about cognition, and its influence on most aspects of psychoanalytic theory have been relatively neglected, Piaget (1945) and Wolff (1967) being conspicuous exceptions. One sign of this neglect is the vague and ambiguous way in which the term is used in the psychoanalytic literature. It can mean memory image, idea, concept, and sometimes even perception—any content of subjective experience, whether immediate and concrete or general and abstract. The ambiguity is even greater when it comes to *unconscious* representations because these are viewed at times as specific contents of experience in an unconscious state and, at other times, as an inferred psychological organization (Beres & Joseph, 1970), a schema (Sandler & Rosenblatt, 1962) underlying the recurrent and organized aspects of any thought, action, or behavior.

The main purpose of this chapter is a critical reexamination of the concept of unconscious mental representations and its relevance to some central

* This chapter originally appeared in *International Review of Psychoanalysis*, 2, 1975, pp. 171–187. Reprinted with permission.

issues in contemporary psychoanalytic theory. In the first part of the chapter I shall examine Freud's assumptions about perception and memory and indicate how they directly influenced his concept of mental representation and its relation to external reality and to drives. I will try to show that Freud follows the principles of association psychology and a view of cognition which is essentially nonmotivational and nondevelopmental. He also starts out with a rationalistic bias, which takes adult, objective, impersonal cognition as the baseline and implicit model for all thought processes and views action only as the outcome of some prior ideation. The burden of transforming this point of view into the motivational and developmental approach which characterizes psychoanalysis rests on the superimposed concept of drive energy, its different modes of discharge, and ways of cathecting the contents of mental representations.

In the second part of the chapter, I shall indicate how Freud's assumptions about cognition and mental representations, although seemingly peripheral to his primary interests and discoveries, have had a profound influence on some of the central issues of psychoanalytic theory, such as the distinction between conscious and unconscious, primary and secondary process, and external and psychical reality. In the third part, I shall briefly indicate the discrepancy between Freud's theory of cognition and the data and concepts of contemporary developmental psychology.

In the last part of the chapter, I shall conclude that the concept of the unconscious as a storage container of specific images and memories may no longer be tenable or even necessary. In line with some more recent views, I shall suggest that it may be more legitimate to infer unconscious sensorimotor organizers of action at a preideational as well as preverbal level, without postulating that behind the various observable manifestations of an inferred unconscious motive lies an unconscious image or fantasy. Such an approach may help to reconsider the meaning of the unconscious–conscious dimension in terms of the ways in which originally unconscious action patterns become represented in consciousness at different levels of symbolic functioning (from concrete images to abstract relationships), the conditions which make the construction of such symbolic representations possible (beyond the negative view of merely lifting the veil of repression from an already preexisting image or thought content), and their effect in modifying the very expression and structure of a motive or drive.

Throughout the chapter my primary aim will be to provide a critical review, a stocktaking, which may help delineate some central issues and provide a clearer perspective for needed reformulations. Thus, my review will be somewhat schematic and cannot do full justice to the complexity of Freud's thought and the creatively unsystematic and changing ways in which he made use of his basic assumptions and concepts, particularly when dealing with clinical data. Many points of my review will sound familiar (so I have dispensed with the use of extensive quotations), but they have usually been considered in isolation and their overall implications have rarely been explored.

MENTAL REPRESENTATION AND THE COPY THEORY OF PERCEPTION

Let us first consider the basic meaning of mental representation—leaving aside, for the time being, the question of unconsciousness and drive cathexis. The term that Freud used is *Vorstellung*. This term is a familiar concept in German philosophical and psychological writing, and Freud saw no particular need to specify or question its meaning. This basic meaning is well summarized by the definition in a standard German philosophical dictionary:

> The image in consciousness of an object or event in the external world without its objective presence (as in the case of perception). It always involves the reappearance in consciousness of the contents of a perception, although in modified form, or of the subjective combination of the contents of several perceptions. It always refers to a concrete object or thing even when its image is vague and blurred. (Schmidt, 1934)

Such images are viewed as the basic elements and building blocks of mental or psychical processes, beyond the immediacy of perception from which they originate. By contrast, the more abstract and complex relations formed by associative networks between these elements are usually termed thought (*Gedanken*), although the distinction is a relative one and Freud is not explicit or always consistent on this point.*

Because representations originate from perceptions, Freud's view of perception has to be considered first. For Freud, in line with the association theory of the nineteenth century, perception is essentially the passive, temporary registration of a specific external object. The perceptual apparatus functions like the receptive surface of a slate or the lens of a camera. In order to keep its unlimited receptive capacity for new registrations, it retains no permanent traces of them; it is "without the capacity to retain modifications and thus without memory" (1900, p. 539). This means that

* *The Standard Edition* translates *Vorstellung* as "idea," in the sense of "association of ideas," in the tradition of Locke and Hume. However, I believe "idea" has too much of the connotation of an abstract and conceptual process for the modern reader. I prefer the term "mental representation," which, despite its ambiguity, stresses the fact that one is dealing with an experience that "represents" or stands for an absent object, not a perceptual presence. Although the term "mental representation" is somewhat broader than that of "memory image," I shall use the two interchangeably because a memory image is, for Freud, the basic model and usual referent of the term *Vorstellung*.

perception is uninfluenced by past experience and not subject to a developmental and learning process.

Freud often equates the two terms "perception" and "external reality" and uses them interchangeably.* Such a view (sometimes labeled a "copy" theory of knowledge or the principle of "immaculate perception") implies an innate capacity for veridical objective registration of discrete external objects, and a direct and intrinsic correspondence between the "real" external object and the perception of it. Let us note in passing that here we have a "primary autonomy" of the perceptual apparatus which considerably antedates Hartmann and goes much beyond what he probably had in mind.

Every perception, while itself temporary, produces a lasting memory trace, so the experience of the perceived object continues to endure as a specific memory image or mental representation. The influence of the past on later experience depends on the existence of these lasting memory images of absent objects, as a built-in feature of the mental apparatus from the beginning of its existence. For Freud, the only way in which the continuity of past and present can be maintained is through the automatic storage of memory images of specific objects of past experience.

In their original undistorted form, memory images duplicate the content of the objective perception of an external object or event. There is a direct correspondence, or isomorphism, between the real external object, the momentary perception of this object, and the permanent memory trace or mental representation left behind by the perception: "[A]ll representations originate from perceptions and are repetitions of them. Thus, originally, the mere existence of a representation was a guarantee of the reality of what was represented" (Freud, 1925b, p. 237).†

In short, Freud does not question a theory of cognition which takes for granted, from the start, the capacity for objective, veridical perceptions and their automatic storage as undistorted memory contents. How could such a theory serve as the basis for an approach which focuses on the subjective, irrational, drive-dominated aspects of mental functioning—on the work and struggle to separate wishful fantasy from reality? The answer is clear and familiar: by assuming that the distortions of initially objective and impersonal contents are the result of motivational factors, of wishful thinking, of drives and their inherent discharge tendency (pleasure principle).

* The reality referred to is not an absolute one, but rather is conditioned by the nature of the sensory apparatus of the human organism (involving some scaling down of the intensity of external stimuli by a "stimulus barrier"). But this epistemological Kantian position is not extended to a psychological level—namely, the relativity of reality to the developmental stage and motivational state of the perceiver.

† "..daß alle Vorstellungen von Wahrnehmungen stammen, Widerholungen derselben sind. Ursprünglich ist also schon die Existenz der Vorstellung eine Bürgschaft für die Realität des Vorgestellten" (*Gesammelte Werke*, *14*, p. 14). English translation by Schimek.

Drive is defined as energy seeking discharge or "satisfaction," which, biologically, can only bc provided by an external object. The presence of a suitable external object simultaneously provides both an experience of drive discharge and a perceptual registration. This co-occurrence leads to a stable associative link between the internal perception of the somatic-affective experience of satisfaction and the memory image of the object which made the drive discharge possible. By this association, the memory image becomes a drive-cathected representation or wish. Drives become directional, object-seeking forces bridging the border between the somatic and the psychical. The originally objective memory content acquires subjective and personal meaning; it becomes the representation of a drive and subject to its vicissitudes.

A drive seeks discharge by cathecting the mental representation of the lost object of satisfaction; this primary, uninhibited discharge process cathects the memory content to full hallucinatory intensity (hallucinatory wish fulfillment). Thus, the basic and primary effect of a drive is the confusion between perceptions and hallucinated memory images. This lack of "reality testing" does not by itself imply that the contents of perception and memories become changed and distorted, but merely that, in the earliest stages of mental development, the infant is incapable of distinguishing whether the source of the contents of his momentary experience is external or internal; he does not know that the content of his perception originates from a separate, permanent, external object.

To account for changes in content—for the unrealistic, "distorted" contents of mental representations—requires another assumption, that of "defense," or forces opposing the inherent tendency of a drive to seek discharge by the shortest path possible. When the direct path is blocked, the mobile drive cathexis will be "displaced" on to the nearest associated mental content available and the contents of several representations will become "condensed" in order to find access to consciousness in a substitute or disguised form. This process is at the core of Freud's well-known formulation of the dream work, the transformation of latent into manifest content, and serves as the model for the process of symptom formation in general.

The progressive establishment of reality testing and of the secondary process is essentially a partial undoing of the distorting effect of unchecked drive discharge; it is conceptualized in economic terms as binding of cathexes, inhibition of discharge. Wishful memories are no longer cathected to full hallucinatory intensity and their contents remain stable, no longer merging according to the momentary shortest discharge path available. Thus, the previously existing objective contents can reemerge and be used for adaptive drive satisfaction, based on reality constraints. The focus is on the progressive reinstatement of cognitive contents, which were already there but had been immediately buried by the distorting power of drives.

In brief, Freud's theory of cognition implies a three-stage process: first, objective perceptions and memory images; second, their distortion through the discharge tendency of drives (mobile cathexis, primary process); and third, the partial undoing and restraining of this distorting process in the service of adaptation to reality (bound cathexis, secondary process). Stage one, of course, does not exist as a distinct developmental stage but is merely the assumed cognitive input for stages two and three.

I have so far briefly examined the relationship of mental representations (as inner copies of external objects) to external reality and to drives (as agents of distortion and providers of personal subjective meaning). These assumptions lead to important consequences for the relation of drives to external reality and to action. Drives do not directly influence the perception of the external world but only through their effects on mental representations. Freud has no concept of a drive organization of perceptions analogous to what Rapaport (1950) has called the "drive organization of memories." Drives distort the content of memories and cathect their contents so that they supersede or at least interfere with the objective information provided by perceptions.

Reality (perceptions) and fantasy (drive-cathected mental representations) are, for Freud, like two different and competing languages or currencies—the constantly shifting dominance between the two depending on economic factors, the relative strength of drive cathexis, and defense countercathexis. Economic and dynamic factors determine not the contents of perceptions but the extent to which these contents are used in regulating behavior. The contents of objective perceptions can be selectively attended to (hypercathected) or actively ignored (denied). In certain states, such as sleep or psychosis, the mental apparatus can loosen its relation to external reality by decathecting the perceptual system.

This point of view is most explicitly illustrated in Freud's papers dealing with the reality principle (1911) and the turning away from reality in neurosis and psychosis (1924). For Freud, the basic mechanism of psychosis is a withdrawal from unbearably painful external reality to a narcissistic world of wishful hallucinatory fantasy (the mechanism which the state of sleep allows for in dreams). However, Freud concludes that this same mechanism operates also in neurosis, only in a more limited, circumscribed, and disguised fashion. Even in psychosis, a veridical picture of reality is never lost but merely buried under, creating what Freud (1938) came to call a "split in the ego" (p. 202).

To anticipate a later point, most contemporary views reject such a dichotomy between objective reality and subjective fantasy. The emphasis is more on a continuum of levels of interacting with the outside world and of constructing a selective picture of external reality. The more primitive levels of such a continuum have a "reality" of their own (including often socially shared myths and delusions) and can be described as subjective and distorted only when an impersonal, scientific, or technological construction of reality is taken as the absolute, fixed standard of "objectivity."

What is the relation of drives to action? In line with the reflex arc model (which clearly separates sensory input, memory storage, and motor output), action is conceptualized by Freud as motor discharge following prior perceptual and memory inputs. The problem of action becomes that of the delay or timing of motor discharge (what Rapaport, 1950, has called the control of the "sluices of motility"). This timing is also mediated through the influence of drives on mental representations. To the extent that wishes are taken for real and perceptions ignored, there will be premature motor discharge and maladaptive action. The change from random motor movements to adaptive action is reduced to an economic explanation—the change from mobile to bound energy which makes possible a suitable delay until the wished-for object has been found in the external world.

Drives express themselves as wishes, as the seeking of a lost object which previously had provided satisfaction. Drives seek discharge by the shortest path possible and this path always starts with the cathecting of a mental representation—originally as a hallucinatory wish fulfillment and later as a "purposive idea," an image of the wished-for object which guides the search for this object in the external world. Hallucinatory wish fulfillment is the first stage and basic model for drive discharge from which both thought and action are derived.* Wishes always precede action. Action is the enactment of a wishful fantasy—first through hallucination and then through goal-directed behavior toward the external world, which Freud calls a necessary detour or "roundabout path" toward the fulfillment of a wish. In more general terms, cognition precedes action; for Freud, organized, goal-directed action requires a cognitive representation of the goal prior to the action. Within the framework of his theory, Freud has to postulate unconscious mental images to account for the goal-directed and organized aspect of actions.

The assumption that drives operate on mental representation inside a spatial model of the mental apparatus—and influence the interaction with reality only indirectly—is expressed by such statements as "in the *Ucs.*, there are only contents cathected with greater or lesser strength" (Freud, 1915c, p. 186), and "the id, cut off from the external world, has a world of perception of its own" (1938, p. 198). It is reflected in an overall aspect of psychoanalytic theory which Rapaport (1960b) has called "the essential duality between psychical and external reality," between the contents of intrinsically objective perceptions which represent external reality, and drive cathected mental representations, which represent the psychical reality of drives.

* Freud sometimes refers to an even more primitive but essentially physiological mechanism of the reflex-like discharge of the tension of somatic needs by random motor movements (e.g., screaming and kicking in the hungry infant).

While this dichotomy follows directly from the assumptions about cognition which I have just reviewed, it also reflects more generally Freud's dualistic philosophical approach to human behavior—his view of external reality as a constraining frustrating power, as implacable Necessity, in eternal opposition to the individual seeking the unlimited expression of his drives (themselves the expression of cosmic forces).

The relative neglect of the problem of action and the implicit assumption that ideation always precedes action must be seen within the context of the clinical and historical basis of Freud's theory. The immediate data of clinical psychoanalysis are primarily verbal communications in a standardized one-to-one situation with a minimum of nonverbal interaction. The patients were mainly neurotics, people who could "maintain themselves in life" (1938), but were troubled by intrusive thoughts, uncontrolled affective reactions, and relatively circumscribed and private symptomatic acts and rituals. The focus of the therapeutic technique and the theory was on the repressed, the ego-alien, the dissociated, and the attempts to interpret their hidden meanings in order to facilitate their reintegration within the rest of the personality. The normal development—as well as the condition of the overall impairment—of the individual's predominant action patterns in everyday life remained rather peripheral in comparison to the search for the repressed, unconscious determinants of symptomatic acts and their ideational manifestations. Freud was well aware of this selective emphasis, as his statement on the last page of *The Interpretation of Dreams* (1900) indicates:

> Actions and consciously expressed opinions are as a rule enough for practical purposes in judging men's characters. Actions deserve to be considered first and foremost; for many impulses which force their way through to consciousness are even then brought to nothing by the real forces of mental life before they can mature into deeds. (p. 621)

THE EFFECT OF FREUD'S ASSUMPTION OF VERIDICAL PERCEPTION

Leaving aside a specific critique of Freud's assumptions about cognition, I would like to point out how these have created difficulties and ambiguities within the framework of Freud's own formulations and may have contributed to an ever increasing lack of integration between the basic explanatory concept of psychoanalysis and its clinical point of view. I shall deal mostly with three topics: the meaning of unconscious mental representations, the nature of primary and secondary process thoughts and their relation to consciousness, and the question of the reality basis of infantile fantasy.

It is important to consider the concept of unconscious mental representations, not only in terms of its underlying theoretical assumptions but also in relation to its observational base within the clinical psychoanalytic situation. It then becomes evident that unconscious mental representations are first and foremost hypothetical constructs of the psychoanalyst as he interprets the verbal communications of the patient. Their first empirical reality comes from conscious ideas in the analyst's mind. Freud (1938) states it this way:

> We have discovered technical methods of filling up the gaps in the phenomena of our consciousness, and we make use of those methods just as a physicist makes use of experiment. In this manner we infer a number of processes which are in themselves "unknowable" and interpolate them in those that are conscious to us. And if, for instance, we say: "At this point an unconscious memory intervened," what that means is: "At this point something occurred of which we are totally unable to form a conception, but which, if it had entered our consciousness, could only have been described in such and such a way." (pp. 196–197)

In other words, we do not know in what form unconscious memories as such exist within the mind of the patient, but we describe them, by analogy, in terms of the contents they would have if they were conscious and verbalized. An unconscious memory is a conscious memory which has undergone a special fate (due to repression, primary process transformations, etc.).

The logic involved and the need to make inferences about unconscious mental processes are not in question; however, it does not follow that these processes have to be conceptualized as contents of unconscious memories. It seems very likely that Freud chose this approach because of the combined influence of the theory of cognition, which he took for granted, and the nature of the clinical hypotheses he was trying to formulate. Within Freud's general assumptions about cognition and memory, the only way the influence of the past can survive is in the form of a storage of memory images of specific objects of past experience, as I said earlier. In line with association psychology, conscious thought processes consist of the establishment of associative links between specific, discrete "ideas" or memory contents; when no rational conscious link can be found, when there is "a gap in the phenomena of consciousness," such a link has to be provided by an inferred unconscious content interpolated to complete the associative chain.

The clinical basis of this formulation is directly related to the view of neurotic symptoms as substitutes for repressed memories of past traumatic events. Repressed memory contents were the clinical paradigm for the concept of unconscious mental representations (and remained so even when the memories referred to fantasies rather than real events). Forgotten memories were once conscious and could become conscious again; thus, to speak of unconscious memories, by analogy with conscious ones, maintained the continuity of psychical processes (Freud, 1915b).

Freud essentially tried to explain why the conscious becomes unconscious and how this process can be reversed (for instance, through the work of the psychoanalytic method). While at a theoretical level, Freud stated that the unconscious was much broader than the repressed; his working clinical model of the unconscious is of contents which were once conscious and, having undergone repression, were submitted to a special fate. Are these repressed contents identical with those that have never reached consciousness because of "primary repression"? I believe this is Freud's assumption and that thereby the complex issues of the clinical and developmental aspects of different kinds of consciousness and symbolic representations were oversimplified or bypassed.

But for Freud, unconscious mental representations were not only interpolated cognitive contents in an incomplete text. In the form of drive cathected representations (or, in more clinical terms, unconscious wishes, memories, or fantasies), they were the original and primary way in which drives expressed themselves beyond the somatic level. Their role in the system was that of causal agents—active forces which "set the apparatus in motion." On many occasions in Freud's writings (cf. 1923b, p. 111), they were equated with the drive itself. The methodological cautiousness about inferred processes "in themselves unknowable" was not maintained.

The unconscious representation, from a construct in the conscious thinking of the analyst, became reified as an entity existing in the unconscious mind of the patient as the true undisguised expression of his conscious thoughts. As an unconscious wish, a representation is endowed with a power and life of its own, almost like a demon seeking to leap out from the depths of the mental apparatus to create havoc with the orderly processes of rational thought and action. While such a view has considerable metaphorical power in expressing the way people often consciously experience their fantasies and impulses, it leads to much ambiguity when used as an explanatory concept. One of the main underlying methodological difficulties is Freud's attempt to reduce relationships of meaning and signification to causal processes.*

* A representation is a content of experience that stands for something that is not immediately present at a sensorimotor level (e.g., an image represents a past experience, a word represents a concept, etc.). A representation always involves cognitive symbolic processes and functions as a signifier that has a relationship of meaning to a signified. This relation cannot be reduced to a simple causal explanation, nor can the representation be equated with or seen as a mere copy of what it represents. In this sense, a drive representation is a cognitive content, which may refer to a past experience of satisfaction, somatic processes, or energy displacements but is not identical with them or simply caused by them. But in another (and, for Freud, dominant) sense, a drive representation (*Triebvorstellung*) is merely the expression or manifestation (here Freud uses interchangeably the words *Repräsentanz*, *Vertretung*, and *Ausdruck*) of the drive discharging its cathexis through a causal mechanistic process; it represents the drive somewhat in the way in which red spots on the skin can be said to "represent" measles.

Freud's assumptions about cognition created difficulties in his formulation of primary process thinking. One can distinguish two relatively unintegrated, if not contradictory, approaches (Schimek, 1974; Chapter 13, this volume). The main formulation views primary process as a distortion or disguise of already existing organized rational contents; this distortion is in the service of the shortest path toward discharge, under the obstacle of censorship or defense. The mechanisms of displacement and condensation are made possible by the mobility of drive cathexis, but they require the presence of defensive barriers as an integral part of the process as the reason for distortion or disguise.

A different view of primary process thought begins to emerge in Freud's writings, approximately 15 years after the original writing of *The Interpretation of Dreams* (1900), although it was never formulated in a very explicit or consistent manner. Here the focus is on "formal regression" in dreams to "primitive methods of expression and representation" (p. 548), implying a universal language whose structure and formal organization cannot be reduced to improvised drive discharge under the barrier of censorship. Thoughts are "represented symbolically by means of similes, metaphors, and images resembling those of poetic speech" (1901a, p. 659). "In every language concrete terms, in consequence of the history of their development, are richer in association than conceptual ones" (1900, p. 339). The main referent here is the issue of symbolism, especially because symbolism cannot be viewed as the creation of the dream work. "Even if there were no dream-censorship, dreams would still not be easily intelligible to us, for we should still be faced with the task of translating the symbolic language of dreams into that of our waking thought" (1916, p. 168).

Although Freud admitted the broad and basic significance of symbolism somewhat reluctantly, he did view it as tied to archaic levels of the development of language and to methods of representation which dominate the conscious thought of children and primitive people (1913, 1939). He seems to have been aware of the difficulty of accounting for symbolism within the framework of the economic explanation of the primary process. Although now often listed as one of the characteristics of primary process ideation, symbolism is not on a par with the concept of displacement and condensation (it was never included in the theoretical formulations of the seventh chapter of *The Interpretation of Dreams*). Freud showed a tendency to reduce symbolism to universal, fixed, sexual contents and to prefer an explanation of recurrent meanings in terms of phylogenetic, inherited contents. Here, again, he was confronted with the basic problem of reducing a relationship of meaning between symbol and symbolized to the language of causal and associative connections to which he was committed.

An alternative view would have been to treat symbolism as a universal ontogenetic stage of the development of thought, a basic method of representation and communication with variable individualized contents. With such a view of symbolism, easily extended to primary process ideation in general, conflicts between impulse and defense become factors motivating regression to already established patterns of primitive thought organization rather than the causal agents that create this organization and method of expression. The emphasis on the stable, structured aspect of primitive thought as a developmental stage of human symbolic processes (rather than a drive-induced distortion of rational objective contents) is in keeping with the main contemporary approaches to the development of thought and language, and has become increasingly dominant in writings on the psychoanalytic theory of thinking (e.g., Holt, 1967b; Rapaport, 1960a; Wolff, 1967).

The same ambiguity is naturally also carried over to Freud's formulations of the secondary process and his persistent difficulties in developing a theory of consciousness. Here, again, as stated earlier, the main explanation is in economic terms, the secondary process being a partial undoing of the distorting effects of the primary process, in the service of biological survival and through the mechanisms of inhibition of drive discharge or binding of energy. However, we also find the view that the secondary process involves a "higher level of mental organization," the creation of new relationships.

In 1900 Freud wrote of the system Conscious as creating "a new process of regulation which constitutes the superiority of men over animals" (p. 617). He was well aware that the specifically human trait of the acquisition of language plays a crucial role in the higher level of organization which characterizes preconscious mental processes, although he never settled the question as to whether language was the defining characteristic of these processes. He distinguished

> thinking in pictures...only a very incomplete form of becoming conscious [which] stands nearer to unconscious processes [and involves] only the concrete subject matter of the thought [from] thinking in words [which can express] the relations between the various elements of the subject matter. (1923b, p. 21)

But Freud's formulation of the acquisition and functioning of language was limited to the simple association concept of the linking of a "thing representation" to a "word representation." Such a learning of labels for objects of immediate experience hardly accounts for the development of abstract thought and relational structures, in addition to being grossly inadequate as a linguistic theory (Wolff, 1967). Nor did Freud carry very far his attempt to explain higher levels of thought in economic terms by using the concept of hypercathexis.*

* This attempt was carried out systematically by Hartmann and, particularly, Rapaport; however, I believe that they were unable to resolve the issue with which Freud had already struggled: Namely, how can a basically quantitative concept like cathexis account for structures or, more specifically, for higher levels of organization and different systems of symbolic representation?

These issues are closely tied to the rationale of psychoanalysis as a therapeutic and interpretive technique. For instance, let us take the concept of the interpretation of the dream—and, by extension, of any neurotic symptom. The "manifest" content of a dream is a distorted translation of a preexisting, organized, "latent" content—as the famous rebus analogy makes clear. A rebus requires a prior verbal statement, which is then translated into pictorial form, without a change in meaning. Interpretation is described by Freud as the deciphering of a rebus; it does not create new meanings but restores a prior buried meaning from its disguised and incomplete surface manifestations.*

Empirically, however, the latent content is the result of the work of interpretation, and this transformation of manifest into latent provides the model for the dream work. By postulating that the process of interpretation is the reverse of the dream work, Freud was able to equate the two in principle and to attempt a causal mechanistic explanation of dream formation as a justification of his method of interpretation. As I shall stress later, such an inference is very questionable and should be contrasted with a view of interpretation as the selective construction of new meanings, of broader and more abstract symbolic relationships.

The same point of view is reflected more broadly in the predominantly reductionistic formulation of the analytic process, as an archaeological digging for the causes of present symptoms in the form of memory contents preserved under layers of distortion and defense. Whatever modifications Freud made in the technical implementation of this basic principle, he held it consistently. In 1914a, he summarized the aim of the technique of psychoanalysis as "descriptively speaking, to fill in gaps in memory; dynamically speaking to overcome resistances due to repression" (p. 148).

In one of his last papers dealing with the subject, he stated, "What we are in search of is a picture of the patient's forgotten years that shall be alike, trustworthy and in all essential respects complete" (1937, p. 158). In this paper he also emphasized that such a picture is often not discovered, does not reemerge in its original form, but is a product of a "construction" of the analyst's interpretive and abstracting activity. He even admitted that such a construction, once it has become convincing and meaningful to the patient, can have the same therapeutic effect as the actual recovery of memories and, he added wistfully, the question of how and under what circumstances this is possible remains "a subject for further research."

This brings us to the basic issue of the reality or truth of unconscious memories (whether recovered or reconstructed). Here, too, I believe that Freud's initial assumptions about cognition, particularly the view of perceptions and memory as passive objective registrations, as inner copies of

* The dream work "restricts itself to giving things a new form," and the work of interpretation tries to restore the old form.

external events, had a significant influence. I think they predisposed him to believe in the factual reality of his patients' memories of sexual trauma and thus to view them as etiological causes of their neurotic symptoms. It is well known that after 1897 he realized that these memories of seduction were often only wishful fantasies—more specifically, screen memories for infantile masturbation and its accompanying oedipal fantasies. This change paved the way for the discovery of infantile sexuality and more generally shifted the focus from external trauma to conflicts around the expression of biologically determined factors.

Less attention has been paid to the fact that this change in Freud's thinking was never complete; he kept debating this issue until his very last writings and often reverted to some form of his earlier views (even though clinically he tried to dispose of the issue by stating repeatedly that it did not matter whether the unconscious wish was based in reality or in fantasy). It seems that Freud struggled with the difficulty in accounting for the source and causal effects of an unconscious fantasy within the framework of his original postulates about cognition and drive. The problem was not with conscious memories and fantasies; these could easily be accounted for as disguised expressions of unconscious fantasies to which they have essentially the same relation as the manifest to the latent dream content.

But what about the content of the original unconscious fantasy? The immediate answer is that it originates from the drive. But how can a drive—as a somatic need, a quantity of energy, or even an inner sensation of pleasure or unpleasure—create the content of a fantasy? We have already seen that, in Freud's original model, a drive acquires ideational content from the memory image of the object that produced the experience of satisfaction. It was difficult to maintain this formulation without assuming a real object or actual event that gave content to the drive.

After 1911 (probably in part under the repudiated influence of Jung), Freud tried to solve this problem by the speculation that the basis of universal unconscious fantasies (for instance, primal scene, castration, Oedipus complex) originated in actual events that had occurred before the individual's lifetime and had become phylogenetically inherited memories. He maintained his belief in the core of "historical truth," not only in social and religious myths (1913, 1939) but also in dreams, fantasies, and delusions (1918, 1937). He described (1918) "the core of the unconscious" as an "instinctive knowledge" and "phylogenetically acquired schemata" which categorize the data of immediate experience and transform them when necessary into fantasies that fit the schemata. (For instance, the child will create a primal scene fantasy from any available experience; the real experience merely triggers or may add details to a fantasy whose main content and meaning are biologically predetermined.)

In this line of thought, a drive as unconscious wish or unconscious fantasy already comes equipped with ready-made cognitive contents and their cathexes—so we have yet another implicit definition of drive which is difficult to reconcile with the more familiar ones. The idea of inherited memory contents gained little acceptance in Freud's days or in our own (Jungian and Kleinian theories being conspicuous exceptions). But the notion of drives as schemata (although not provided ready-made by heredity) organizing and categorizing experience (but not only fantasy) is very much part of contemporary thought. Freud seems to have been hampered by his belief in the originally veridical nature of the contents of perception and memory and the dichotomy between factual and psychical reality. He retained the concept of immaculate perception rather than assuming that perception always involves the interaction between the "objective" features of the external stimuli and the "subjective" drive or schemata of the individual, which selectively organize and give meaning to immediate experience.

With this latter point of view, there is no difficulty in dealing with the role of actual deeds in the content of childhood memories—if these events are defined, not in terms of adult objective "reality" but in terms of the "actuality" of the child's world and experience (Erikson, 1962). For instance, the memory of an infantile seduction need not be a fantasy but can refer back to actual interactions with a parental figure which the child—and often the adult—perceived, experienced, and reacted to as a seduction at the time, even if they do not meet adult criteria of a seduction (e.g., deliberate genital contact). Such a point of view is obviously in keeping with the spirit of Freud's clinical thinking, but his theoretical assumptions about cognition and reality did not allow for an adequate conceptual formulation of this problem.*

In the ambiguities and inconsistencies of the issues reviewed in this part of the paper, one can see the reflection of two conflicting trends which pervaded Freud's thinking: a dominant intent to explain mental phenomena in terms of forces and quantity derived from a causal mechanistic model of a "mental apparatus"—in contrast to the search for connections of meaning at different levels of symbolic expression, through a new method of interpretation. While the former trend is more explicit in his metapsychology and the latter pervades the spirit of his clinical discoveries, the struggle between these two approaches is evident at all levels of Freud's formulations, whose enduring richness can never be reduced to a tightly knit consistent system.

* Freud came closest to such a point of view when he suggested that female oedipal fantasies of seduction by the father "touch the ground of reality" by referring back to real experiences of libidinal stimulation provided by the normal maternal care of the child's bodily needs (1933).

SHOULD THE CONCEPT OF UNCONSCIOUS MENTAL REPRESENTATION BE ABANDONED?

It is time to summarize the ways in which Freud's view of cognition and the theory of motivation that is closely interlinked with it are in conflict with some of the main trends of contemporary developmental psychology.

I do not plan here to go into a detailed critique of association theory. Suffice it to mention that such a theory begs the question on the main developmental issues. How does experience get organized as the stable discrete units which associationism takes for granted from the start? Where do the categories which determine the formation of associations (contiguity and, particularly, similarity) come from? Association theory has to assume that they are provided ready-made by external reality—which, in fact, usually means reality as defined by some external observer and his presumably scientific, objective point of view and standards.

The complex issues involved in Freud's drive concept fall outside the scope of this chapter and I shall merely refer to the relevant critiques in the literature (e.g., Holt, 1967a; Klein, 1967; Loewald, 1971a). From these reexaminations, one can draw the overall conclusion that the economic principles of quantities of energy with different processes of discharge have little explanatory value (except as a questionable metaneurology) and can at best be used as a kind of shorthand or set of metaphors for describing clinical phenomena.

With regard to Freud's assumptions about cognition, it is clear that the concept of immaculate perception, of a passive objective registration of external reality, is totally discrepant with modern psychological data and concepts. Contemporary developmental psychology assumes that the contents of primitive perception are diffuse and global, with no clear differentiation between separate objects, between object and self, and between external sensorimotor stimulation and internal visceral affective reactions. The subjective or motivational valence of an object is an intrinsic, inseparable part of immediate perception and not something tacked on to an objective sensory content. When objects become differentiated, they are first perceived as "things of action." The experience of the external world in terms of separate, stable objects which can be "contemplated" (Werner & Kaplan, 1963) outside the context of immediate action and the subject's momentary state is an active construction of the mind, the product of a long developmental process involving memory as well as symbolic and conceptual functions.

Such a view of perception already had been taken for granted 30 years ago by some of the main systematizers of psychoanalytic theory, such as Fenichel and Rapaport. Yet, they mostly ignored the implication that such an approach forces a reevaluation of Freud's theory of cognition and thought. If the early experience of satisfaction is global and undifferentiated and does not involve, as Freud assumed, the perception of a particular object, a wish is no longer the search for an object but merely the desire to reexperience a diffuse pleasurable sensorimotor-affective experience. How does one account for the shift from the (hallucinated) recall of a global state to the wish for a specific object? Freud's model of the wish takes for granted that the infant has the capacity for the perceptual registration of an object differentiated from the global experience of satisfaction, as well as the capacity to recall a memory image of the original perception and to use this image as an anticipatory signal and magical hallucinatory substitute for the experience of satisfaction.

If the contents of immediate perception are the result of an active selective construction process, the same has to be true for memory images. A memory image is then not a mere copy or replica of the past object, but the selective reconstruction of certain aspects of past experience in terms of the needs and cognitive capacities of the present. The capacity to recall the past in the form of memory images is probably the result of a complex developmental process. It is preceded by the capacity merely to recognize objects of past experience and to react to the absence of an object in a specific familiar situation which previously included this object as an integral part.

While much remains to be known about the earliest preideational stages of memory, it is likely that they are at a predominantly motor-action level, including motor imitation of the object and repetition of actions toward the object despite its absence. (From an adult point of view, one could describe this as "magical" procedures to make the object appear, which may be somewhat the motoric equivalent of Freud's hallucinatory wish fulfillment.)

I shall now summarize the reasons why the further development of psychoanalytic theory requires the abandonment of the concept of unconscious mental representation: (1) This concept rests on a theory of cognition which is contradictory to most contemporary developmental data and concepts; (2) It is directly linked to the idea of psychic energy, the economic drive discharge model, and all its problematic aspects; (3) With the unconscious as a container of encapsulated mental contents, the dichotomy between psychical and external reality, the separation of motor action from the ideation which always precedes it, it becomes difficult to account for unconscious processes as directly regulating perception, communication, and interaction with the outside world; (4) It tends towards a reductionistic emphasis in psychoanalytic theory, with the implicit assumption that by interpretation we can rediscover past experience in its original form; (5) It does not provide an adequate approach to the problem of the different levels of consciousness, their influence on behavior and their relation to symbolic processes and language.

Any reformulation will have to take into account the observations which Freud's concepts of displaceable quantities of energy and unconscious mental representations tried to account for. I am referring to such issues as variations in the strength and salience of various motives and behavior patterns, the continuity of function and meaning between phenotypically extremely different activities and thought contents, and the general difference between more peremptory and reactive actions and those which are mediated by processes which common-sense language describes as will, judgment, and choice.

ACTION, MEMORY, AND UNCONSCIOUS IDEATION

We must now examine some of the consequences of rejecting Freud's hypothesis that the primary and original form of the unconscious is an ideational one—namely, contents of memories or fantasies which, by acquiring drive cathexis, become causal agents of behavior. What is at issue is not a determination of the nature of the unconscious as a thing or substantive entity inhabiting some mental apparatus. We are talking about a change in the "intellectual scaffolding," to use Freud's expression, which helps integrate and give meaning to clinical observations. The main empirical referent of the unconscious is the concept of interpretation, the process by which psychoanalyst and patient construct new meanings and relationships from the patient's symbolic, predominantly verbal productions.

I can merely indicate the direction and general point of view which a reformulation may take (and, I believe, has already taken), with various degrees of explicitness and specificity, in the writings of Erikson and other contemporary writers (e.g., Klein, 1967; Loewald, 1971a; Mahl, 1970; Rosen, 1969; Schafer, 1972). Let me first state that Freud's way of conceptualizing the unconscious as ideational contents, by analogy with the contents of conscious verbal experience, has become not only obsolete but also basically unnecessary. The idea that "thought processes are in themselves unconscious" or that "thought is an unconscious activity of the mind" (to use one of Piaget's favorite quotations, which he attributes to Binet) has become very much part of contemporary thought in many fields beyond psychoanalysis, including developmental psychology, linguistics, anthropology, and the like. One can make the assumption that the contents of immediate experience are conscious, but that the regulating processes, reasons, and long-range antecedents of these experiences are normally unconscious—and can only become conscious to a limited extent by a reflective process involving a conceptual and symbolic reconstruction of immediate experience.

To put it more simply, I am conscious of what I am perceiving or thinking at the moment but not of the underlying processes that made me think or perceive this way or of all its antecedents and implied meanings. To take an analogy from linguistics, our language is regulated by rules of syntax, yet the child and most adults are unconscious of these rules, not only in Freud's sense of preconscious, but also because they are unaware of following rules and, unless they are linguists, quite unable to formulate them.

If we use Freud's model of unconscious representations, we would have to say that the rules of syntax as formulated by linguists exist in similar form in the child's mind but in an unconscious state. Or to use an analogy which comes closer to the Freudian paradigm of the relationship between the unconscious infantile wish and adult behavior, Piaget has tried to show the developmental continuity and formal similarity between the sensorimotor activity of the infant—ordering, classifying objects in his immediate experience through his motor actions—and, at the other extreme, the activity of a logician constructing relationships between abstract concepts. It is neither necessary nor very meaningful to assume that the child's behavior is regulated by the mental operations of the adult logician existing in his mind in an unconscious regressed state.

As I have already indicated in earlier parts of this chapter, Freud's concept of unconscious mental representations is derived mainly from the theory of cognition and the general theoretical postulates that dominated his thinking. I am referring to the assumption that the influence of the past can only be carried through the contents of stored memory images, and the related postulate that the organized, repetitive, and goal-directed aspects of thought and action can only be accounted for by assuming that they are the enactment of the contents of a prior wishful memory or fantasy. The data of modern development psychology, of Piaget (1945), in particular, support the conclusion that organized, goal-directed action patterns, which can be carried over to new situations and become modified by them, occur at an age when we have no reasons to believe that the child already has the capacity to recall the past in the form of mental images.

For Piaget, such action patterns or sensorimotor schemata are based on inborn reflex structures, which become progressively differentiated and modified as part of interaction with the external environment. An external object or event is given personal meaning by being assimilated to such a schema, and the schema itself accommodates to the object and becomes modified thereby. There is no assumption of unconscious cognitive contents and images preceding these action patterns and regulating them. As Wolff (1967) puts it, "The earliest forms of thought are sensorimotor actions—the sensory event and the motor response constitute one integral unit" (p. 324). The influence of the past is carried on through the modification of these action patterns, not through memory images of absent objects.

We may make the assumptions that unconscious motives can operate on a prerepresentational level at all stages of development. The fact that a child (or adult, for that matter) repeats and generalizes (usually with some modifications) salient aspects of his interactions with the mother to other people does not require postulating the persistence of an unconscious image of his mother. Once the capacity for evocative memory has developed, this repetition may be accompanied by an image of the mother, and the pattern itself may be carried out entirely at the level of thought or fantasy or by actions which are only symbolic substitutes for the original concrete behavior. But the persistence of memory images is based on the continuity of prior action patterns rather than the reverse.

Such organized action patterns are "ways of going at things," tendencies to seek or avoid specific experiences and situations; they do not require any mental representation of past experience as their anticipated goal. They would express the earliest and most basic level of any motive, truly unconscious in the sense of not yet being capable of achieving any symbolic representation. The general concept of prerepresentational unconscious organizers of action (which is exemplified in some way by Piaget's sensorimotor and affective schemata or Erikson's modes and modalities) has the same methodological status as Freud's concept of unconscious mental representation. It is an inferred construct to account for relationships between observables; it does not refer to some unconscious experiential content of the observed subject and also leaves open the question of the neurological mediation of the observed processes.

Such an approach is more parsimonious than and less contradictory to other areas of observation than the view of the unconscious as an encapsulated storage container of images of the past within which drive energies find their most immediate expression. Action patterns have their roots in the biological interaction between the organism and environment, including the mode of functioning of various organs, but they rapidly go beyond this and should be considered as a psychological rather than a biological concept.

As Piaget has amply demonstrated, they involve cognitive processes and an active ordering and classifying of experience—even if it is only the coordination, at a here-and-now level, of perceptions, motor actions, and bodily sensations. Such activity includes the construction of basic categories of experience (e.g., the permanent object, space, time, etc.) and the establishment of a relationship between objects where one functions as an anticipatory signal for the immediate presence of another—activities which can be seen as the precursors of later mental operations and symbolic relationships. We are no longer limited to Freud's alternatives that the unconscious has to be conceptualized as purely somatic processes or as the mental contents of unconscious images.

No longer taking for granted the existence of mental representations from the beginning of development may allow one to reconsider some core issues of the psychoanalytic approach, particularly the unconscious–conscious dimension and the process of "making something conscious." Freud dealt with these issues mostly in terms of the dynamics of repression (assuming a force that pushes toward consciousness, as part of the natural path of drive discharge, and becomes pitted against the counterforce of repression) and the difference between primary and secondary processes of drive discharge. The process of something becoming conscious can both create conflict and help resolve it; but does it still remain the same process? Freud was aware that consciousness is not a unitary phenomenon—that there are different levels of consciousness involving transformations in the content and organization of experience—but he was never able to formulate this relationship even to his own satisfaction.

A different approach to the development of cognition is clearly needed, an approach that distinguishes different stages and levels of symbolic (or, more accurately, semiotic) functioning as the key to the meaning of the unconscious and conscious aspects of everyday experience. A consideration of the development of the symbolic function must obviously include the central role of language and the motivational and interpersonal aspects of such development. The normal developmental sequence of symbolic processes has been extensively studied (by Piaget, 1945, and Werner & Kaplan, 1963, in particular) and cannot be reviewed here. I shall merely refer in a schematic way to the three main developmental stages involved.

The first stage—already mentioned earlier and the one which does not exist in Freud's model—is the prerepresentational level of concrete action schemes. Conscious awareness is limited to perceptions of here-and-now experience, and objects can function as signals or clues within a specific action sequence.

The second stage includes the beginnings of true representation, the capacity for the symbolic evocation of absent realities through memory images, fantasy, and by also giving a symbolic—instead of a purely pragmatic, action-oriented—meaning to external events. This level of representation tends to be "iconic," to be based on some concrete similarity between the representation and what is represented—a similarity often derived from the specific past experience and personal frame of reference of the subject. Such a representation can often function as an evocative affective substitute for the "presence" of the absent object. The concept of primary process ideation corresponds to this level, but only in a descriptive and not in an explanatory sense.

At the third stage, that of logical abstract thought, a representation (e.g., a word) has no concrete similarity to what is represented; the relationship is "arbitrary" (i.e., based on a learned system of consensual impersonal relationships between the signifier and the signified concept). Representations refer to general concepts rather than specific experiences and imply the construction of invariant structures relatively independent of specific contents. Language—indispensable for the abstract level of representation but probably not for the iconic one—can be and is constantly used at both levels; hence, there is the ambiguity, multiple connotations, and dependence of meaning upon context which characterizes much of language and forms the basis for the technique of interpretation and free association.

Psychoanalysis and developmental psychology agree that the three levels of representation are not just developmental stages that become superseded, but that they remain as coexisting aspects of adult experience. When we state that a patient is "unconscious" of the relation between his infantile wishes and some aspect of his conscious adult thoughts, it is useful to keep in mind that such a relation can only be established through a process of abstracting and conceptualizing activity. This may not be available to the patient, quite apart from the reasons why he may not want to establish such a relationship. As mentioned earlier, some contemporary writers have already redefined unconscious mental representation as an inferred psychological organization or schema, but becoming conscious of a regulatory principle is quite a different process from remembering the contents of a forgotten memory.

The main point I want to stress here is that the different levels at which a concrete experience or object can be represented must not be viewed as merely different codes—different systems of labels attached to the same object (as implied by the rebus analogy). Each level of symbolic representation changes the experience of the object represented, its meaning, function, and relationship to other objects. It is an organizing abstracting process, the construction of a "higher level of mental organization," which cannot be reduced to the distortion or disguise of the contents of a lower level. A dream or fantasy is already a higher level of conscious representation of a motive than the enactment of this motive as concrete action patterns; the "interpretation" of a dream is, in turn, a new, more abstract, higher order construction.

Each level makes possible a different way of interacting with the environment, of giving meaning and valence to external events. The kind of symbolic representation or level of consciousness which a motive or drive achieves changes the nature of the motive itself and its influence on behavior. At each higher level, something is added but something is also partially lost—namely, the immediacy and uniqueness of concrete experience.

With such issues we are back to the basic postulate of the psychoanalytic method: that transforming the unconscious into conscious, through interpretation and insight, can change the integration and self-regulated autonomy of an individual's actions and self-experience. The study of symbolic functions probably holds the key to a better understanding of this point of view. To be clinically relevant, such understanding must be able to specify the motivational and interpersonal factors that influence the development of symbolic processes and the constant shifts in their range of functioning in a specific individual.

What accounts for specific deficits in the development of the symbolic function, for the lack of integration between different coexisting levels, and the inability to use the symbolic construction of a specific situation (whether in the abstract or concrete direction) which is most adaptive to its interpersonal context? I believe that the clarification of some of the central problems of the clinical theory of psychoanalysis—particularly such concepts as repression, the nature of insight* and its role in changing behavior, the development of internalization, and the meaning of "thought disorder"—depends on the answer to such questions.

One of the strongest points of psychoanalytic theory has traditionally been the demonstration of the persistence of basic infantile drives and wishes and the continuity between them and many aspects of adult behavior and thought. A long-standing weak point of the theory has been the problem of accounting for the specific individualized manifestations of these quasi-universal motives and conflicts, their range of expression, and different effects in the individual case (e.g., "the choice" of neurosis or defense, grossly different degrees of pathology even when the inferred content of the underlying conflict seems similar, etc.).

Invoking differences in ego strength or drive intensity does not provide much more than labels for this problem. There is clearly a need for greater emphasis on the level of symbolic representation that a motive achieves because it is largely this representation which gives a motive its individualized aspect and mediates its specific effects on behavior. Is a motive expressed only by repeated action and reaction patterns to here-and-now stimuli? Is it capable of symbolic representation in fantasy, memory, and dreams? Or can it also be conceptualized and experienced by the patient as an enduring goal or organizer of his actions, as his intent, and as his way of acting and thinking?

Several trends in contemporary psychoanalytic thought begin to converge on these issues: (1) A greater interest in the diversity of the "manifest" and its specific context (including detailed descriptions and reconstructions of the experiential world of the patient), with less of a tendency to reduce all levels to equivalent manifestations of an unconscious infantile wish; (2) Less emphasis on contents and more on recurrent structures, modes, and configurations, relatively independent of specific contents; (3) A close analysis of the assumption and steps of the process of interpretation, including the nature of the observed manifestations from which the unconscious underlying processes are inferred and the degree of inferential distance and interpretive construction required for different kinds of data. This involves

* Maybe insight does not precede change but follows it. A limited change, first enacted unconsciously in the concrete interaction with a specific object (for instance, the analyst), may then, by achieving a higher level of symbolic representation, get generalized, estranged from its concrete origins, and adapted to other situations, and thus become internalized as a conscious motive, integrated with the patient's self-image as an active agent. Maybe by paying closer attention to the creation of a new language and new levels of symbolic representation in the patient–analyst interaction, we can get a better understanding of such familiar but vaguely specified processes as "working through" and "the resolution of the transference" (beyond the limitations of an explanation merely in terms of the lifting of resistances).

paying greater attention to the specific and unique nature of the psychoanalytic interaction, where the analyst can observe the patient's total range of actions directly only in one context—namely, that of the psychoanalytic situation—and knows about other areas of a patient's life only insofar as they have already achieved some symbolic representation in the patient's verbal communication; (4) Since speech plays the central role in the psychoanalytic process, the need to deal with linguistic problems, including the various functions of language and its capacity to carry simultaneously multiple levels of meaning and symbolic relationships. (Freud, 1900, already had spoken of the "predestined ambiguity" of words.)

Such trends require a drastic revision of Freud's assumptions about cognition and unconscious thought, but may help give new meaning and a better conceptual basis to psychoanalysis as an investigative and clinical method. One may view as a paradoxical proof of Freud's lasting originality the fact that, starting with a rationalistic and nondevelopmental view of cognition, he ended up creating a primarily motivational and developmental approach to human behavior. He showed how "irrational" cognition had meaning and lawfulness and constitutes a basic system of expression and communication grounded on the human capacity for different levels of symbolic functioning. He thus made a decisive contribution to the contemporary outlook on problems of cognition, and indirectly demonstrated the inadequacy of the very assumptions about cognition that he took for granted in many of his theoretical formulations.

Chapter 11

Affective schemas

Toward a structural view of cognition and affect*

In this chapter, I want to touch upon three aspects of the relevance of Piaget to psychoanalysis. The first deals with Piaget's critique of Freud's theory of cognition, the second with Piaget's concept of affective schemas and its potential relevance to psychoanalysis, and the third with the inherent limitations of Piaget's approach when applied to the understanding of the multilevel aspects of the cognitive performance of the individual (in contrast to a generalized human mind).

Piaget highlights the ways in which Freud relied on the principles of the association psychology of his times. Freud incorporated within his dynamic psychology a view of rational and objective cognition which is essentially nonmotivational and nondevelopmental. He seems to take for granted, from the beginning of development, the capacity for veridical perception as a passive, camera-like registration of discrete external objects and for the automatic storage of these perceptions in the form of memory images. Such objective information is used and distorted by primary process drive expression (and the need for censorship and defense), which leads to a confusion between memories and perception (hallucinatory wish fulfillment) and the selective condensation and distortion of the contents of memories. The construction of an objective view of reality is brought about by the progressive inhibition or taming of the distorting power of wishful thinking, learned through the hard knocks of necessity and frustration. As Wolff (1967) has summarized it, Freud's epistemology implies

> a direct correspondence (an isomorphism) between the event as objectively described, the event as registered in memory, and the event as recalled under appropriate dynamic conditions, as if from the start of development the experience were identical with the physical event. (p. 312)

* This chapter was originally presented at the Piaget and Freud Symposium, Philadelphia, 1978.

For Freud, some form of ideation or representation always *precedes* any organized, goal-directed action as the seeking in the real world of perceptions that will match the wished-for memories of lost or absent objects of satisfaction. In sharp contrast, for Piaget, the earliest forms of thought *are* sensorimotor actions; they precede and are the basis of later evocative memory and higher forms of representation. Objective reality is a selective construction through a series of schemes and mental operations, not a passive registration and accommodation to what is externally given.

The central issue for Piaget is this: How does the human mind *construct* a stable, objective, impersonal representation of external reality? Or, more specifically, what are the origins of logical-mathematical operations as the most powerful and advanced tools for such a construction? For Freud, the question is this: How do our desires, wishes, and fears *distort* the contents of our objective perceptions and memories? What can we infer about unconscious wishes and drives from theses distortions? The issue is not how we acquire objective knowledge, but how it gets distorted and overruled and how this distorting influence of the primary process gets limited and inhibited through the secondary process, in the service of adaptation.

Freud's assumptions about cognition and memory have shaped many aspects of his thought—particularly the belief in the possibility of recovering the forgotten past, as a kind of archaeology, and the assumption of a dichotomy between objective external reality and purely subjective internal, drive-dominated fantasy. These issues have been elaborated in earlier papers by Wolff (1967) and others (Litowitz & Litowitz, 1977; Chapter 10, this volume).

It has been said that Piaget's critique is no longer relevant in the light of contemporary developments in psychoanalysis. Indeed, many analytic writers, partly influenced by Piaget, have put great emphasis on the dynamics of the development of the differentiation between self and object, from an original state of egocentrism or lack of boundaries. They have also highlighted the issue of the slow achievement of object permanence or constancy.

Many aspects of severe psychopathology have been viewed in terms of impairments in the acquisition and maintenance of self/object differentiation and object constancy. Yet many psychoanalytic writers refer to infantile hallucinatory wish fulfillment as an empirical fact (Mahler). More generally, in their reconstruction of the *preverbal* past from the adult transference, they tend to attribute to the infant powers of omnipotent, elaborate fantasy constructions which hardly fit with our present knowledge of cognitive development.

So far we have reached two main conclusions from Piaget's critique of Freud's theory of cognition. First, Piaget provides us with a model of the development of rational, objective thought far superior to the passive registration and association model assumed by Freud. Objectivity is the result of a selective construction, not just the inhibition of drive-dominated distortions. Second, the continuity between past and present should be viewed not in terms of the conservation of charged memory images contained in the unconscious as some dark storehouse, but as the persistence of organizing schemes of action and thought that influence our ongoing construction and experience of outer and inner reality. Summarizing Piaget, we can say that the unconscious could be seen as a system of operations and action schemes, whose development and interrelationships have to be studied—rather than as a reservoir of memories that one can hope to retrieve and to invoke as an explanatin of present behavior.

Piaget (1945) makes a reference to the interrelationship between an individual's motor, intellectual, and affective schemas as constituting the basis of his "character" (p. 189). But he does not try to address the complexity and the dynamics of this interrelationship. Yet it is precisely this issue that psychoanalysis has struggled with and is essential for the understanding of individual behavior, even—or maybe especially—in its cognitive aspects. This aspect of cognition has always remained peripheral to Piaget's main interests, almost a bothersome topic which could not be altogether avoided and had to be somewhat disposed of. This makes it even more remarkable that some of Piaget's contributions in this area are of potential relevance to psychoanalytic theory.

The whole area of wishes, motives, and interests is lumped by Piaget under the vague overall label of "affectivity." Piaget never tires of repeating that all cognitive operations have an affective component and vice versa. He also constantly emphasizes that this affective component has a limited effect on the development of intelligence and the organization and structure of cognition. Although affectivity is constantly at work in the functioning of thought, it does not create new structures of reasoning: "Affective life, like intellectual life, is a continual adaptation, and the two are not only parallel but interdependent, since feelings express the interest and value given to actions of which intelligence provides the structure" (1945, p. 205).

Piaget thinks of affectivity mostly as a variable quantity of energy which fuels our actions and influences the *choice* of the activities we engage in and the *intensity* with which we pursue them. This idea of affectivity as energy was a familiar one in European psychology (Janet, Claparede) and has a strong similarity with one main aspect of Freud's concept of drive as a displaceable quantity of energy, investment, or cathexis.

Piaget will grant that affectivity can influence the individual timing of the stages of intelligence. But whether accelerated or slowed down, the sequence and organization of the stages remains invariant and universal. But, at times, he goes beyond this very general and not particularly useful concept of affectivity as fuel or energy for cognitive schemes. In a few passages, mostly in the 1945 book on symbol formation, he introduces the concept of affective schemas. Although mostly ignored since then, this concept is, I believe, one of the more promising bridges between the structural aspects of Piagetian and psychoanalytic thought. Affective schemas are modes of acting, feeling, and thinking which form organized and self-maintaining structures. They are derived from the child's interaction with the primary people in his early environment—rather than the manipulation of physical objects. They involve not momentary interests and goals but what Piaget (1945) calls "intimate permanent concerns, secret often inexpressible desires" (p. 175). These schemas remain centered around the individual's construction of the interaction with particular people and intense bodily sensations and activities.

Structurally, such schemas stay at the level of preoperational intelligence; they show a predominance of assimilation and deal with concrete, not decentered, relations rather than conceptual ones:

> The first personal schemas are afterwards generalized and applied to many other people. According as the first inter-individual experiences of the child who is just learning to speak are connected with a father who is understanding or dominating, loving or cruel, etc., the child will tend (even throughout life if these relationships have influenced his whole youth) to assimilate all other individuals to this father schema. On the other hand, the type of feelings he has for his mother will tend to make him love in a certain way, sometimes all through his life, because he partially assimilates his successive loves to his first love which shapes his innermost feelings and behaviors. (p. 207)

Such a point of view is almost identical with Freud's reference to patterns of loving and hating, which every individual develops early in life and then "transfers," in more or less modified form, to many later personal situations and experiences.

Basically, Piaget's affective schemas are a close equivalent to the system of persistent unconscious wishes, fantasies, and scenarios which psychoanalysis uses as a central, but often inadequately formulated, explanatory concept (with the Oedipus complex as a prototypical example). Piaget seems right in thinking of such a system of unconscious fantasies not as charged images or memories, but as underlying organizing structures which can manifest themselves in patterns of action, in the contents of conscious thoughts and feelings, and in the personal meaning and value we give to our experience, at various levels of representation.

Freud uses the concept of the Oedipus complex as an organizing structure (a self-regulating totality capable of multiple transformations while maintaining its overall organization, to use Piaget's definition), centered around a limited set of categories and relations (parent–child, male–female, love–hate, etc.). Many different and changing experiences and people can be fitted within individual versions of these general scenarios—categories, and roles—if they are "subjectively analogous," to use Piaget's expression. This not only takes place in fantasy but also is used to give meaning to actual interactions.

Piaget's concept of affective and interpersonal schemas as transformational structures also fits with the psychoanalytic emphasis on psychological reality. I mean that schemas, affective or cognitive, are not simply learned or conditioned behavior patterns and habits merely reflecting the environment (e.g., the child's actual interaction with the parents). They represent the assimilation, the selective symbolic construction of the external reality input, in terms of the child's desires and fears and his striving for consistency and equilibrium. On this crucial point, Piaget and Freud are clearly on the same side, in contrast to behaviorism and social learning theories (and even the renewed one-sided emphasis on early environmental factors and deficits which characterize many contemporary neo-Freudian formulations).

But now we also face some of the basic limitations of Piaget's approach. First, we may ask *why* these affective schemas remain relatively permanent, rigid, and impervious to accommodation. Piaget alludes to the fact that they represent "permanent intimate concerns," but he does not elaborate this crucial point. Psychoanalysis focuses on the role of such permanent intimate concerns and their ongoing effects on mental life and behavior. Individuals have a vested interest in clinging to their affective schemas as their earliest patterns of gratification and security and as the basic wishes, hopes, and compensatory mechanisms (even if they are somewhat illusory from an objective point of view) necessary for their inner equilibrium and self-cohesiveness.

Second, Piaget does not mention that such affective schemas do not have a clear-cut, unambiguous, compelling external reality to accommodate to. At the sensorimotor level, we get immediate and clear feedback from our action; at the operational level, there are unambiguous definitions of true and false, right and wrong. This is not the case in the realm of fantasy or even in the realm of social and personal reality, where situations are ambiguous and open to multiple interpretations. Furthermore, affective schemas and irrational or nonobjective beliefs and attitudes may fit with the beliefs and myths of the individual's social reference group and thus find external confirmation and validation. People also often act in a way which will bring external validation to their personal schemas. (If we believe that someone is hostile to us, we may act in a way that may bring confirmation of our initially false assumption.)

A more fundamental limitation comes from the fact that Piaget, within the framework of his theory and data, is interested only in the highest level of mental operation that the individual is capable of under optimal circumstances at any particular stage. He is not interested in the fact that the individual's actual behavior and cognitive performance (to use Chomsky's term) at any one time will involve the *coexistence and interaction* of many simultaneously operating schemes—which all contribute to our individual experience of reality (our perception of the field) and our actions in relation to it.

Piaget talks of the mutual accommodation and integration between different schemes as an intrinsic part of the developmental process. But such an interaction remains part of our functioning at any level, including the adult one. We always function at several levels simultaneously. Different schemes may be dominant in a particular situation or state; the accommodation between different schemes may be insufficient, leading to various degrees of compromise, conflict, and defense. Piaget makes some reference to such issues of conflict and contradiction between the organization of action and thought, but purely in terms of our understanding of the physical world (and mostly in his last works). Even in the most optimal, least conflicted situation, we need the ongoing support of intuitive, figurative, and preoperational schemes to make use of formal operations. Abstractions need some ultimate anchoring in the examples and motives of our personal experience.

We do not think purely rationally or simply regress to a prior irrational, affective level. We strive to construct and maintain some equilibrium between often conflicting schemes and constructions of reality. And I would like to suggest that this search for equilibrium constantly constructs new, although often unstable and temporary, structures whose manifestations range from maladaptive symptoms to creative works. Piaget's basic assumption that affectivity does not influence the structure of cognition but only its contents can only be maintained as an abstract principle, within the specific limits of his data and his concepts. The very distinction between structure and contents is an abstraction which acquires empirical content as part of development and only truly holds at the formal operational level. In the individual's actual functioning, the interaction between impersonal rational schemes and more personal affective ones constantly creates new structures, change, and novelty, bringing about new systems of classification, connections, and meaning. Logical thought is only one of our most powerful tools; it can be used in the service of a paranoid system as well as a scientific theory.

It is not surprising that Freud's theory of cognition and Piaget's views on motivation and conflict are the weakest links in their respective systems. But it is in these areas that each approach can make a contribution to the other—toward the goal of understanding the overall functioning of actual human beings rather than just a generalized human mind striving for objectivity and abstraction or a mental apparatus seeking the best available discharge for drive tensions.

Freud and Piaget used very different data for different purposes. They shared an exceptional ability for the close observation of behavior and for picking out crucial and previously neglected details. Neither of them stayed at the level of conscious experience and manifest behavior; they based their theories on the assumption of inferred unconscious structures and rules which organize cognition and behavior. In both theories, such structures, anchored initially on the biological level, involve the transforming, symbolizing capacity of the mind—without which we could construct neither illusion nor reality.

Chapter 12

Notes on the psychoanalytic theory of consciousness and reflective awareness*

PERCEPTION AND CONSCIOUSNESS

At the present time, psychoanalytic psychology does not have a systematic theory of consciousness. Freud approached the problem of consciousness from several different angles, changing his emphasis through the years and leaving many of his ideas fragmentary and unintegrated. This historical development has been reviewed in detail by Rapaport (1958). In this chapter, I shall first restate some of the basic principles and concepts involved in Freud's thinking, stressing throughout the possibilities and difficulties they present for a unified theory of consciousness. After these fundamentals, I shall mention some other aspects of Freud's theory of consciousness and the questions they raise. In the second part of this chapter, I shall deal mostly with the specific and unique characteristics of consciousness of our inner thought processes, which set it further apart from perceptual awareness. Finally, I will elaborate on the notion of reflective consciousness and try to place it in the context of some broader aspects of mental functioning and personality development.

As is well known, Freud gave three different meanings to the dimension of conscious–unconscious, each one intended to account for a somewhat different area of observations and data (1900, p. 615). The first meaning is the *descriptive* one, consciousness as awareness, as an immediately given quality of mental experience. Even superficial observation shows that this quality is "fugitive," temporary, and strictly limited in its range of content at any one time (what academic psychology has called the attention span): "Everything else psychical [except consciousness] is in our view 'the unconscious'...This reminds us that consciousness is in general a very highly fugitive state" (1938, p. 159). Freud made the bold assumption that "the psychical is in itself unconscious" (p. 158) and that the quality of consciousness is something extra added to certain mental contents temporarily and under special circumstances—a "hypercathexis" available in limited

* This chapter was originally presented to the Rapaport-Klein Study Group, June 1964.

quantity. This leads to the question of the nature of this hypercathexis and the conditions of its deployment.

The second meaning, which, like the third, is unique to psychoanalytic theory and data, is the *dynamic* one. It is contained in the concept of repression and countercathexis and based on the observation that certain mental contents are systematically excluded from consciousness and require the overcoming of resistances and expenditure of psychic energy to become conscious. Using this criterion, Freud (1923b) distinguished between the preconscious, which is capable of becoming conscious relatively easily, and the repressed, which is "the prototype of the unconscious" (p. 15).

The third meaning, usually called the *topographic* one, is really "double barreled." Based originally on the analysis of dream work, parapraxes, and neurotic symptom formation, it assumes that unconscious mental processes obey different laws than conscious ones. Conscious, preconscious, and unconscious represent different stages or levels of mental organization along a continuum from primary process dominated drive representations to secondary process organized reality representations.

Freud originally assumed that the distinction between conscious, preconscious, and unconscious as different levels of mental organization could be used as the main criterion for dividing the mental apparatus in three different systems or agencies. However, when he tried to coordinate this *topographic* meaning with the *dynamic* and *descriptive* ones, most explicitly in the 1915(c) paper, "The Unconscious," he encountered major difficulties. He found that many highly organized contents were subject to repression and descriptively unconscious. This was particularly true for some of the defensive activities, clinically described as resistances, which are an essential attribute of the system preconscious. He concluded that "consciousness stands in no simple relation either to the different systems or to the process of repression" (p. 192).

In 1923, when Freud reformulated his view of the mental apparatus, the three systems, ego, id, and superego, had no intrinsic, simple relation to consciousness as a mental quality. Insofar as the topographic point of view refers to the three systems Unconscious, Preconscious, and Conscious, it was thus superseded after 1923 and replaced by the structural model; however, the principle of a relationship between the experience of consciousness and the different levels of organization was never relinquished, as some of the formulations of 1932 and 1938 clearly show. Yet neither was it further developed or integrated with the new structural concepts. This problem, mostly ignored in subsequent analytic writings, has been clearly emphasized by Rapaport.

Let me return briefly, now, to the descriptive meaning of consciousness. Freud saw no special need to define the experience of consciousness; he felt that it was self-evident, the same as the "consciousness of philosophers and everyday opinion" (1938, p. 159). But it is also evident in all his writing, from the 1895 *Project* to the 1938 *Outline,* that he considered immediate perceptual awareness as the prototype of the experience of consciousness: "The process of something becoming conscious is above all linked with the perceptions which our sense organs receive from the external world" (1938, p. 161).

Freud did not develop an explicit theory of perception, but it is clear that he considered conscious perception as an active, selective process tied to the function of "attention." Conscious perception actively samples the external world, focusing on those aspects of it which are most paramount for the biological survival of the individual and most relevant to his personal needs and interests. Conscious awareness is "the function of attention. Its activity meets the sense-impressions half way, instead of awaiting their appearance" (1911, p. 220).

Because perceptions of external stimuli and of bodily sensations of pain and pleasure have prime importance for biological survival, it is obvious why Freud considers them the most fundamental content of conscious awareness and attention cathexis.* There is no evidence to suggest that Freud ever modified or expanded this view of conscious perception as a mobile and functionally selective process, although the specific concept of attention fades out of his writing after 1911—except for a dubious reference in 1915.

How do internal thought processes become conscious? Not directly, but by being transformed into external perceptions through linkage with memory traces of perceived (heard) words— that is, through the acquisition of speech, which Freud always considered the most specific, if not exclusive, characteristic of preconscious mental contents. In line with this perceptual theory, the process of consciousness is conceptualized as the function of "an overlying sense organ," which can perceive external stimuli, bodily sensations, and those internal mental processes which have come linked with word presentations.

This supersense organ is called the *Cs.* in *The Interpretation of Dreams* (1900): "The psychical apparatus, which is turned towards the external world with its sense-organ of the *Pcpt.* systems, is itself the external world in relation to the sense-organ of the *Cs.,* whose teleological justification resides in this circumstance" (pp. 615–616). After 1916, Freud no longer distinguished between the perceptual system and the system *Cs* but combined

* Because of the renewal of interest in attention cathexis following Rapaport's (1953) emphasis on this concept, it might be useful to put it in historical perspective. The concept of attention was very popular in the academic psychology of the turn of the century (for instance, in the writing of James and Ribot). It was probably a necessary counterpart to theories that viewed perception primarily as a passive, unselective registration, the results of which are then filtered out by shifts in the function of attention. One may speculate that Freud's early emphasis on attention reflects most directly the teaching of Brentano and the view of perception as "an intentional act."

them as the system Perceptual-Conscious (*Pcpt-Cs*). The important and sometimes forgotten point is that this system Perceptual-Conscious survived the structural reorganization of 1923 and remained, then and later (1933), as a subregion of the ego, its outermost surface part through which the mental apparatus is in contact with external reality.

> We can best arrive at the characteristics of the actual ego, in so far as it can be distinguished from the id and from the superego, by examining its relation to the outermost superficial portion of the mental apparatus, which we describe as the system *Pcpt.-Cs.* This system is turned towards the external world, it is the medium for the perceptions arising thence, and during its functioning the phenomenon of consciousness arises in it. It is the sense-organ of the entire apparatus; moreover it is receptive not only to excitations from outside but also to those arising from the interior of the mind. (1933, p. 75)

The attempt to use perceptual awareness as the model of consciousness leads to several unresolved problems. The most basic one, in my opinion, comes from trying to conceptualize consciousness of inner thought processes as merely a special case of perceptual registration. It is clear, even from Freud's formulations, that perception of external stimuli (or of body sensations) is structurally, genetically, and dynamically different from the perception of our own thought processes. Perceptual awareness is direct and immediate, depending only on the shifting of attention cathexis; awareness of one's own thought contents is a second-order, reflective process necessitating a relatively high level of development, the learning of speech, and the presence of various other aspects of preconscious secondary process organization. I shall deal further with the issue of inner thought processes in the second part of this chapter.*

The second problem, also stressed by Rapaport (1953), concerns the forces which command the deployment of hypercathexis, or what I would call the difference between passively or actively determined awareness. By "passively determined awareness," I am referring to external stimuli which compel our attention because of their intensity or suddenness as well as ideational contents with high drive cathexis which intrude upon awareness in a peremptory fashion (for instance, obsessional ideas, certain fantasies, hallucinations, etc.). The theoretical prototype for this type of awareness is hallucinatory wish fulfillment (Freud, 1900, 1911).

* Relevant here is the distinction that Freud particularly stressed in his early writings—in the *Project* and *The Interpretation of Dreams*—between the perceptual systems whose temporary stimulation is immediately conscious and, on the other hand, the memory systems, in which the lasting traces of temporary conscious perceptions are stored—traces which in themselves are unconscious and have to be made conscious through linkage with verbal residues of previous perceptions.

By contrast, when perception and attention hypercathexis are viewed as active, selective, and reality-oriented ego functions, this implies the capacity for focusing awareness on any stimulus relevant to dominant ego interests and goals—even if the stimulus is of low intensity, low drive cathexis or associated with painful affect. Of course, we are dealing again with a continuum broadly defined by the terms "primary" versus "secondary process" or the pleasure versus the reality principle. The main problem here is that this double aspect spreads and dilutes the phenomenon of consciousness over the whole range of mental levels and leaves it without any specific distinguishing features.

The third problem deals with the question of perception without consciousness. This question, while peripheral to Freud's theory of consciousness, is particularly important in view of recent research interest in "subliminal" perception and attempts to formulate it in relation to psychoanalytic concepts. Freud's usual view is that perception and consciousness are intrinsically linked, which seems to exclude the idea of unconscious perception. But it does not exclude registration of external stimuli at a level below conscious perception. Many brief passages scattered throughout Freud's writings (1895, 1900, 1920, 1925a, 1925b) suggest that he was toying with the idea of a hierarchy of screening systems for the reception of external stimuli (the stimulus barrier, the sense organs, the perceptual systems, and the overlying system Conscious), which would parallel the hierarchy of "censorship," or levels of organization of inner drive representations and thought processes.

This idea remained embryonic in Freud's writing, probably partly because it was outside his main area of interest and possibly because it seemed to contradict his view of the mental apparatus as being in contact with the external world only by its outermost layer, the system Perceptual-Conscious. However, this view has been developed and expanded by Rapaport (1951) and, particularly, George Klein (1959).

Klein has made the assumption that external stimuli can be registered at all levels of awareness, ranging from concentrated wakeful attention to sleep. The structural and dynamic conditions of the state of consciousness or level of mental organization at which the external stimulus is registered will determine not only its clarity but also its mode of expression (for instance, as part of a perception, fantasy, dream, etc.) and its meaning in terms of the drive organizations or conceptual organizations in which it becomes embedded. Such a formulation seems very promising, but it clearly views the mental apparatus as an "open system" communicating with the external environment on all levels and not just through the uppermost layers of the ego—a view which seems to require a modification of many of Freud's concepts. This would lead us into problems quite beyond the scope of this chapter.

CONSCIENCE, CONSCIOUSNESS, AND REFLECTIVE AWARENESS

In trying to clarify and integrate some aspects of the many-sided theory of consciousness, it would be useful to start with two basic distinctions. The first is between consciousness as a function or agency of the mind and "being conscious" as a content or result of the activity of this function or agency. A similar distinction has been made by Eissler (1962). Or, to put it differently, consciousness is always consciousness of something; it involves a relationship between a subject and an object, between an observing function and an observed content—even if both belong within the psychic structure of the same individual. For instance, in Freud's terms, the active observing function is the system Perceptual-Conscious, whose object (of awareness) can be external stimuli, bodily sensations, or inner thought processes. So, when we talk of what is conscious or repressed or has a specific level of mental organization, we should specify whether we mean the observing function or its observed contents.

The second distinction is closely tied to the first and starts off as a matter of definition. The term *consciousness* is often used in the broad sense as synonymous with any mental state or process, as equivalent to the capacity to respond and discriminate between external stimuli (for instance, in such expressions as "states of consciousness"—from coma to full wakefulness—"loss of consciousness," etc.). As we have seen in the first part, Freud's distinction between unconscious and conscious, in the dynamic and topographical sense, applies primarily to inner mental processes or "psychical reality" and not to the perceptual awareness of external stimuli—despite Freud's attempts to link the two at a purely theoretical level. Therefore, I shall limit myself here to the more restricted definition of consciousness as the awareness of our own mental states and reactions (ideas, memories, fantasies).

If we follow through on Freud's assumption that these processes are "in themselves unconscious" and even that "the most complicated and most rational thought-processes, which can surely not be denied the name of psychical processes, can occur without exciting the subject's consciousness" (1900, p. 612), it becomes clear that the psychoanalytic theory of consciousness deals essentially with consciousness as a reflective function—the mind's unique capacity to take itself as its own object of observation and to become aware of its own contents and activity—at least some of them, some of the time. This is clearly stressed by Freud in the aforementioned quote that "the psychical apparatus, which is turned towards the external world with its sense-organ of the *Pcpt.* systems, is itself the external world in relation to the sense-organ of the *Cs.*, whose teleological justification resides in this circumstance" (pp. 615–616).

The psychological and clinical meaning of the term *unconscious* and the very concept of repression directly assume the view of consciousness as a reflective function. For instance, what does it mean, in terms of actual experience, to have an unconscious memory, fantasy, or idea? It is not the content of the unconscious memory which has disappeared from our mind because it continues to influence our thoughts and actions, and the very fact of the selective defense against its emergence into consciousness implies some knowledge of it. What is missing is the knowledge that we have this memory and that it is part of our experience: We know something but we do not know that we know it.

What is experienced at one mental level cannot become the object of awareness for a higher observing level; its links to other parts of the mental apparatus are absent, having been lost or never established. Thus, awareness of our own mental processes—or, for short, reflective consciousness—means "to know that we know": not just to have an experience but rather to be aware of ourselves as having this experience. To use Rapaport's (1951) expression, it is "an awareness of awareness" (p. 385).

In varying degrees, reflective consciousness involves a capacity to take distance from an immediate, concrete experience or reaction, to see it in a subjective perspective as our own experience, and to place it in a network of relationships to other experiences and ideas—a network in which our self is the main stable reference point. In terms of the object of awareness, the distinction is that between a response to a stimulus (whether internal or external) or the whole stimulus–response sequence becoming itself a stimulus for a higher level of response.

At the risk of belaboring this, I shall illustrate this crucial distinction by two concrete, if oversimplified, examples. Imagine that I look out of a window and see a tree. This is a direct perception: The object or content of my awareness is the tree "out there." But I can also become aware of my perception—that is, of myself as looking at the tree—in which case the object of my awareness is "myself in a room in the act of looking at a tree," which is a different content or level of awareness than the direct perception of the tree.

Or, to take a less purely cognitive situation, imagine I am angry at someone, X; the immediate content of my awareness is X seen in a certain light: as somebody unfriendly, dangerous, to fight with, to avoid, and so on. But when I become conscious of my anger, the object of my awareness is "myself in a state of anger toward X," which, again, is a different state that is one level removed from the immediate concrete emotional reaction and likely to occur only when the heat of the anger has already somewhat calmed down. (In case this example seems too artificial, one need only remind oneself of the difference between a patient actually expressing anger in the content of his speech and behavior and the one who talks about his "feeling angry," the causes and effect of it, etc.)

The most unique and specific aspect of reflective consciousness is that it brings about a kind of split in the mind between one part observing and the other part being observed, one part of the mental apparatus taking the other as an object of its awareness. This fact has often been belabored by philosophers but mostly ignored by psychologists. How are we to account for it within the psychoanalytic model of the personality, particularly from a structural and genetic point of view?

In 1932, Freud talked specifically about the ego's ability to take itself as an object, but he then dealt with self-awareness and self-observation primarily as functions of the superego. In an earlier formulation of the relationship of self-observation to conscience and the ego ideal, he talked of "a critically observing agency—which becomes heightened into conscience and philosophic introspection" (1914c, p. 97). He added a most significant footnote: "I cannot here determine whether the differentiation of the censoring agency from the rest of the ego is capable of forming the basis of the philosophic distinction between consciousness and self-consciousness" (p. 98). In many ways, what follows can be seen as an attempt to find a psychological basis for such a distinction.

Let us then assume that reflective consciousness is a function of a differentiated substructure of the ego having many similarities to the superego, principally, that of being capable of viewing the rest of the ego as an external object. The immediate difficulty with such an assumption is that Freud, in most of his formulations, emphasized the punitive and restricting aspects of the superego and consequently viewed self-observation mostly as a preliminary phase to self-criticism and punishment. However, some of the just mentioned passages from the paper "On Narcissism" (1914c) and the *New Introductory Lectures* (1933) are an exception to this and seem to take a broader view of self-awareness and self-observation.

Also, in his 1927 paper, "Humor," Freud speaks of the more benevolent aspects of the superego; there he describes how, by viewing a situation as humorous, the superego comforts the ego in the way a benevolent parent would a child. It does this by helping it take distance from the immediate situation, judging it in a broader context, and, from this higher vantage point, keeping a sense of mastery and superiority over temporary unpleasantness and suffering. We see this also in papers by Sandler (1960) and Schafer (1960).

One could therefore view reflective consciousness as a broadening or "neutralization" of the judging function of the superego, a self-observation which is not limited to self-criticism or self-praise, but is capable of more objective observation. Such a formulation has been made by Waelder (1936, 1960), who speaks of "a formal superego function" that he views as the underlying characteristic of all superego activities as well as a basis of symbolic language, objective knowledge, and the distinguishing mark between men and animals. The potential danger of such a broad formulation is that it may blur the specificity of reflective consciousness and fail to distinguish it from secondary process, conceptual thinking, and ego organization in general.

In pursuing the analogy between reflective awareness and the superego, let us consider the genetic point of view. How does the split in the ego between an observer and the observed come about? It is likely to be based on an internalization of the relation between the observing parent and the observed child, but a somewhat different aspect of this relation than the one usually assumed to form the core of the superego. In other words, the emphasis here is not so much on the parent in a judging and punishing role, but on the parent observing the child in order to learn to understand it, to know what the child "is up to," in order to try to anticipate its needs and actions—or simply the parent who, by vigilant observation, expresses his interest and love for the child just as, in an internalized fashion, reflective consciousness gives a person useful knowledge and can provide reassurance and narcissistic gratification.

This hypothesis would have to be confirmed and specified by developmental observations and genetic reconstruction (for instance, attempts to relate the degree and kind of self-awareness a patient manifests in analysis to specific aspects of his early parental relationships as well as to the functioning and origins of his superego). One would have to examine to what extent the development of reflective consciousness parallels the formation of the superego or is a later "neutralized" derivative of it. (One is reminded here of Nietzsche's view of objective and neutral judgment as derived from guilt and "ascetic ideals.") Of special importance would be the child's early experiences of being looked at, the resulting sense of shame or approval, the feeling of being "self-conscious," and, at later stages, the relationship between guilt, self-criticism, and more neutral objective self-appraisal.

Just as the superego encompasses not only parental attitudes but also, later, admired authorities and social influences, reflective consciousness also probably involves an introjection not only of the observing parents but also of later significant observers, their point of view, and their image of us—or, rather, what we think it to be—so that we see ourselves through their eyes, so to speak. There are many clinical observations suggesting a relationship between a strong superego and the capacity for reflective awareness and introspection. We could, perhaps, think of a continuum ranging from self-observation in the exclusive service of self-criticism, self-doubt, and self-punishment to reflective consciousness as a wider, more objective, and adaptive source of self-awareness and self-knowledge.

In the preceding section, I have stressed the internalized relationship between an observer and the observed inner contents as the most essential characteristic of consciousness. There are, of course many other factors involved, particularly structural and genetic ones, which can be viewed as necessary but not sufficiently prerequisite to reflective consciousness. They overlap with broader aspects of ego functioning such as the development of the secondary process, of "the inner world" of language and conceptual thinking, and of the differentiation between the self and nonself.

To be conscious of one's inner experiences, one has first to be able to take a certain distance from them; this means to delay action and immediate drive discharge (binding of energy). A further step, both a result and an instrument of this binding, is the establishment of a network of stable relationships between separate experiences, a process in which words and language play a crucial, if not exclusive, role (which, in general, is characteristic of higher levels of ego organization). Putting a word or label on a specific concrete experience means abstracting certain features of this experience, representing it in terms of its relation to other similar experiences, and thereby seeing the immediate unique event in a broader perspective and making it easier for it to become a differentiated "object" of awareness. (As mentioned earlier, Freud repeatedly stressed the importance of "word presentations" for consciousness, but more in terms of his perceptual theory of consciousness—thought processes have to become like perceptions before they can become conscious—than as an aspect of higher levels of mental organization or synthesis.) Language also being an essential aspect of social communication helps us become aware of the other person's point of view which, in internalized form, contributes to self-awareness.

The capacity for reflective consciousness is tied to general intellectual and cognitive development, particularly the progressive differentiation between inner and outer and between self and object representations. Piaget has studied in detail this progressive and interdependent development of object and self concepts in its succeeding stages ranging from global motor actions and perceptions to concrete and then conceptual thinking. For a broader psychoanalytic survey of this development, let me refer to Jacobson's (1954) study. One is also reminded that Freud stressed bodily sensations of pleasure and pain as the most fundamental inner perception and the body ego as the nuclear core of the ego. Body representations probably play a crucial role in the development of self-awareness because the body is felt as very much part of our self, but can also be viewed as a physical object extended in space which our consciousness can observe almost as an external object.

The development of reflective consciousness is only a small part of these broader aspects of ego development; it is both a result of and an agent in it. It is likely that every factor that increases the differentiation and stabilization of self and object representations and of different aspects of self-representations also increases the ease and scope of reflective awareness; reflective awareness, in turn, helps further binding and differentiation of the inner world. Reflective awareness can occur at many levels and does not presuppose a completely stabilized self-representation or sense of identity; it is more likely that personal identity is itself a high-order integration of a long developmental sequence of experiences of reflective awareness of our own inner experiences. Conversely, it is likely that every factor that hinders the development of the differentiation between self and nonself and between different agencies with the mental structures itself also hinders the development of reflective consciousness.

Through its effect on this differentiation, conflict (both external and internal) plays a dual role. The frustrating impact of external reality is essential in the differentiation of self from the environment; internal conflict will increase the split between different parts of the mental apparatus and heighten the potential for awareness of opposing forces, choices, and alternatives. On the other hand, to the extent that internal conflict is handled by denial and repression, it represents a primary obstacle to the functioning of reflective consciousness.

SUMMARY AND CONCLUSIONS

I shall sum up by referring again to the distinction between consciousness as a mental function or agency and the contents or results of this activity. I believe that some of the difficulties in reconciling the different facets of the psychoanalytic theory of consciousness stem from the failure to make such a distinction. I have been suggesting that consciousness of our inner mental contents be viewed structurally as a function of a subsystem of the ego. This follows the lines of Freud's 1900 formulation of the superordinate system Consciousness, but, in this case, a system more closely tied to the superego than to the perceptual apparatus.

This system corresponds to a high level of mental development and is probably the product of a relatively late stage consolidated only after puberty; it remains embryonic in many people, is pathologically overgrown in some, and is easily impaired and subject to regression in most. Its degree of autonomy, "neutralization," and objectivity depends on the vicissitudes of individual development about which we know little, except that certain aspects of early parental identifications (for instance, the way the individual feels he was looked upon by his parents and later substitutes) play a crucial role. Consciousness and the observing agency need not and usually is not conscious, in the descriptive sense. In principle, it can become aware of mental content from any level; in practice, however, the degree of structural organization and the amount of countercathexes to be overcome will determine the ease with which a content becomes an object of awareness for the observing agency. Consciousness as a subsystem of the ego is probably also an essential part of that aspect of ego autonomy which Rapaport (1958) describes as the capacity to supply "inner nutriment" for higher ego processes and combat regression in case of external sensory deprivation or overstimulation.

On the clinical side, the evaluation of a patient's initial and potential capacity for reflective awareness is essential for psychoanalytic treatment. Insight therapy presupposes that the patient's reflective capacity should be fairly well developed, even though its functioning is impaired in specific areas of neurotic conflict by repression and other defenses. The less this prerequisite is fulfilled, the less interpretation and "insight" are likely to be effective therapeutic tools and goals.

It has been stated many times that one of the goals of psychoanalytic treatment is not just a temporary lifting of repression in specific areas, but also a general and lasting broadening of the capacity for more realistic self-observation. This most likely comes about by an identification with the analyst in his actual role as benevolent and neutral observer—a process which is basically similar to what I have assumed to be the genetic prototype of the origins of reflective consciousness: namely, the introjection of parental figures as benevolent but realistic observers. These familiar clinical observations and practices are mentioned here only to illustrate the fact that they need to be grounded on a systematic theory of consciousness—a theory which in turn will have to be able to encompass them.

While in the preceding I have stressed that consciousness is always to some extent a reflexive function, I hope I have not given the impression that this applies only to the relatively special case of highly developed or deliberate introspection and self-observation. The general approach suggested here can be stated in terms that apply to a whole continuum of levels of self-awareness and is not tied to a unitary concept of consciousness or to the tripartite division of the mental apparatus. It rests on the basic psychoanalytic assumption of psychical functioning as a hierarchy of levels of mental organization—levels which correspond to stages of genetic development but are never completely superseded and consequently coexist and interact in varying proportions in any adult mental state or process.

Rapaport has attempted to apply this principle systematically to the whole range of experienced mental states (from dreams and fantasy to attentive wakefulness) and their various pathological variations. Each state has certain recurrent structural characteristics, its own balance of drive expression versus drive control, inner versus external representations and, most relevant here, its own degree of self-awareness. This implies that each of these mental conditions is itself multiply layered and includes, in varying degrees, a differentiation between an observing part and an observed one—for instance, "It is a commonplace that waking consciousness is characterized both by being aware of a content and by the possibility of becoming aware of the fact of this awareness" (Rapaport, 1951, p. 394).

I would therefore define consciousness as the cognitive relationship between any two levels—or aggregates of them—of mental functioning with the higher or more organized level taking the lower one as an object or content of awareness. One would assume that the higher observing level cannot be simultaneously observer and observed, subject and object; however, it can potentially become in turn an object of awareness for a still higher level. As Rapaport states it: "The lower orders of reflective awareness are mirrored in the higher ones" (personal communication).

The subjective quality of any conscious experience, including its passive or active, compelling or detached character, can be expressed in terms of the distance between the observing and the observed level. This distance corresponds to a continuum from the intensely gripping external stimuli or drive representations, which allow for practically no distance at all and where any distance between self and nonself, between perceiver and perceived is temporarily obliterated and any experience is lived in its absolute and immediate concreteness—at the extreme, to systematic introspection and broad-range dispassionate self-observation. This dimension is obviously not primarily a cognitive one but is directly related to the range of drive control, choice, and anticipation available at any level. Probably reflective consciousness is most adaptive when the distance is in the middle range, with enough detachment and perspective for judgment and enough closeness of action and control.

This could be clinically illustrated by the various types of "awareness," in the sense of open verbalized content, which have no therapeutic effectiveness because they involve not enough or too much distance (for instance, the content bursting out of the psychotic state or drowned out in hysterical histrionics or kept isolated by obsessional intellectualization). By contrast, "insight" assumes the establishment of new or forgotten connections between different levels and stages of one's experience and the acceptance of them as part of oneself—instead of their remaining hidden or dissociated foreign bodies in our mental organization.

I have tried to view consciousness as a unique, specific function and also as an integral part of psychic organization, an expression of the degree of inner differentiation and of communication or synthesis between different levels of mental processes. I have had no new data or concepts to offer, merely some evidence of the need for a better integration between existing ones and, I hope, some suggestions to further this goal.

Chapter 13

Signorelli

The parapraxis specimen of psychoanalysis*

The interpretation of parapraxes played an important part in Freud's explanation of the origins and meaning of neurotic symptoms and dreams. The dynamics of parapraxes are usually less complex than those of neurotic symptoms or dreams and share with dreams the advantage of being part of "the psychopathology of everyday life." Among the hundreds of examples mentioned by Freud, his own experience of forgetting the name of the Italian painter Signorelli deserves special attention. Not only is it the first interpretation of a parapraxis that Freud published, but it is also the one he analyzed most extensively, devoting an entire paper to it (1898b) only a few weeks after its actual occurrence and also the whole first chapter of *The Psychopathology of Everyday Life* (1901b). Thus, the Signorelli example has the claim of being the prime specimen of a "Freudian slip," playing a role similar to that of the Irma dream, but in a minor key.

In this chapter I shall present a detailed reexamination of Freud's interpretation of this example of motivated forgetting. In addition to the data and arguments specifically included by Freud, I shall make use of information about the broader context of the event in terms of Freud's life circumstances and the development of his thinking at the time using mostly the published Fliess letters (Freud, 1887–1902) and some of the autobiographical information included in *The Interpretation of Dreams* (1900).

I shall try to show certain omissions, inconsistencies, and strained arguments in Freud's analysis that seem motivated by the same conflicts, defenses, and compromise formations manifested in the name-forgetting itself. Freud's explanation hinges on the crucial role of external "superficial associations" and the exclusion, or at least the minimizing, of the need for deeper connections of meaning between the forgotten name and the repressed ideas. The theoretical interest of this example lies in the concept of external associations, which is based on Freud's "economic" assumptions (primary process, displacement of mobile cathexes) and the use of

* This chapter originally appeared in *Psychoanalysis and Contemporary Science*, 3, 1973, pp. 210–230. Reprinted with permission.

the framework of association psychology. In the last part of the chapter, I shall indicate how the difficulties that Freud encountered with the concept of external associations are directly relevant to the clarification of concepts such as defense and primary process as persistent issues within contemporary psychoanalytic theory.

THE FORGETTING OF A NAME AND ITS EXPLANATION

First, let us review the highlights of Freud's account of the incident. It took place during his summer vacation of 1898. Freud was 42 at the time:

> I was driving in the company of a stranger...to a place in Herzegovina: our conversation turned to the subject of travel in Italy, and I asked my companion whether he had ever been to Orvieto and looked at the famous frescoes there. But the artist's name escaped me and I could not recall it. I exerted my powers of recollection...I was able to conjure up the pictures with greater sensory vividness than is usual with me. I saw before my eyes, with special sharpness, the artist's self-portrait—with a serious face and folded hand...My continued efforts met with no success beyond bringing up the names of two other artists who I knew could not be the right ones. These were Botticelli and, in the second place, Boltraffio...I had for several days to put up with this lapse of memory and with the inner torment associated with it which recurred at frequent intervals each day, until I fell in with a cultivated Italian who freed me from it by telling me the name: Signorelli. (1898b, pp. 290–291)

Freud starts the analysis with a categorical and strangely unsupported statement: "The reason why the name Signorelli was lost is not to be found in anything special about the name itself or in any psychological characteristic of the context in which it was introduced" (1901b, p. 2). He continues:

> Light was only thrown on the forgetting of the name when I recalled the topic we had been discussing directly before, and it was revealed as a case in which *a topic that has just been raised is disturbed by the preceding topic*. Shortly before I put the question to my traveling companion whether he had ever been to Orvieto, we had been talking about the customs of the Turks living in Bosnia and Herzegovina. I had told him [my traveling companion] what I had heard from a colleague practicing among those people—that they are accustomed to show great confidence in their doctor and great resignation to fate... I assume that the series of thoughts about the customs of the Turks

> in Bosnia, etc. acquired the capacity to disturb the next succeeding thought from the fact that I had withdrawn my attention from that series before it was brought to an end. I recall in fact wanting to tell a second anecdote which lay close to the first in my memory. These Turks place a higher value on sexual enjoyment than on anything else, and in the event of sexual disorders they are plunged in a despair which contrasts strangely with their resignation towards the threat of death. One of my colleague's patients once said to him, "*Herr,* you must know that if that comes to an end then life is of no value." I suppressed my account of this characteristic trait, since I did not want to allude to the topic in a conversation with a stranger. But I did more: I also diverted my attention from pursuing thoughts which might have arisen in my mind from the topic of "death and sexuality." On this occasion I was still under the influence of a piece of news which had reached me a few weeks before while I was making a brief stay at *Trafoi.* A patient over whom I had taken a great deal of trouble had put an end to his life on account of an incurable sexual disorder. I know for certain that this melancholy event and everything related to it was not recalled to my conscious memory during my journey...But the similarity between "Trafoi" and "Boltraffio" forces me to assume that this reminiscence, in spite of my attention being deliberately diverted from it, was brought into operation in me at the time [of the conversation]. (pp. 2–4)

So far, Freud's argument is that the forgetting was due to the interference of a consciously suppressed thought in the immediately preceding conversation, and that, in turn, this thought had been suppressed because of its relation to the repressed painful news about the patient and its connection with the broader topic of "death and sexuality."

But what connection does the forgotten name Signorelli have with the topics of the Turks and death and sexuality? Freud makes a rather strange statement about the likely relevance of these topics to the frescoes painted by Signorelli:

> The affinity between their content...in the one case The Last Judgment, "Doomsday," and in the other, death and sexuality—seems to be very slight; and since the matter concerns the repression of a name it was on the face of it probable that the connection was between one name and another. (1898b, p. 292)

This statement then justifies the construction of the chain of "external associations" which becomes the core of Freud's explanation:

> Now *Signer* means *Herr* and *Herr* is also present in the name Herzegovina. Moreover, it was certainly not without relevance that both the patient's

> remarks which I was to recall contained *Herr* as a form of address to the doctor. The translation of *Signor* into *Herr* was therefore the means by which the story that I had suppressed had drawn after it into repression the name I was looking for. (1898b, p. 292)

SOME QUESTIONS ABOUT FREUD'S EXPLANATION

This explanation is far from convincing. Are we to believe that it is such a chain of associations that actually drew the name into repression, by a process that Freud himself describes as constructed "in most arbitrary fashion by making use of a roundabout associative path which has every appearance of artificiality" (Freud, 1901b, p. 14)? Freud (1900) defines external associations as those established "by assonance, verbal ambiguity, temporal coincidence without connection of meaning" (p. 530), adding that "considering the low standards expected of an association of this kind one could be established in the great majority of cases" (1901b, p. 6).

It is even harder to agree that there is no connection of meaning between the topic of death and sexuality and frescoes depicting heaven and hell—especially when we observe that the content of these frescoes consists in large part of an apocalyptic vision of hundreds of naked bodies in various postures of lust or torment. Even before examining what personal meaning the Orvieto frescoes may have symbolized for Freud, his unsupported statement of the lack of connections of meaning has some of the earmarks of what he was later to describe as the defense of negation. ("You ask who this person in the dream can be. It's not my mother." 1925b, p. 235)

Freud himself seems to have become increasingly doubtful about his initial denial of any significant connection between the frescoes and the repressed topics, but he acknowledged his doubts reluctantly and as a kind of afterthought. At the very end of his second extensive presentation (1901b), he says:

> There is, however, the profounder question...whether some more intimate connection between the two topics is not required. On a superficial consideration, one would be inclined to reject the latter demand and accept as sufficient a temporal contiguity between the two, even if the contents are completely different. On close inquiry, however, one finds more and more frequently that the two elements which are joined by an external association (the repressed element and the new one) possess in addition some connection of content; and such a connection is, in fact, demonstrable in the Signorelli example. (p. 6)

But Freud does not go on to demonstrate such a connection or to revise his formulation accordingly. In fact, in the next chapter, after having discussed another case of forgetting, he returns to the Signorelli example and to his original formulation that the repression was entirely due to external associations furnished by "temporal contiguity," as if he had forgotten his remarks in the previous chapter. But then, at this point, he adds a footnote that is a kind of return of the suppressed:

> I am not entirely convinced of the absence of any internal connection between the two groups of thoughts in the Signorelli case. After all, if the repressed thoughts of the topic of death and sexuality are carefully followed up, one will be brought face to face with an idea that is by no means remote from the topic of the frescoes at Orvieto. (1901b, p. 13)

We may now ask ourselves why it was so difficult for Freud to admit the existence of inner connections of meaning and why he tried to maintain an explanation exclusively in terms of external associations.* The answer, as I shall illustrate in the remainder of this chapter, is that Freud had deep personal motives for denying the relevance of inner connections of meaning (i.e., the content of the Signorelli frescoes) and also a strong investment in external associations as a crucial explanatory concept within his theory of dream and symptom formation.

But, first, I must deal briefly with another point of Freud's argument. He stated that although he could not remember the name Signorelli, the content of the frescoes (including the self-portrait of the artist) emerged in his mind with unusual sensory vividness. This, for Freud, is further proof that the content of the frescoes was unrelated to the topics of death and sexuality because it was not subjected to repression. He assumes that the vivid recall of the content of the frescoes was due merely to their connection with the repressed name, thus constituting a further step in the displacement of cathexis to a safer and even more removed substitute.

Is it not more likely that the unusual sensory vividness of the content was largely due to its being especially meaningful and overdetermined, rather than a case of mere external superficial displacement? This would be not only closer to the data, but also in line with Freud's explanation of sensory vividness in dreams as the result of condensed multiple meanings (for instance, the word *trimethylamin* in the Irma dream). The unusually vivid recall of the sensory contents may be seen as a compromise formation which also has a clear defensive aspect. The contents can be recalled

* An understandable reluctance to reveal in print the details of his personal conflicts about death and sexuality does not really provide an answer. The overall connection between the content of the frescoes and death and sexuality is clear enough without further specification and Freud could have mentioned his initial denial of these connections as a broader example of defense, a continuation of the mechanism that led to the forgetting in the first place.

in every concrete detail as long as their meaning, their connection with repressed topics, is cut off; the captured attention, the narrow focusing or concentration on specific pictorial contents, is indeed suited to this defensive purpose. Twenty-five years later, Freud (1926a) described the defense mechanism of isolation in the following terms:

> The experience is not forgotten but instead it is deprived of its affect and its associative connections are suppressed or interrupted so that it remains as though isolated. The elements that are held apart in this way are precisely those which belong together associatively...The normal phenomenon of concentration provides a pretext for this kind of neurotic procedure. (pp. 120–121)

TRANSFERENCE AND THE GUILTY THERAPIST

A brief summary of Freud's life circumstances at the time may give us a better understanding of the motives Freud labeled as concern about "death and sexuality," particularly in their relation to the repressed news of Trafoi, to the anecdotes about the Turks, and, ultimately, to the content of the religious frescoes.

We know that the years 1897 and 1898 were a period of intense crisis and crucial discoveries in Freud's life. He was in the midst of his self-analysis, struggling with the discovery of infantile sexuality and the Oedipus complex, and formulating his theory of neurotic symptoms, dreams, and unconscious processes in general. In this struggle, he vacillated between intense loneliness, discouragement, confusion, and the conviction and excitement of unraveling hidden secrets and making important discoveries. He made Fliess the confidant of his moods and discoveries and tried to view him as a guide and mentor, repressing some increasing doubts about Fliess's competence and theories.

In 1896, Freud's father died, a death that he described as "the most poignant loss in a man's life" (1900, p. xxvi) and the trigger for his self-analysis. In this year Freud also makes repeated references to various neurotic symptoms from which he was suffering: primarily his concern about his health and his fear of premature death. Freud also had many doubts and misgivings about the new method of treatment he was developing. Was he being effective in his treatment? Was he neglecting organic factors? Or was he being irresponsible and overambitious in prematurely testing his new discoveries upon his patients? Was he damaging or destroying them by forcing upon them his "solutions" and interpretations? What would happen to his professional reputation and his ability to support his large family?

Of course, the issue was much broader than one of professional responsibility and success. The results of Freud's work with his patients, the findings of his own self-analysis, and his ambition to discover new laws and principles of the mind were so closely linked that success or failure in one area had direct consequences for the others.

Some of these concerns are well illustrated in Freud's letter to Fliess, written just before the journey on which the Signorelli incident occurred:

> The secret of my restlessness is hysteria. In the inactivity here and the lack of any interesting novelty the whole thing has come to weigh heavily on my mind. My work seems to me now to be far less valuable, my disorientation is complete and time—a whole year has gone by without any tangible advance in the principles of the thing—seems hopelessly inadequate for what the problem demands. On top of it, it is the work on which I have staked my livelihood. True, I have a good record of successes, but perhaps they have been only indirect, as if I had applied the lever in the right direction for the line of cleavage of the substance; but the line of cleavage itself remains unknown to me. So I am running away from myself to gather all the energy and objectivity I can, because I cannot throw the work up. (1887–1902, letter 95)

But it is clear that Freud was not able to "run away" from himself during his vacation, especially after being hit by the news of the patient's suicide. The patient's suicide and the anecdotes about the Turks share a common reference to "death and sexuality," but in a very specific context—that of doctor–patient relationships. Good and bad patients and, by implication, good and bad doctors are being contrasted, suggesting what would now be called transference and countertransference issues. The anecdotes about the Turks contain an implicit comparison between the Turks as patients and Freud's own patient, as well as between Freud as a doctor and the older doctor who had treated the Turks. The telling of the first part of the anecdotes ("The Turks treat doctors with special respect and they show, *in marked contrast to our own people,* an attitude of resignation towards the dispensations of fate," 1898b, p. 292; italics added) can be seen as a kind of wishful undoing of the effect of the news of Trafoi. It is almost as if Freud had said, "If only my patient had had more faith in my ability to cure his sexual disorder, or at least more resignation toward his fate, instead of taking matters into his own hands by committing suicide."

But the second part of the anecdote can be seen as a return of the repressed because the attitude expressed—"better die than have a disturbed sex life"—fits directly the behavior of Freud's patient. Clearly, the Trafoi news put Freud in the role of the bad doctor, the false healer who does not save his patients, does not deliver the promises of curing sexual problems through his new methods and psychological discoveries.* But Freud, too, was a patient; he describes himself as neurotic, suffering from various "hysterical" symptoms, among which fear of premature death was particularly prominent—symptoms whose sexual etiology he was in the process of painfully discovering through his self-analysis.

Thus, Freud identified with the patient role. He was his own patient in his self-analysis, and transference aspects were expressed by his very close and increasingly ambivalent relationship with Fliess. Also related to such transference issues may be the fact that the traveling companion to whom Freud told one of the anecdotes about the Turks was a Berlin lawyer with whom Fliess could have been acquainted, because Freud mentions his name to Fliess. Furthermore, the anecdotes themselves originated with an older respected doctor whom Freud refers to as a friend and colleague ("lieber Kollege"). To sum up, in the sequence leading up to the forgetting of the name, there are clear references to Freud's concern about his own as well as his patient's health and survival and indications of his guilt, worries, and doubts and the issue of his therapeutic, intellectual, and sexual potency.

RELIGIOUS THEMES AND INFANTILE SEXUALITY

The themes we have discovered so far are still only indirectly related to the religious content of the Signorelli frescoes. It may be worthwhile to take a closer look at the frescoes themselves. In Italian art books, they are generally entitled "The Preaching and Deeds of the Antichrist," "The End of the World," "The Resurrection of the Flesh," "The Fate of the Damned," and, finally, "The Coronation of the Chosen." The main theme is obviously the classical religious one of false knowledge versus true faith, salvation versus damnation; the frescoes form a sequence or progression depicting the travel or journey of the soul. Let us note that it is the first fresco (the Antichrist) which contains the portrait of Signorelli that Freud remembered so vividly; the painter is represented standing in the far corner as witness to, but not participant in, the frenzied action. It is also interesting to note that in the center background of the same fresco is a scene of miraculous healing as one of the deeds of the Antichrist.

Could these religious themes have had any personal meaning for Freud? I believe an examination of the context of Freud's visit to Orvieto will provide some answers. Freud had visited Orvieto exactly 1 year before, while traveling on a summer vacation with his brother. Some of the letters suggest

* It is interesting to note that Freud's first report of the Signorelli incident, in a letter to Fliess (letter 96), is followed by a reference to a "conflict with my medical conscience" involving the wish to use a medical consultation as a pretext to visit Fliess in Berlin.

that Fliess is the one who had stimulated Freud's interest in this kind of art work. Freud dates the beginning of his self-analysis to this summer of 1897. Just before this vacation, he had been struggling with a formulation of the etiology of neurosis resting on the belief in the reality of infantile seductions, particularly by the father ("I wish to pin down the father as the originator of neurosis," 1887–1902, letter 64). As part of his self-analysis, based in large part on his dreams, Freud was beginning to be aware of memories of his own childhood, particularly of sexual wishes toward his mother and hostility toward and competition with his father.

Something important is likely to have happened during the 1897 vacation with respect to these issues because, immediately after his return, Freud wrote his famous letter to Fliess (letter 69) announcing that he no longer believed in the predominant role of actual seductions as the cause of neuroses:

> Let me tell you straight away the great secret which has been slowly dawning on me in recent months. I no longer believe in my neurotica... Now I do not know where I am, as I have failed to reach theoretical understanding of repression and its play of forces...but...I have a feeling more of triumph than of defeat...

In the next letters, Freud reports some of the discoveries from the analysis of his own dreams. These bring us closer to the topic of religion and sexuality and the special meaning of Freud's viewing of the frescoes at that time in his life:

> [M]y "primary originator" [of neurosis] was an ugly, elderly but clever woman who told me a great deal about God and hell, and gave me a high opinion of my own capacities...later...libido towards *matrem* was aroused; the occasion must have been the journey... [in which] I must have had the opportunity of seeing her *nudam*... (letter 70)

He also adds that he was quite fond of the old woman who "provided me at such an early age with the means for living and surviving..." at a critical period of his childhood when his mother had just given birth to his first sibling. Freud was so impressed by his rediscovery of the memories of the old Catholic nurse that he checked them with his mother, who provided the following information:

> [She was] an elderly woman, very shrewd indeed. She was always taking you to church. When you came home you used to preach, and tell us all about how God conducted His affairs...she turned out to be a thief, and all the [coins] and toys that had been given you were found among

> her things. Your brother Philipp went himself to fetch the policeman, and she got ten months. (letter 71)

In the preceding letter, Freud also reports a dream about this nurse:

> She was my instructress in sexual matters, and chided me for being clumsy and not being able to do anything...The whole dream was full of the most wounding references to my present uselessness as a therapist...she encouraged me to steal [coins] to give to her...The dream can be summed up as "bad treatment." Just as the old woman got money from me for her bad treatment of me, so do I now get money for the bad treatment of my patients... (letter 70)

It is not too far-fetched to view this passage as establishing a direct link between the religious imagery, the important and ambivalent figure of the nurse during Freud's oedipal period, and, even more crucial to our purpose, a connection between sexual ignorance and impotence and uselessness as a therapist with the theme of bad and dishonest treatment—received from the nurse and given to patients.

In the same context, a letter written a few weeks later recalls a memory of the same period of Freud's early childhood: When, during a journey, he saw for the first time the gas jets of street lights in a big city, he was terrified, believing they were "souls burning in Hell." It is clear that Freud was impressed by the Signorelli frescoes at a time in his life when he was dealing with reawakened childhood memories in which religious symbolization of guilt and sexuality played a central role. It is also not difficult to see how the context and content of the name-forgetting sequence, occurring exactly a year later during a similar vacation, was well suited to reawaken some of the underlying themes symbolized by his earlier viewing of the Signorelli frescoes.*

It is not surprising that the religious themes suggested by the frescoes would be among the ones most strongly defended against. Erikson (1954) has pointed out how childhood religious themes are usually most staunchly defended against in people who are nonbelievers and for whom the repudiation of collective religious solutions is an important part of their adult identity. In Freud's case, the material mentioned before can give us some idea why, for him, religion meant infantile submission to authority as well as being seduced and deceived by such an authority. Freud's writings show an active and persistent interest in religion—but as an institution to be repudiated for representing the regressive pull of infantile dependence and

* Jones, in his biography of Freud (1955), makes a highly relevant though somewhat enigmatic reference to the Signorelli example: "As I hope to expound in a revised edition of volume I of this biography, it was connected with a significant episode that must have played an important part in the inception of Freud's self-analysis" (p. 335).

submission to father figures and authorities. Religion stands in the way of the discovery of individual truth. Added to this is the obvious fact that Freud grew up as a member of a Jewish minority in a Catholic culture and that anti-Semitism was a permanent part of his and his family's experience.

*FLECTERE SI NEQUEO SUPEROS, ACHERONTA MOVEBO**

In the Signorelli example, religious issues seem most strongly denied and transference issues (Freud and his patients, Freud as patient, and his relation to older doctors and authorities—with the shadow of Fliess most prominent among them) are only hinted at. I cannot resist speculating that the figure of Signorelli played an important part in these transference issues. It may have provided an identification figure for Freud, a symbol for the creative solution of his infantile as well as contemporary life conflicts. I am referring to Signorelli as the painter of the frescoes and, more particularly, to his self-portrait, which was so vivid in Freud's mind ("with a serious face and folded hands," standing aloof in one corner of the scene depicting the deeds of the Antichrist, 1898b, p. 291). In his exploration of unconscious forces, Freud often described himself as a lone explorer traveling through a mysterious and dangerous land—with courage and determination but also awe, fear, and ignorance of the ultimate outcome of his journey. He speaks of the image of Dante traveling through the inferno and compares himself to a conquistador who will either return in triumph or be totally discarded. This feeling could well be symbolized by the picture of Signorelli, who creatively depicted and evoked the powers of heaven and hell and represented himself as part of the scene but not as part of the crowd of the damned or the saved. The theme of finding one's own individual salvation—not by following the false security and seductiveness of accepted truths, but by a lonely journey into darkness, hopefully leading to the discovery of new light—may well be symbolized here.

The end point of the association chain started by the name Signorelli is the word *Herr* (the Turk's way of addressing the doctor). The term *Herr*—especially when followed by the intimate form of address, *du*—seems well suited to express the filial respect and blind faith which the child in us grants to God, fathers, and doctors. We may now speculate that the external link between the name Signorelli and the word *Herr* represents not only the most superficial and defensive connection but at the same time some of the deepest layers of wished-for conflict resolution and adaptiveness.

It becomes clear that the forgetting is not just another example of repression as a passive attempt to master anxiety. The immediate consequences of the forgetting show that it was also a successful attempt to reestablish

* "If I can't influence the gods in heaven, I will invoke the forces of hell."

active control by creative intellectual mastery over the very conflict that led to the repression. In a letter to Fliess written just before his vacation (letter 94), Freud had already attempted to understand another instance of name forgetting and indicated the relevance of this kind of analysis to his formulation of the mechanism of repression and symptom formation. Thus, this small instance of motivated forgetting had provided Freud with sought-after material to further his understanding of unconscious processes and justify his methods and concepts. It was in itself a microcosmic example of creating success out of failure and finding salvation by mastering the powers of darkness.

SIGNORELLI AND THE IRMA DREAM

The reader familiar with the Irma dream and its interpretation by Freud (1900) and Erikson (1954) will already have noticed some points of similarity between the themes underlying the dream and the name-forgetting. I would like to spell out briefly some of these rather striking similarities. The Irma dream was dreamt and analyzed by Freud 3 years earlier than the occurrence of the Signorelli incident. But the Fliess letters again tell us that Freud was working on the first chapters of *The Interpretation of Dreams* (and the Irma dream is Chapter 2, at least in the final version) just before this summer vacation of 1898. The Irma dream was used by Freud to illustrate "the method of interpreting dreams," especially how the use of free associations to the separate elements of the manifest content can reveal the meaning of a dream as a disguised wish fulfillment.

The Signorelli example was meant to illustrate the unconsciously motivated aspect of forgetting and, more specifically, the way in which a chain of external, superficial associations can serve as the model for the process of displacement in dream and symptom formation. It is therefore not surprising that we encounter some of the same theoretical issues in both cases.

Turning to more specific aspects of content, the Irma dream deals with displacement of guilt for the bad treatment of Irma and, more generally, with what Freud (1900) labels as "concern about my own and other people's health—professional conscientiousness" (p. 120). We have seen ample evidence of similar themes in the present example. Erikson has also suggested the presence of a hidden religious theme, in the Irma dream, around the issues of joining the believers and the safety of dogma and authority versus facing the guilt and rewards of being an ambitious, lone explorer and outcast. As I have tried to show, such themes are probably at the very core of the dynamics of the Signorelli example.

Finally, in both instances, Freud's interpretation both reveals and hides some of the underlying meanings and thus has simultaneously an expressive as well as a defensive function. In the Signorelli example, the emphasis on external association serves in part to deny the relevance of the content of the frescoes as symbols of infantile religious themes concerning guilt and sexuality. In the case of the Irma dream, the documents published by Schur (1966) make clear that Freud's interpretation expressed some of the same motives present in the dream itself—namely, displacement of guilt—but now in reference to Fliess's actual bad treatment of Irma, the implications of which Freud was struggling to deny as part of his "transference" conflicts.

EXTERNAL ASSOCIATIONS, DEFENSE, AND THE PRIMARY PROCESS

This extended analysis has mainly amplified the clinical principles of Freud's approach. It has shown that the forgetting must be understood as part of an extended sequence, including the steps preceding and following the actual symptomatic event. In this sequence, we have encountered a continuity of underlying themes expressed at a variety of levels, from current and specific preoccupations to broader, deeper meanings and their infantile sources. In the constantly shifting balance among conflicting motives, a whole range of defensive operations was involved (including repression, suppression, negation, and isolation).

I have tried to stress how each step in the sequence possesses simultaneously expressive, defensive, and adaptive functions. An act that seems, on the surface, primarily a defensive avoidance of a conflicted topic can, at the same time, serve as the expression of deeper levels of the very same conflict. For instance, when Freud deliberately suppressed the sexual part of the anecdote about the Turks (which had become unconsciously connected with the recent news about the patient's suicide), he defensively shifted the topic to the apparently innocent and remote subject (the frescoes of Orvieto). But this new topic unconsciously continued the trend of thought that had motivated the defense; the memory of the frescoes was well suited to symbolize and re-evoke, at a deeper level, some of the basic conflicts, of which Freud's reaction to the news of Trafoi and his telling one (but suppressing the second) anecdote about the Turks had all been only relatively limited and surface manifestations. Freud centered his explanation on the role of external or superficial associations, but the present, more detailed analysis puts the role of these external associations in a rather different perspective. It is time to reexamine Freud's formulations about external associations and to suggest the relevance to broader theoretical issues.

Freud's view of the theoretical importance of a chain of external associations is most explicitly stated at the end of the 1898b paper:

> The example elucidated here receives an immensely added interest when we learn that it may serve as nothing more nor less than a model for the pathological processes to which the psychical symptoms of the psychoneuroses owe their origin. In both cases we find the same elements and the same play of forces between those elements. In the same manner as here and by means of similar superficial associations, a repressed train of thought takes possession in neurosis of an innocent recent impression and draws it down with itself into repression. (p. 295)

This explanation clearly rests upon a theoretical model of the primary process as displacement of mobile drive cathexis. If a drive-cathected content meets a defensive barrier, the cathexis will flow into whatever channel is available at the time, following the path of least resistance. Whatever is nearest in time or space will be chosen in a completely arbitrary and contingent fashion, as long as it can provide the shortest path to discharge. It is important to note that, in this model, it is the path of external associations which actually determines the direction of the displacement and the choice of substitute drive object. There need be no prior connection of meaning between the originally repressed thought and the substitute (for instance, the name Signorelli has no intrinsic connection of meaning with the topic of the Turks and the thoughts of death and sexuality). According to this view, primary, or "drive-organized," thought processes are like a seething cauldron, without structure, constantly changing, and all contents that provide drive discharge being interchangeable.

In this model, defense and drive are clearly separated as parts of two different systems and operate in alternation: The flow of drive energy meets a defensive dam or barrier and it is then deflected into another channel until it meets a further defensive barrier that deflects the drive in yet another direction, and so on. Defense has an independent existence of its own as a dam or barrier, presumably made up of solidified anticathectic energy. It should be noted that this model assumes that the chain of external associations occurred before the forgetting or symptom, so the external associations (occurring, in fact, afterward during the process of interpretation) retrace the steps by which the symptom was formed. The emphasis in this model is not so much on interpretation, in the sense of giving meaning to symptoms or manifest dream content, as on uncovering the causal process by which symptoms or dreams are produced. It is essentially Freud's attempt to give a causal, "scientific" explanation and justification for his method of interpretation.

It is this model that dominated Freud's metapsychological formulations and was particularly emphasized by Rapaport. Yet, as can be shown even in this limited example, Freud did not systematically adhere to such a model, particularly when dealing with the complexities of clinical data. It represented only one of the organizing polarities of his thinking.

As I have illustrated at length, there is no lack of inner connection of meaning between the forgotten name and the context in which it occurred. There is no need to construct a chain of external associations to account for the symptomatic act and even less evidence for assuming that such a chain was created unconsciously before the occurrence of the forgetting. It is clinically more meaningful to view the construction of such a chain of associations as a temporary compromise formation occurring at one stage of the process of interpretation.

From Freud's account, we have reason to believe that he constructed such a chain of associations after having already decided that the forgetting was due to the influence of the previous topic and that the name Signorelli had no connection of meaning with this topic. It is almost as if he constructed such a chain to justify or rationalize his conclusions. It is difficult to consider such a chain as an example of free association; it looks more like a somewhat contrived intellectual attempt to solve a riddle, following certain rules given in advance: Connect two topics without using meaning or personal relevance, but in a way that will be immediately understandable to anyone.

Nonetheless, we can assume that the use of such a chain of external associations was overdetermined and served several purposes for Freud. First, in its defensive function, it does away with the necessity for dealing with deeper levels of meaning and conflict; second, it provides an illustration and justification of a method of interpretation and theoretical explanation in which he had a vested interest; and, third, in the choice of the end terms that this chain links (Signorelli and *Herr*), it may well have expressed a very significant, unconscious meaning.

In a well-known passage of the seventh chapter of *The Interpretation of Dreams,* one finds a formulation of the function of superficial, external associations that is much closer to clinical evidence. In this passage, Freud justifies the use of the method of free association by the basic assumption that "no influence that one can bring to bear upon our mental processes can ever enable us to think without purposive ideas...when conscious purposive ideas are abandoned, concealed purposive ideas assume control" (1900, p. 528). He then justifies the existence of sequences of thought that seem meaningless or arbitrary as follows:

> Whenever one psychical element is linked with another by an objectionable or superficial association, there is also a rational [my own translation of *korrekt*] and deeper link between them which is subjected to the resistance of the censorship. The real reason for the prevalence of superficial associations is not the abandonment of purposive ideas but the pressure of the censorship...[that] has resulted in a displacement from a normal and serious association to a superficial and apparently absurd one. (pp. 530–531)

In this formulation, the role of external associations has been downgraded, both clinically and theoretically. They no longer represent the arbitrary and contingent discharge path by which substitutes are chosen, symptoms are formed, and "innocent impressions are drawn into repression." The presence of external associations is the result of censorship or defense and serves to disguise already existing inner connections of meaning between the ideas they link. Such associations are not necessary to create the symptom or substitute but are merely added on, as a part of increased resistance during the process of interpretation; "the longer and more roundabout the chain of associations the stronger the resistance" (1933, p. 13).

A chain of external associations is an overdetermined compromise formation, like a smoke screen that both hides and betrays an already existing path or connection. The external and arbitrary quality of such a chain represents a striving toward randomness, a purely temporal sequence wherein each associative link appears independent of the anticipation of the following one and devoid of any overall meaning. The unconscious purposive idea (i.e., the already established deeper link between the two end terms of the chain of superficial association) expresses itself by influencing or biasing the choice of associations, making them drift in a certain direction toward a preestablished goal.

Whether created by censorship or drive discharge, what claim does such a chain of external associations have as the model of "primary" thought organization? The sequence is established not in terms of the meaning of words as signifiers but by finding similarity between the words themselves as "things," as patterns of sound or shape (for instance, rhyming words in complete disregard of their meaning). This way of treating words has a certain formal similarity with the way language is used to express multiple personal connotations in primary symbolic processes (early developmental stages of language, dreams, "regressive" states, poetry, etc.): "In every language, concrete terms, in consequence of the history of their development, are richer in associations than conceptual ones" (Freud, 1900, pp. 339–340).

In contrast to the use of words as fixed lexical signs with a specific, clear-cut, consensual meaning, in this use of language, each word is a personal symbol, rich with multiple connotations, and often embodied in the concrete physiognomic features of the word and their similarity with the signified. This way of connecting words to deep, personal, and stable meanings is essentially different from a chain of "superficial" associations where the sound of a word is used only to link it to the sound of another word in order to disguise meaning. But external associations as compromise formations may reflect, in a disguised and caricatured way, not only the unconscious meaning but also some of the formal aspects of the style of language in which this meaning was originally expressed.

To view external associations as compromise formations is clinically meaningful, but leaves unresolved a basic issue in Freud's conceptualization of the primary process. If we take Freud's view that external associations are a model of primary-process ideation (mobile discharge and drive organization of thought) alongside his formulation that they are primarily a function of the degree of defense or resistance, we end with the theoretical problem that the degree of primary-process organization is a direct function of defense or, to put it more bluntly, *that defense is the cause of primary processes*. It is the familiar view that the dream work is primarily due to the needs of the censorship and that the primary process is a distortion operating only on repressed thoughts.

When Freud (1900) speaks of a defensive "displacement from a normal and serious association to a superficial and apparently absurd one" (p. 531), he is referring to the dream work, the transformation of latent into manifest content. But what is the nature of the latent content of the "correct and deeper links"? Here we have two competing points of view. The first assumes that the latent dream thoughts or deeper meanings exist originally in rational, logical, immediately understandable form and then become "distorted" by primary discharge processes made necessary by censorship. The final rational interpretation of a dream or symptom undoes the distortion and reestablishes the latent thoughts in the original form (or approximates this goal).

The alternate view stresses the existence of "archaic primitive methods of expression and representation" (1900, p. 547) as a language in its own right, with its own rules and organization that cannot be reduced to improvised drive-discharge processes under the barrier of censorship. In this language, "colorless and abstract expression…[is] being exchanged for a pictorial and concrete one" (p. 339). Thoughts are "represented symbolically by means of similes and metaphors, in images resembling those of poetic speech" (1901a, p. 659). The reemergence of this primary language is closely tied to the concept of regression and altered states of consciousness—a regression that can and usually does have defensive and adaptive functions. Within this framework, interpretation is no longer primarily the removal of distortions, the breaking of an improvised code, but the construction of new meanings, "a higher level of mental organization." This "higher," "secondary-process" level is a more explicit, logical, abstract, and impersonal construction, which necessarily loses some of the richness and immediacy of the more "primitive" medium of expression and way of organizing experience.

Clearly, these issues, which have been in the forefront of some of the later reformulations of psychoanalytic theory (Holt, 1967), need more extensive consideration than they can be given here. My aim was only to show the relevance of this early classical example to some of these basic and lasting issues. Even this limited example reminds us again of how closely personal "clinical" motives and "metapsychological" concepts are interwoven in Freud's thinking. It also illustrates the inseparable mixture of unlimited richness and unavoidable ambiguity that characterizes both the data he explored and his insights into them.

Chapter 14

The Interpretation of Dreams revisited

Interpretation, primary process, and language

The Interpretation of Dreams (1900) is one of Freud's major works and one of the few he kept amplifying and revising over almost 20 years. It presents his fundamental rationale for the interpretation of both dreams and neurotic symptoms and also his basic concepts about the functioning of the "mental apparatus." Because of its scope and richness, it includes many complexities and ambiguities, often increased rather than resolved by his later revisions. Many of the major ideas in the book have become extremely well known—in some cases, almost part of popular language. But in this process, they have also become simplified and solidified, often reduced to the level of frozen clichés. Thus, they have lost much of their complexity, richness, and ambiguity and become open to one-sided and biased interpretations, both positive and negative. The issues involved are still highly relevant and controversial today and by no means only of historical and biographical interest.

My aim in this chapter is to examine what I consider some of the major concepts and contributions of Freud's *The Interpretation of Dreams*. In doing so, I will try to use the perspective of a reader of around 1900 (to the limited extent that this can be done) as well as of a contemporary one, a century later. We now read the work very differently, with our knowledge and understanding of Freud's later writings and with a selective perspective influenced by the many post-Freudian developments in psychoanalysis.

Freud begins the book—at the beginning of each of the first two chapters—by making the fundamental assumption that a dream has meaning and can be interpreted. In Chapter 1, he writes: "every dream reveals itself as a psychical structure which has a meaning and which can be inserted at an assignable point in the mental activities of waking life" (p. 1). And, again, beginning Chapter 2, he reiterates: "for 'interpreting' a dream implies assigning a 'meaning' to it—that is, replacing it by something which fits into the chain of our mental acts as a link having a validity and importance equal to the rest" (p. 96). And he immediately adds,

> The scientific theories of dreams leave no room for any problem of interpreting them, since in their view a dream is not a mental act at all, but a somatic process signalizing its occurrence by indications registered in the mental apparatus. (p. 96)

We can note here that this scientific dismissal of dreams as epiphenomena of altered brain functioning during sleep (as indicated by specific patterns of brain waves, rapid eye movements, etc.) is very much alive today. The issue, as Freud is well aware, does not apply only to dreams, but also to many observed mental phenomena (neurotic symptoms, parapraxes, delusions), as well as to behaviors that seem incomprehensible, or at least bizarre and irrational to the observer. One either assumes that these phenomena are essentially random and meaningless by-products of altered and/or pathological brain functioning, or one has to infer some sort of hidden, unconscious meanings and organizing motives behind these seemingly incomprehensible observables. This is the crossroads from which Freud starts, and this is the most basic postulate of psychoanalysis in all its versions and offshoots.

In the second chapter, Freud refers briefly to two distinct popular methods of dream interpretation. One interprets the dream as a whole, as a symbolic allegorical story. Such a method is completely intuitive, cannot be used with confused and disjointed dreams, and is illustrated mostly by artificially constructed dreams, such as those in the Bible and later literature. The second method is based on a decoding of each separate major component of the dream according to a fixed key applied to all dreams (although the use of such a dream book is sometimes fitted to the character and circumstances of the dreamer). Such a method rests on the choice and presumed validity of a particular dream key.

The method that Freud presents also sees each element of the dream separately. But instead of the interpreter using a fixed key, the *dreamer's* associations to each element are the basis for unraveling its meaning. Here Freud immediately acknowledges that his method is derived from his prior attempts to interpret and remove neurotic symptoms. And he states that this

> taught me that a dream can be inserted into the psychical chain that has to be traced backwards in the memory from a pathological idea. It was then only a short step to treating the dream itself as a symptom and to applying to dreams the method of interpretation that had been worked out for symptoms. (p. 101)

This is already a hint that in both cases—of the dream and the symptom—the ultimate clinical goal of interpretation will be the uncovering of a repressed early pathogenic memory. We can also note that in his previous writings about the treatment of neurotic symptoms, Freud had not yet explicitly highlighted the crucial role of *interpretation,* but rather he focused on the *lifting of repression,* in bringing about the emergence of repressed memories. Freud then describes, for the first time, in explicit detail, the procedure of asking the patient/dreamer to relinquish voluntary control over his thoughts and to allow an altered state similar to that before falling into sleep or to hypnosis.

But how do such "involuntary thoughts" lead to interpretation? Does a unitary hidden meaning spontaneously emerge from them? Having postulated *that* dreams can be interpreted, Freud will naturally go on to show us *how* they can be interpreted and what the main results of such interpretations are. After the first chapter, which is an extensive review of the prior literature on dreams, the subsequent three brief chapters (2, "The Method of Interpreting Dreams: An Analysis of a Specimen Dream"; 3, "The Dream as Fulfillment of a Wish"; and 4, "Distortion in Dreams") serve as a kind of rough preliminary answer and overview of these questions.

Freud will tell us that dreams are to be interpreted by obtaining the dreamer's associations to each separate element of the dream report (the manifest content, Chapter 2); by the end of Chapter 4, he will give us the broad conclusion that "*a dream is a (disguised) fulfillment of a (suppressed or repressed) wish*" (p. 160). We may wonder as to what kind of wish, and even exactly what Freud means by wish, and *why* the dream always has to be a wish fulfillment. Is the method of interpretation simply the getting of associations, and are the results of such a method enough to reach the general conclusion of dreams as wish fulfillment? We will want to get a closer look at the analysis of a particular dream (the Irma dream) that Freud has given us. But let us first briefly anticipate how Freud deals with these questions in the remainder of the book. We will find, of course, many dream examples, the most extensive ones being Freud's own dreams with all the advantages and limitations that such a choice brings.

The important point is that the detailed spelling out of Freud's theory of dreams will be focused not on interpretation as such, its rationale, and technique, but rather on what the results of interpretation tell us about the material and sources of dreams (Chapter 5), on the way dreams get constructed through the "dream-work" (Chapter 6), and, finally in Chapter 7, on some general considerations about the psychology of the dream process and the general picture of mental functioning that these imply and illustrate. The understanding of the function of dreams and the process of dream formation may provide a rationale for the process of interpretation. This, however, assumes that interpretation travels in reverse and can undo the distorting effects of the dream-work, and that the process will be essentially the same in either direction.

One nearly forgets that the manifest content of the dream and the process of interpretation are the empirical realities on which the theory of the process of dream formation rests. The path from manifest to latent is observable, at least in principle; the reverse path from latent to manifest is a reconstruction and an inference. I believe and hope to make clear that this seemingly obvious point touches upon a major, if not *the* major and most lastingly controversial issue of the whole of *The Interpretation of Dreams.*

Freud does not seem primarily interested in teaching the reader the details of the technique of dream interpretation; nor is he particularly interested in convincing us of the primacy of repressed infantile sexual wishes as the ultimate meaning and source of dreams. This point is made explicit only at the end of the book, almost as if it were an afterthought. The argument that dominates Freud's exposition is that the hidden meaning of a dream can be found by using a particular method of interpretation, which is objective, content free, and neutral as to the meaning that will be found. The model, at least ideally, is that of a message in code or in a foreign tongue, which we can decode or translate if we know the necessary rules (of the code or of the syntax and vocabulary of both languages). By such a method, the preexisting meaning will be found.

An alternate view that kept haunting Freud as an unwelcome intruder, which he was never quite able to dismiss, is that interpretation depends to a large extent on the point of view of the interpreter, thus giving rise to multiple possible interpretations. How much is interpretation the refinding or decoding of a prior set meaning and how much is it the present retroactive creation of meaning? In actuality, these two views need not be completely exclusive, especially within our more contemporary framework. But, in part because of his view of science (and also archeology), Freud was strongly committed to the first position, and this commitment dominates much of his presentation and arguments in *The Interpretation of Dreams*—as I will try to show in more detail in various contexts.

Freud proceeds to give us a first illustration of his method by the "analysis of a specimen dream," the since famous Irma dream. He gives us as a "preamble" a summary of the immediate circumstances and context of the dream, then the dream itself, and then concludes that "no one who had only read the preamble and the content of the dream itself could have the slightest notion of what the dream meant" (p. 108). This is a rather dubious statement. In the preamble Freud has told us that he had been concerned the night before with self-criticism and doubts about the outcome of his treatment of his patient Irma and felt a need to justify himself to some of his medical colleagues (Otto and Dr. M, who appear directly in the dream). I think most readers would agree that these themes are pretty openly and directly reflected in the dream, without the use of further associations and interpretations.

Freud then gives us his extensive, but admittedly selective, associations to various elements of the dream. These reveal a good deal about Freud's current life, interests, hopes, concerns, and worries. They give us more details about the various characters in the dream, and the personal context and meaning of seemingly obscure and arbitrary words such as *trimethylamin* (directly related to Fliess and his sexual theories and, by implication, Freud's versions of them).

But what is the overall interpretation? A summary of common themes in the associations: "concern about my own and other people's health—professional conscientiousness" (p. 120). The main conclusion is that "the dream acquitted me of the responsibility for Irma's condition by showing that it was due to other factors" (p. 118) and by shifting the blame to various medical colleagues. The dream was "*the fulfillment of a wish and its motive was a wish*" (p. 119)—presumably the wish to be above reproach medically and not to feel guilty. But such a wish was already present and consciously salient before the dream (see Preamble), and it is clear enough in the dream itself, with the associations mostly amplifying and specifying it. So this early specimen is not very enlightening as to the crucial role of associations. In a broader sense, it leaves unanswered the exact relationship between associations and interpretation.

Is getting associations sufficient for interpretation? Does a hidden meaning spontaneously emerge from converging themes in the associations? Or are associations only a necessary first step toward interpretation, extending the material of the dream report, but then having to be further subjected to selective interpretation from among a wide range of possibilities? A fundamental issue which underlies much of our discussion of all the topics of *The Interpretation of Dreams* is the extent to which hidden meanings emerge spontaneously, are simply recovered by a particular procedure, such as free associations, or are always also a selective creation of the interpreter.

Many attempts at "deeper" interpretations of this dream have been made, but they are not directly relevant here. Let me mention only one obvious issue. In terms of Freud's main formulation of dream formation, as presented later in *The Interpretation of Dreams*, the reaction to Otto's reproaches of the preceding day and the guilt triggered by them must have been quite strong and gotten reinforcement from deeper and broader issues in order to trigger a dream. So one may ask what the guilt was about, because it had to be denied so strenuously and projected in the dream content. Freud himself gives a hint of personal sexual issues, perhaps about voyeurism and phallic intrusiveness underlying his forceful exploration of the sexual basis of his patients' neurotic conflicts.

But more interesting is the fact (relatively recently discovered in the Fliess letters) that, at the time, Freud had real, major reasons to feel guilty about Irma. He had handed her over to Fliess, who performed an almost fatal surgery on her nose; he must have been struggling with strong guilt as well as ambivalence toward his close and admired friend, Fliess. (The relevant letters show desperate attempts to deny such feelings.) If this event is taken into account (which, of course, Freud could not do publicly and apparently not even acknowledge to himself), Freud's relatively superficial interpretation of the Irma dream hints at and, at the same time, occludes "deeper" more threatening issues, and it is a typical compromise formation which both reveals and conceals. One may further speculate about some return of the repressed in Freud's choosing, 4 years later, this particular dream as "the specimen dream" in a major work of which the manuscripts were sent to his friend Fliess.

In Chapter 3 ("A Dream Is a Fulfillment of a Wish"), Freud seeks to give further proof of dreams as wish fulfillment. But his examples deal only with ongoing, potentially conscious wishes, more or less directly reflected in the content of the dream. Children's dreams are some of his main examples. This illustrates only how the content of ongoing wishes (in the most surface, conventional sense, such as a child's wish for strawberries) may be one of the topics reflected fairly directly and convincingly in the content of a dream. This is not yet the true meaning of wish for Freud, as will become clear later on.

In the next chapter (4, "Distortion in Dreams"), we are introduced to the idea that it is the latent content (the dream as interpreted) and not the manifest content (the remembered and reported dream) which contains a wish fulfillment. The multiple meanings and levels of this seemingly simple distinction will be discussed later. The wish in the manifest content is disguised and distorted by censorship and may appear unpleasant or even anxiety producing. (This is the first of Freud's many, ultimately unsuccessful, attempts to fit anxiety dreams within the postulate of the pleasure principle.) But the reasons for this censorship are not spelled out and remain rather vague and superficial, such as the avoidance of unpleasant or socially undesirable thoughts (e.g., not wanting to think ill of a friend).

To go back to the Irma dream: Why should the conscious wish to be a responsible physician, to be free from guilt and criticism, be censored and disguised in the dream? Clearly, because Freud has not yet referred to wishes as primarily repressed expressions of infantile sexuality, he cannot give a strong or specific justification for censorship at this point. Freud has given us the preliminary conclusion that dreams are the disguised expressions of wish fulfillment. But what does he really mean by wish and why the strong need for disguise?

The contents of these introductory chapters illustrate Freud's skillful and no doubt deliberate method and style in introducing his ideas to a new, presumably skeptical reader. Freud goes from what seems most evident and least controversial to what is more inferential, difficult, and potentially shocking to the reader. It is not simply that he goes from the easier to the more complex issues as a basic didactic device. Rather, most of the issues are brought up repeatedly at different levels of complexity. In particular, the concept of "wish" goes from surface to depth, from commonsense, everyday meaning to a highly specialized one, from recent, conscious, easily retrieved wishes to unconscious "infantile" ones, depending on interpretation and reconstruction.

As I will show, this applies also to the concept of latent content and dream-thoughts. In general, because Freud cannot always maintain a clear and consistent separation (which would be difficult and artificial) between the different levels of his presentation, a good deal of ambiguity is introduced. As an example, it is unclear as to the kinds of wishes to which he is referring and the level of evidence and inference at which he is working. This problem is increased by the many layers of additions and revisions to the text that Freud introduced over the years. When Freud is quoted out of context or read very selectively—which is unfortunately too often the case—I think these aspects of the exposition may lead to a good deal of misunderstanding and to dubious interpretations.

Some of these problems become particularly evident in the lengthier Chapter 5 ("The Material and Sources of Dreams"). This material ranges from somatic stimuli during sleep to recent (and often indifferent) events to memories from childhood. Where does this material come from? How is it obtained? First and foremost, it is obtained from the dreamer's associations. For the first two categories, the link with the dream content is fairly direct and often self-evident: An event or experience of the day before, or at least a part of it, appears in the dream.

The connecting of the dream content to such recent sources can hardly be considered interpretation and, as the associations expand in various directions, their connection to the manifest dream becomes more tenuous. Freud has to invoke "superficial" links, usually selected or constructed through interpretation. Here, for the first time (in *The Interpretation of Dreams*), Freud invokes the concept of displacement (p. 177) and "intermediate links" (p. 175), based on seemingly arbitrary far-fetched links characteristic of a "primary" process different from normal thought. These are all ideas that will be elaborated in the last chapter of the book, "The Psychology of the Dream Process."

The issue of the role of interpretation in finding the sources of the dream is even more crucial in the case of "infantile material" and the one of most interest to Freud. The associations sometimes include memories from childhood, as Freud illustrates from some of his own dreams. But Freud admits that "as a rule the childhood scene is only represented in the dream manifest content by an allusion, and has to be arrived at by an interpretation of the dream" (p. 199). This is, of course, the typical clinical situation with which Freud is dealing (Dora and the Wolf Man being the most detailed examples).

So we can already assume that there is more to interpretation than getting the dreamer's associations. Such associations essentially become further manifest material to be interpreted. But are there specific rules of interpretation? If so, what are they? When and how is Freud going to reveal them? These are some of the main questions that the reader may ask at this point.

We may notice already—and this will be true throughout the book—that the most extensive dream associations are provided by Freud himself, using his own dreams as examples. This means that we have the special case where the dream, the associations, and the interpretations are all provided by the same person and are thus hard to differentiate.

CHAPTER 6: "THE DREAM-WORK"

In Chapter 6, the longest chapter (almost of book length by itself), Freud sets himself the task "of investigating the relations between the manifest content of dreams and the latent dream-thoughts, and of tracing out the processes by which the latter have been changed into the former" (p. 277). Let us note in passing that, just before this statement, Freud has referred to the latent dream-thoughts not as the meaning of the dream, but as something "between the manifest content of dreams and the conclusions of our enquiry...It is from these dream-thoughts that we disentangle its meaning" (p. 277).

This would suggest that the dream-thoughts are not the end point of interpretation but are themselves subject to further interpretation or, to put it differently, that there are several levels of depth and interpretation to the dream-thoughts, all the way down to the "infantile wish," or Scene—as will become clear in the last chapter of his book.

Freud (in Chapter 6) then compares this task to one of translation between two different languages. "Or, more properly, the dream content seems like a transcript of the dream-thoughts into another mode of expression [a primarily pictorial, visual one], whose characters and syntactic laws it is our business to discover by comparing the original and the translation" (p. 277). The implication of this comparison is that once we have discovered these laws, we should be able to interpret dreams readily and objectively, just as someone who is familiar with two languages can reliably translate one into the other:

> The dream-thoughts are immediately comprehensible, as soon as we have learnt them. The [manifest] dream-content, on the other hand, is expressed as it were in a pictographic script, the characters of which have to be transposed individually into the language of the dream-thoughts. (p. 277)

Freud then gives the analogy of a picture rebus. This is a puzzle consisting of a seemingly nonsensical sequence of pictures. When each picture is replaced by a corresponding word or part thereof (for instance, the picture of half a goat may translate as the word *go*[at]), a hidden verbal text or message will emerge.

This often quoted metaphor for interpretation and the dream-work makes several assumptions: First, that the original dream-thoughts are like a pre-constructed, directly "comprehensible" verbal text. Yet, as we will see, there are many levels of dream-thoughts and many depths of interpretation. Second, that this text has been translated or encoded into a different language, and that, except for this change in mode of expression, the two texts are essentially equivalent. This also implies that there is only one original text and one correct interpretation. Thirdly, it assumes tht it is possible to find regular laws which allow a decoding or re-translation into the original. And finally, it assumes that these laws will be similar to the syntax and vocabulary (lexicon) of a language, a point on which Lacan anchored his famous "return to Freud."

The metaphor of decoding an unknown language by comparing a text in that language to its translation in an already known language clearly refers to the decoding of hieroglyphics through the discovery of the Rosetta Stone, to which Freud, with his passion for archeology, refers explicitly in other passages. But this appealing metaphor does not really apply to Freud's own method. We cannot compare the translation to an original when we do not have this original—which is just the case in dreams. We have only the manifest content. The "original" latent content can only be established as the result of the very process of interpretation, the laws of which are supposed to be provided by a comparison of an initially given original text with a translated version.

Freud's use of such a linguistic metaphor expresses his ideal goal of finding formal laws of interpretation which can be applied in a consistent, stable, objective, and consensual manner to reveal an unambiguous correct hidden meaning. Thus, interpretation would have a "scientific" basis and would not require preestablished assumptions and theories about the nature of the hidden content.

Nowhere in Chapter 6, on the dream-work, will Freud present rules of interpretation—beyond the already stated need to get the dreamer's associations to the elements of the manifest dream. He compares the manifest dream to the contents revealed by associations and interpretations. (Chapter 5 has already provided a good deal about the "material and sources.") He then tries to describe and classify the nature of the links and transformations between the latent and manifest content.

Freud will present a theoretical justification for these processes in the last chapter of the book. The dream-work is known only through the work of interpretation, which it is supposed to account for and justify. Freud's implicit but fundamental assumption is that interpretation travels the path of the dream-work in reverse, undoes the transformations created by it, and restores the original—even though this goal may be only partly achieved in any single instance.

I think that this is a basic postulate which, while logical and plausible, is impossible to prove or disprove on any empirical, clinical basis. I will also suggest later that such a notion is not essential to make the interpretation of dreams (and the associations they generate) a useful tool for the exploration of the dreamer's unconscious thoughts and motives. But if we accept such a postulate, the understanding of the dream-work, the knowledge of the rules of transformation through which the dream got constructed could provide the basis for interpretation as a self-sufficient decoding method. This is what seems to be Freud's goal.

In reviewing the main components of the dream-work, we will have to keep asking ourselves if they really provide an encoding system which would allow us to predict or at least to account for the transformations from a given latent content to a specific manifest outcome. I maintain that this is not the case. We will see that Freud's emphasis is more on the *why*—on the motives for the dream-work—rather than on the *how*—on what determines the choice of some specific transformation and outcome.

The two primary aspects of the dream-work are condensation and displacement. To what do they refer? First and foremost, they are general descriptive labels based on a comparison of the manifest dream and the latent dream-thoughts (at various levels). The dream report can generate a great number of associations and interpretations, which obviously expand its meaning and connotations, so that the dream can thus be viewed as a compressed or condensed expression of them. Thus, because interpretation is expansion and amplification, the dream-work, as the reverse process, must involve compression and condensation. This, of course, as we have seen earlier, is based on Freud's basic assumption that associations and interpretations take the reverse path of the dream-work and restore the original preexisting dream-thoughts.

Even more broadly, when we compare the manifest dream with that of the dream-thoughts, they appear markedly different in content, sequence, and emphasis. What seems quite salient and central in the manifest dream (e.g., the botanical monograph), no longer plays a significant role and can even disappear completely in the dream-thoughts. Thus, through the transformations of the dream-work, massive displacements have occurred. Freud refers to displacement as the "essential portion of the dream-work" (p. 308). All other aspects of the dream-work—such as condensation, change in modes of representation (from verbal to sensory and concrete), and secondary revision—result in various forms of increased displacement. It is not accurate to view condensation and displacement as separate "mechanisms" involving different principles (e.g., similarity/metaphor for condensation and contiguity/metonymy for displacement).

Displacement is also used by Freud as a general explanatory concept, based on the economic/dynamic model of the mental apparatus spelled out in the last chapter. In the context of the dream-work (Chapter 6), Freud speaks of displacement of "psychical intensity," referring somewhat vaguely to the "value or the degree of interest of an idea" (p. 306). Thus, displacement tends to put the emphasis on quantitative changes in interest and intensity rather than on transformations of content, more typical for condensation. Displacement is in the service of censorship and is mainly responsible for the distortion of the latent dream-thoughts. It is necessarily involved in condensation and is part of all the processes of the dream-work.

Yet it is noteworthy that, while Freud labels displacement as "the essential portion of the dream-work" (p. 308), he devotes only a 4-page section to it in his 235-page chapter on the dream-work. He has no need to give any specific examples, presumably because all the numerous dreams presented in the rest of the chapter involve some form of displacement—condensation as composite figures evoking several elements of the dream-thoughts simultaneously by artificially combining some of their attributes. Words can also be condensed to create neologisms. Even when the manifest dream element corresponds to a real person or experience (e.g., Irma, the Botanical Monograph), the associations may show that it has become the condensed expression or representation of multiple thoughts and meanings.

What is the *basis,* rather than the overall *purpose,* of condensation and displacement? Is it a strong objective or subjective, but lasting, similarity between the two elements? Or is it more that some often indifferent and accidental day residue is available and will be used by presently pressing concerns to express themselves by transferring their affect and some of their contents onto it on the basis of the most superficial, partial, and artificial links? Perhaps it is a mixture of both.

It is impossible to predict, from the latent dream-thoughts, the manifest dream and what specific paths displacements and condensations will take. Unlike a linguistic or symbolic system, Freud's description of the dream-work does not provide specific rules of transformation which will allow us to go from the original, even if it were known, to the manifest. Freud recognizes this (p. 341) but then strangely concludes that this is no more a problem than in deciphering hieroglyphics. Back to his linguistic model! Only the specific associations can, in principle, unravel the specific condensations and displacements by traveling the paths of the dream-work in reverse and thus reveal the various latent elements that have been transformed by it.

The closest thing to a fixed code, a basic transformational language (though still somewhat context dependent, as is true for all natural languages), will be symbolism, which is not present in the 1900 model and which I will discuss further on. Freud's rationale rests on the assumption that the associations are guided by an unconscious "purposive idea" (p. 527) (as is true in more or less disguised ways for all the patient's material, particularly in the altered states of sleep and free association) and that, because the associations start with a dream element, they will be specifically linked to the dream. But this linkage to the specific manifest content gets more and more remote and inferential as the associations expand and diverge.

In principle, this is a *post hoc, prompter hoc* fallacy which Freud tries to address in the section on condensation and then again in Chapter 7, Section A ("The Forgetting of Dreams"). In practice, associations almost always start with recall of recent thoughts or events directly related to the dream content (day residues). They give essentially the personal reference and allusions depending on clear individual context (Irma, trimethylamin). But the most important links, for Freud, are far from obvious. He has to invoke intermediate thoughts and superficial, external links in the service of deeper unconscious links.

Freud admits that the associations may open new paths and not follow those used by the dream-work; however, he claims that this does not matter as long as they reach the same goal—namely, the unconscious dream-thoughts underlying both the dream and the associations. So the associations give us the latent, from which the principles and the mechanisms of the dream-work can be inferred by comparison. The transformations need not be identical both ways, but presumably they have the same starting point and ending point and follow the same general principles. (This issue is discussed in the sections on condensation, on representability, and in Chapter 7, Section A.)

Here, Freud explains that the associations bring in new elements and create new paths, but get back to the "essential dream-thoughts...which completely replace the dream and which, if there were no censorship of dreams, would be sufficient in themselves to replace it" (p. 311). To reconstruct "the process by which the dream was formed" (p. 310), the dream analysis (valuable, even if incomplete) has to be complete and lead to a dream synthesis, presumably requiring the complete context of the neurosis. Because the dream-thoughts have no end, the definition of a complete analysis, which would completely account for the dream, seems only an ideal.

The associations start by being very close to the manifest dream; they then expand and diverge from it more and more, so the links are remote, carried only by (seemingly) superficial links and transitions within the chain or sequence of associations. Yet, underneath this divergence, a converging unconscious theme is expressed—an unconscious theme which is also at the core of the dream thoughts. But at what level of dream-thoughts? Freud also acknowledges that the dream-thoughts (and the associations) have, in principle, no end point: "They are bound to branch out in every direction into the intricate network of our world of thought" (p. 525). This point makes further untenable the model of the latent content as a finite preorganized text.

In the dream book, the examples at best show how, with the use of associations, one is led back to the current life concerns of the dreamer—concerns which also find, more or less directly and convincingly, their expression in the manifest dream. Both with his own dreams and with those of patients, Freud stays essentially at the level of the rational recent dream-thoughts, even if a few retrieved childhood memories occasionally surface. Clinically, the goal for Freud is to get at the repressed infantile sexual conflicts and wishes. Yet, there are no examples of this and no rules of interpretation as to how this is to be accomplished—specifically, how one goes from the associations to the repressed infantile wishes which have been transferred onto the rational dream-thoughts.

The royal road to the unconscious is to the repressed infantile scene, at the deepest level, not only of the dream but also of the neurosis and the personality structure of the individual. However, this ultimate level of interpretation is also the most predetermined by theoretical choices prior to the specific interpretation as its implicit, required starting orientation and its end point. Thus, the interpretation can only aim at specific individual versions and derivatives of a generic theory-based theme, using it as an organizing theme ("narrative structure") for aspects of individual experience.

6C: "THE MEANS OF REPRESENTATION"

This section (6C) and the next (6D: "Considerations of Representability") can be viewed as dealing with further manifestations of condensation, reflecting the fact that the complex and primarily verbal dream-thoughts have to be represented in the primarily pictorial, visual medium of the manifest dream. The focus here is on the limited means which the dream-work has of expressing the abstract logical relations of the dream-thoughts (for instance, such relations and qualifiers as "if," "because," "just as," "although," "either–or," etc., which need the syntactic structure of sentences and the rules of language).

Freud shows that the dream has to rely on concrete aspects of contiguity, sequence, size, and so on in pictorial content of the manifest dream to allude to the more precise and abstract logical structure of the underlying dream-thoughts (e.g., *x* occurring before *y* can suggest that *x* is the cause of *y*). This section extends the discussion and examples of condensation required by the limited pictorial modes of representation of the dream (a picture is worth a thousand words, one may say) and the formation of composite figures.

The need for pictorial representation is specific to the dream, as thinking during sleep (in contrast to other products of condensation and displacement, such as fantasies, delusions, etc.). The pictorial quality of dreams is intrinsic to their being a regressive state. Freud takes for granted that the deepest and most primitive levels of mental functioning are at a primarily concrete and pictorial level.

Freud also makes the distinction, which will become crucial for the theoretical discussion of Chapter 7, between the essential dream-thoughts and thoughts emerging in the associations. The dream-thoughts "could completely replace the dream if there were no censorship" (p. 311) and have "the most intricate possible structure, with all the attributes of the trains of thought familiar to us in waking life" (p. 312). Thoughts emerging in the associations may not have had a share in the formation of the dream and, indeed, may refer in part to events occurring after the dream. Such material

> includes all the connecting paths that led from the manifest dream-content to the latent dream-thoughts, as well as the intermediate and linking associations by means of which, in the course of the process of interpretation, we came to discover these connecting paths. (p. 311)

In Chapter 7, these distinctions, as well as the preceding one between dream analysis and dream synthesis, will be central to the distinctions between external and deep links and between dream-thoughts and infantile wish.

Another important side issue in this section is Freud's not altogether convincing argument that the use of speech and reasoning, even if transformed and distorted in the manifest dream, is irrelevant for the expression of relationships in the dream-thoughts. Freud has to admit an exception for secondary revision, and this will turn out to be an integral part of the dream-work. He may also have a vested interest in the primary, sensory aspect of the manifest dream as part of the ultimate regression to the content of the infantile visual Scenes. Manifest speech and names are likely to be day residues that may acquire different meaning. This seems to be Freud's main argument. But how about the pictorial, metaphoric use of language in the next section?

6D: "CONSIDERATIONS OF REPRESENTABILITY"

Here, Freud brings up another type of displacement and transformation affecting the dream-thoughts. This displacement is at a verbal level; colorless and abstract language is replaced by a concrete and pictorial one. Words are used in a figurative, evocative sense. Freud remarks that in every language concrete terms are richer in associations (personal connotations, we may say) than conceptual and abstract terms. In speech, "words...are the nodal points of numerous ideas" and "predestined to ambiguity" (p.

340) as simultaneous multiple levels of connotative meanings. All of this favors condensation, disguise, allusion, hidden meanings, and so on.

In a very important passage, whose implication he usually ignored (p. 376), Freud mentions, almost in passing, the ambiguity of the interpretation of any specific dream element. Such use of language is not idiosyncratic and arbitrary, but is based on "firmly established linguistic usage..." in contrast to "symbolism arbitrarily chosen by the interpreter" (pp. 341–342). This use of language as a shared and stable (though always context-bound and ambiguous) system of representation and transformation is in contrast to the improvised and personal associations which Freud has, until this point, highlighted as the core aspect of the dream-work. This foreshadows the increasing emphasis, after 1900, on Symbolism as an essential aspect of the dream-work and of dream interpretation. This also raises the whole issue of the role of linguistic relationships in the organization and expression of the Unconscious (e.g., the unconscious structured as a language, one of the basic, if ambiguous, Lacanian formulas).

6E: "REPRESENTATIONS BY SYMBOLS"

While foreshadowed in the previous section (as well as in Section D, "Typical Dreams," in Chapter 5), symbolism is a new dimension, added only in later versions of the book and constantly expanded. It does not fit well with Freud's main model of interpretation through individual associations or with the theoretical model of the dream-work, spelled out in the next chapter, as the expression of an improvised compromise between primary process discharge and censorship. As he acknowledges, it is a version of the traditional popular "dream book" method of interpretation.

Symbolism functions as a form of indirect representation, displacement, and disguise; however, it is based on fixed, shared, quasi-universal methods of representation. Symbolism is not created by the dream-work nor is its use limited to dreams. Freud speculated that it was a regressive remnant of an archaic inherited universal language. But symbols are ambiguous and can have several meanings depending on context; hence, their interpretation should be combined with the use of associations and/or knowledge of the specific context in which the symbol is used. The number of objects or words which can have a symbolic meaning is practically unlimited. While some may be universal, many are culturally and historically specific. And, most important:

> Often enough a symbol has to be interpreted in its proper meaning [a cigar can be just a cigar] and not symbolically; while on other occasions a dreamer may derive from his private memories the power to

> employ as sexual symbols, all kinds of things which are not ordinarily employed as such. (p. 352)

Thus, one assumes a continuum from quasi-universal symbols to those shared by a culture, a group, a couple, or only limited to the private language of an individual. The symbolic meaning of a word or object is only one of its meanings, a meaning that may be more or less dominant, background, or foreground, depending on context and circumstances.

While Freud admits sometimes that what is symbolized need not be unconscious or exclusively sexual, he assumes that in practically all cases, particularly in dreams, it is an expression of repressed sexuality in the broad sense of libidinal issues and concerns. All his examples here and in the *Introductory Lectures* (1917, Chapter 10) on Symbolism and from the same period as this added section to the 1900 dream book are to that effect. Thus, the number of contents and issues that find symbolic representation is quite limited (sexual functions, body parts, basic family figures, etc.); almost any word can acquire some symbolic/sexual connotation. In a more limited sense, Freud's symbols are those words whose sexual connotation is most shared and evident. Thus, symbolism is the closest approximation to the ideal of a fixed translation code that can be applied to the decoding of all dreams. But it is a code that is not content free but rather has a predetermined range of meanings.

Interpretation through symbolism is indeed the "royal road" to the repressed infantile sexual wishes that Freud considered at the core of dreams. But a reader of 1900 could, at most, get only a faint hint of this and only by the end of the book. Freud warned against the exclusive, reductive use of symbolism (usually referring to Jung or Stekel), and stated that it should be used as a supplement to the method of individual associations. Yet it is clear that it came to play a central role in his method of dream interpretation, as is already evident in the Dora case. Symbolism has no explicit place or acknowledged role in the original *Interpretation of Dreams;* yet, in 1917, in the *Introductory Lectures,* Freud will declare to the general public, "Symbolism is perhaps the most remarkable chapter of our theory of dreams" (p. 151).

What kind of language is symbolism? What is the nature of the symbolic relationship? It is based on a comparison, on some common attribute, so that the symbol can at least allude to the symbolized. The basis of this comparison may be obvious, as in phallic symbols, or it may be rather remote and concealed. The comparison is often based on some seemingly superficial aspects such as shape, rather than common, functional features, such as suitability for physical sexual use. But the implicit comparison frequently involves some basic vectorial dimensions or categories such as openings, enclosures, and rhythmic motion, which already represents a certain level of abstraction and classification. One should also raise the question of whether symbolism has to be considered as more than an indirect representation of sexual meanings, but may be a way in which the symbol can become a sexual object in thought and in action.

Symbols as comparisons and substitutions based on partial similarity can readily be viewed as a kind of metaphoric language; insofar as a symbol is stable and commonly used, symbols become a system of what has been called "dead" metaphors. In comparing symbolism to the general primary process mechanisms of condensation and displacement, the latter apply to any content, at least in principle, and are improvised, context-bound compromises; in contrast, displacements based on symbolism are stable and interindividually shared.

61: "SECONDARY REVISION"

Secondary revision is presented as the last and implicitly nonessential part of the dream-work. The material is revised to give it an appearance of cohesion and intelligibility, to make it resemble our waking thought organization. This is the influence of the ego or the system Preconscious, which is brought up explicitly in the next chapter. This system has a need "to establish order in material of that kind, to set up relations in it and to make it conform to our expectations of an intelligible whole" (p. 499). This revision is primarily a defensive distortion, a kind of rationalization, and part of the censorship function.

But, as usual, a closer look shows the issues to be a bit more complex and ambiguous. Freud adds that such a secondary revision cannot be limited to the last stages of the dream-work, but

> that from the very first the demands of this second factor constitute one of the conditions which the dream must satisfy and that this condition, like those laid down by condensation, the censorship imposed by resistance, and representability, operates simultaneously in a conducive and selective sense upon the mass of material present in the dream-thoughts. (p. 499)

Thus, this need for cohesion and an appearance of intelligibility—to create a narrative, if we want to use a more contemporary term—is an integral part at all levels of the selective transformations of psychic material, even at so-called primitive or regressed levels.

The second issue is that Freud states that secondary revision makes use of preorganized material—namely, daydreams and fantasies. Such fantasies have already a basic similarity with dreams, in that they are wish fulfillment and contain impressions of infantile experience, and they have been constructed in a way similar to the dream-work. Freud explains that "the wishful purpose that is at work in their production has mixed up the material of which they are built, has rearranged it, and has formed it into a new whole" (p. 492).

But even more important, although mentioned only incidentally here, is the reference to fantasies as the basis of symptoms. "Hysterical symptoms are not attached to actual memories, but to phantasies erected on the basis of memories" (p. 491). This is Freud's first published statement of the crucial role of fantasies as the basis of symptoms. While Freud did not spell this out in *The Interpretation of Dreams*, he is dealing here with at least two levels of fantasy: First, he is concerned with fantasy as recent, usually preconscious, daydreams, which are part of the dream-thoughts as day residues. They give coherence to the manifest dream and are part of the defensive aspects of secondary revision. Secondly, he is dealing with unconscious fantasies as the basic expression of infantile wishes, and as such, the deepest source of dreams and symptoms.

CHAPTER 7: "THE PSYCHOLOGY OF THE DREAM PROCESSES: A: THE FORGETTING OF DREAMS"

This section deals with two issues and with potential criticisms of this method of interpretation. The first serves as a clarification of the concept of manifest content. Here, for the first time, Freud makes explicit the distinction between the dream as a primarily visual hallucinatory experience during sleep and the dream as a memory and verbal report of this experience during the waking state. This memory of a dream is "not only fragmentary but positively inaccurate and falsified" (p. 512). Furthermore, the report of the dream is not a fixed text but will change on different tellings (e.g., at different times during the analysis).

So how can interpretation be based on focusing on every detail of such incomplete and changeable data? Freud's answer is that the omissions and changes are not random, but a continuation of the dream-work process—specifically, of the censorship. Thus, later additions and changes to the dream report become particularly telling clues of its most important and hidden meaning. Freud even claims that remembered dreams can be easier to interpret after a long period of time has elapsed since their occurrence because the resistance will have lessened in the meantime.

One would think, then, that it is likely that the access to the immediate context and day residues of the dream would be lessened so that the interpretation would deal primarily with the more lasting and stable unconscious wishes at the core of the dream and of many aspects of the dreamer's psychic life, rather than the more specific and temporary aspects of the latent content. Freud also repeats (earlier in Chapter 6, Section A) that, in principle, an interpretation of a dream is never complete because

"The dream-thoughts to which we are led by interpretation cannot, from the nature of things, have any definite endings; they are bound to branch out in every direction into the intricate network of our world of thought" (p. 525).

Thus, again, the dream-thoughts do not constitute a specific, limited, preorganized text simply translated into the manifest content, along the ideal proposed in the introduction to Chapter 6, on the dream-work. The manifest content cannot be reduced to a specific and finite set of elements which would provide the one and only true and complete interpretation as the solution to a puzzle—a metaphor Freud often uses. The fragmentary dream report, our only access to the dream, is enough to get to the essential dream-thoughts; the complete retrieval or reconstruction of the dream itself, as a nighttime experience, may not be possible and "is in any case a matter of no importance" (p. 517).

We begin, progressively, to sense what Freud will conclude by the end of the book—that he is not primarily interested in the dream, as such, or even in a systematic decoding of it, but rather in using the dream report and the associations it triggers as a "royal road to the Unconscious." In the same context, Freud then tries to anticipate the argument—much used since (e.g., Piaget, Spence)—that once we start a chain of associations from one element of the dream, we may be getting an accidental, improvised, and basically aimless chain of thoughts, wherein each element triggers and influences the choice of the next one. We are then likely to read some meaningful patterns into such basically random sequences and assume that these patterns were the thoughts underlying and preceding the dream because the associations were initially triggered by the dream.

Freud's answer is that each association does not simply and superficially trigger the next, but that the whole chain is guided by unconscious "purposive ideas," which steer the associations in a particular direction toward a predetermined end point. He adds that the "intermediate thoughts" linking the latent and the manifest often seem external, superficial, and arbitrary. Such associations are made possible by the mobile displacements of the primary process (discussed in Section E), but they are used as a disguise, a detour, an indirect path because the direct and legitimate one is barred by the censorship. "The real reason for the prevalence of superficial associations is not the abandonment of purposive ideas but the pressure of the censorship. Superficial associations replace deep ones if the censorship makes the normal connecting paths impassable" (p. 530).

Yet there seems to be some ambiguity here. We can have a fairly good idea of what Freud means by normal, serious, and legitimate links in contrast to superficial and external ones, the result of primary process displacement motivated by censorship. But at first the statement seems to imply that there are also direct and normal links between the manifest and the latent dream-thoughts (as in the "Signorelli" example). But it becomes clear that he could only be referring to the links between different aspects of the dream-thoughts, links that can only emerge through interpretation after undoing the distortion and displacements of the dream-work which has made use of these "objectionable or superficial" associations (p. 530). But this would leave the choice of the manifest substitute (manifest dream content and more broadly, symptom) to such improvised and arbitrary associations; these, by Freud's own admission, could be used to link anything with anything.

There is no simple solution unless other factors, mostly derived from Freud's specific earlier examples, are invoked. First, the manifest substitute is chosen because of its suitability for linkage with several elements of the dream-thoughts, through condensation. Second, the manifest content has some fairly direct or easily retrievable links with the day residue aspects of the dream-thoughts—whether important (Irma as Freud's actual patient) or seemingly indifferent (as the botanical monograph). Third, Freud hints (pp. 545–546) that because of the visual and regressed aspects of the dream, some aspects of the primarily visual aspects of the deeper infantile wishes and Scenes may also find direct expression in some of the concrete pictorial details of the manifest content and thus influence the choice of dream images.

It would be the convergence of all these factors in the choice of manifest content, the overdetermined choice, that would make it more serious and legitimate, instead of resting on one particular chain of superficial and seemingly arbitrary links. Freud concludes this section by admitting that the paths from the latent to the manifest are too complex to be "passable both ways [i.e., fully retraceable by interpretation]...fresh daytime material inserts itself in the interpretative chains" (p. 532), which may get back to the dream-thoughts by slightly different paths.

7B: "REGRESSION"

The bulk of this section is devoted to accounting for the hallucinatory aspect of dreams in terms of the quasiphysiological model worked out in the unpublished 1895 *Project*. Essentially, it speculates that during the state of sleep, excitation moves in a backward direction toward the sensory rather than the motor end, thus intensifying memories so that they are experienced as perceptions. This theoretical model is closely tied to the concept of primary process and hallucinatory wish fulfillment as its prime, inferred manifestation (as will be spelled out in the following sections of the chapter).

But then Freud considerably widens the concept, giving to dreams a new dimension which seems to go beyond what the reader may have anticipated from the preceding chapters: "In regression the fabric of the dream-thoughts is resolved into its raw material" (p. 543). Dream-thoughts regress to concrete and pictorial modes of expression, presumably characteristic of early stages of development. The material of childhood memories, mostly as visual scenes, also tends to emerge and to mix with the more recent dream-thoughts and day residues. Thus:

> The transformation of thoughts into visual images may be in part the result of the attraction which memories couched in visual form and eager for revival bring to bear upon thoughts cut off from consciousness and struggling to find expression. On this view a dream might be described as a substitute for an infantile scene modified by being transferred on to a recent experience... (p. 546)

This, of course, anticipates the next section (C: "Wish-Fulfillment"), where we will discover that the infantile wish is the necessary foundation of the dream. In the penultimate paragraph of the section on regression, added in 1919, Freud makes even more sweeping statements: The dream involves a revival of childhood and can even give access to the archaic remnants of the prehistoric stages of the human race (primal fantasies and symbols, etc.). "Behind this childhood of the individual we are promised a picture of a phylogenetic childhood—a picture of the development of the human race" (p. 548).

7C: "WISH-FULFILLMENT"

In this lengthy and complex section, which I will deal with only in a cursory fashion, Freud finally tells us what he means by wish fulfillment. We learn that only a repressed infantile wish can supply the energy and the motive force for a dream. So we are not dealing with obvious wishes of everyday life (Freud's daughter's wishes for strawberries, Freud's wishes for professional success and a professorship), as we may have been led to believe from most of the examples so far. No, the dream-thoughts as preconscious day residues may or may not contain wishes; even when they do, these wishes would not be strong enough by themselves to account for the dream. They only become strong enough as the vehicle of unconscious childhood wishes whose energy has been transferred onto them and whose representative or substitute expression they have become.

Freud also gives us the most general and abstract definition of wish, in the light of a brief outline of his model of the mental apparatus (derived from the 1895 *Project* and also expanded in Section E of the chapter): A wish is the seeking of the object of a prior experience of satisfaction; the most immediate and direct attempted wish-fulfillment is the hallucinatory cathexis of the memory of the object. This is the essence of the primary process, which will have to be inhibited by the secondary process to make any real satisfaction possible. And Freud concludes, "Thought is after all nothing but the substitute for a hallucinatory wish: and it is self evident that dreams must be wish-fulfillments since nothing but a wish can set our mental apparatus at work" (p. 567).

Thus, Freud's model of the mind requires that dreams ultimately be wish fulfillment. But this is rather nonspecific because the same is true, by definition, for all other thought activities, in varying degrees. All motives must ultimately be reduced to the transformed expression of basic early wishes. This is particularly difficult to demonstrate in the case of anxiety dreams, an issue with which Freud struggles repeatedly (including in the following section of this chapter).

7E: "THE PRIMARY AND SECONDARY PROCESSES"

In this section, the dream-work, particularly condensation and displacement, is subsumed under the theoretical concept of primary process. This process assumes mobile, freely displaceable energy seeking discharge by the quickest path available. This leads to displacements and condensations, superficial associations (discussed in Section A), with little regard for the proper meaning and logical relations of the contents. We also see the two meanings or levels of the dream-thoughts in a way which was not made clear before. The dream-thoughts consist of normal, rational waking thoughts, current concerns, and interests.

So far we may have assumed that these thoughts produce a seemingly irrational manifest dream because of the need for visual representation and the action of the censorship—although it was never quite clear why such rational current thoughts, even if at times unpleasant or shameful, needed such systematic censorship. Freud states that "these dream-thoughts are certainly not in themselves inadmissible to consciousness" (p. 593). In the previous section we learned that these dream-thoughts, whether they contain wishes or not, can produce a dream only if an unconscious infantile wish has been transferred onto them. Now we are told that it is this transfer which is the main reason for the abnormal and irrational aspects of the dream-work. The transfer of the repressed infantile wish onto the current dream-thoughts is the main cause of the primary process transformations of condensation, displacement, and censorship to which they are subjected.

Here, Freud increasingly invokes the psychology of the neuroses and the process of symptom formation, which he sees as basically similar to the dream-work, so that each can serve as model for the other. Freud concludes that the repressed infantile wish has to be a sexual one in the case of the neuroses. But he somewhat coyly adds:

> I will leave it an open question [for the reader? certainly not for Freud himself] whether these sexual and infantile factors are equally required in the theory of dreams; I will leave that theory incomplete at this point, since I have already gone a step beyond what can be demonstrated in assuming that dream-wishes are invariably derived from the unconscious. (p. 606)

But let us note that even in Freud's model, the deeper, repressed infantile wishes would be the ones most subject to censorship, most distorted and displaced (through primary process superficial and external links), and most remote from the manifest dream report. One may conclude that, unlike for more recent day residues and dream-thoughts, these deep infantile wishes would also be the most difficult to retrieve, the least likely to emerge fairly directly from the dreamer's associations, and the most dependent on the point of view of the interpreter. They are also assumed to manifest themselves in symptoms and in varying degrees in all aspects of an individual's thought and behavior. Thus, Freud concludes that the interpretation of dreams is the royal road to a *knowledge* of the unconscious activities of the mind—the royal road but not the only one.

In the last section, let us only note the reference to "psychical reality" (contrasted with material reality, but not further defined) of "unconscious wishes reduced to their most fundamental and truest shape" (p. 620). And in the penultimate paragraph of the book, we find an often forgotten reminder: "Actions and consciously expressed opinions are as a rule enough for practical purposes in judging men's characters" (p. 621). Much of behavior is not ruled by unconscious motives, but psychoanalysis focused on those areas of thought and behavior where their role is crucial and claims that their influence, although not a determining one, can be found in all areas. Thus, Freud also leaves us with the complex and unresolved issues of the relation between thought and deed and between psychical and material reality.

SUMMARY AND DISCUSSION

I will review the important aspects of Freud's theory of dreams which, because they are often neglected or misunderstood, I have highlighted in this review of *The Interpretation of Dreams*. These aspects center around the different levels of the dream process, from infantile wish to verbal dream report, and involve the different meanings of wish, latent dream-thoughts, and manifest content.

At the core of the dream is an infantile wish—more specifically a repressed sexual one. This wish is presumably fixed in the Unconscious primarily in the form of the visual contents of a prototypical Scene. Thus, a dream is essentially "a substitute for an infantile scene modified by being transferred on to a recent experience" (p. 546). The assumption that repressed childhood libidinal wishes are at the core of dreams is fundamental to Freud's view of dream interpretation. But, as I have tried to show, these assumptions emerge only at the end of the book; as Freud points out, they are derived from his theory of neurosis as the disguised expression of repressed infantile sexuality, rather than being unique or specific to dreams and to the dream-work.

All aspects of experience and behavior are influenced, in varying degrees, by the transfer of repressed unconscious wishes, always seeking expression or discharge. Dreams only represent a natural regressed state wherein the influence of the unconscious, repressed factors is particularly prominent; Freud concludes that dreams are the royal road to the unconscious, but he believes that all roads lead eventually to the unconscious. Thus, the theory of the neuroses mandates that a dream be the expression of repressed sexual wishes; even more broadly, the assumption that all dreams must be wish fulfillment follows logically from Freud's postulates about the functioning of the mental apparatus (as spelled out most explicitly in the 1895 *Project*) and the basis of all motivation and thought (p. 606, quoted earlier). The unconscious wish is the entrepreneur of the dream, providing the energy for the hallucinatory experience as well as the major need for the censorship.

Thus, a fundamental step in the formation of the dream is the transfer of the infantile wish or scene onto the current dream-thoughts. The dream-thoughts are normal, rational thought processes, capable of any degree of complexity, verbalization, and abstraction, reflecting the experiences, concerns, worries, hopes, and wishes (in the ordinary sense) of current life (day residues). The infantile wishes and primarily visual scenes transfer their intensity and their contents selectivity onto those of the current dream-thoughts; rational processes undergo abnormal transformations—primarily condensation of contents and displacements of intensity and emphasis as expressions of the primary process (freely displaceable energy). This mixture of unconscious, primarily visual contents from the early past (memories, fantasies) with preconscious, rational, heavily verbal, recent material is then subjected to further transformations because of the needs of censorship and the limited means of representation of the dream as a visual, concrete, pictorial medium.

What I want to stress is that the dream-work and the primary process apply to both levels of this process, although Freud deals explicitly only with the second stage—the dream-thoughts to the dream—until the last chapter of the book. Also, he does not differentiate explicitly or consistently between the rational, current dream-thoughts and these thoughts, once the infantile repressed material has been transferred onto them. Both can be said to constitute the latent content of the dream—that is, both the rational dream thoughts (day residue) and the abnormally transformed dream thoughts.

I believe it is important to distinguish conceptually these two different levels of the dream-work, even if there is no reason to assume that they represent a clearly differentiated or linear chronological sequence in the formation of an actual dream. The main point here is that, not surprisingly, these two levels have their counterpart in two levels of interpretation and inference. We have seen that the dream is only retrievable as a selective and often changing memory, subject to secondary revision (as a kind of defensive early automatic self-interpretation) and put in verbal form as soon as it becomes more than a fleeting private memory. Thus, there are four levels of transformation of dream material: level 1, unconscious infantile scenes; level 2, rational dream thoughts; level 3, the dream as dreamt, as thinking during sleep; and level 4, the verbal dream. Among other aspects, these four levels involve a repeated oscillation between the predominantly pictorial unconscious scene (1) and the dream as dreamt (3), and the predominantly verbal and conceptual (reasoning, logical relations) dream thought (2) and verbal report (4).

We have considered the assumption that dreams' having to be wish fulfillment is not intrinsic to the theory of dreams, but rather an extrapolation from the theory of the formation and compromise function of neurotic symptoms. The wish is necessary to provide the energy or intensity—but why only a wish, rather than anxiety, except for the requirements of the discharge model of motivation? Any present-day issue and conflict can be intensified by reverberating with past instances transferred onto it—a process not limited to sleep, but more easily occurring during an altered state with a minimum of immediate reality constraints. And not only wishes require censorship and disguised expression. If "dreams are nothing other than a particular form of thinking, made possible by the conditions of the state of sleep" (p. 506)—a fact that modern sleep research has spelled out and confirmed—then the argument that the infantile wish is always necessary to provide the energy or intensity to produce a dream is not very compelling.

It is easy to accept the assumption that, in the state of sleep, our memories and fantasies will become more dominant (as prime contents of our dream consciousness) than during waking consciousness (which is primarily focused on interaction with the immediate environment). But does this compel us to view infantile wishes and memories as the core and true meaning of the dream? Or, in empirical terms, does this compel us to interpret and reduce the dream to its presumed earliest origins?

Freud, as we have seen, has difficulty in maintaining the decoding or translation model of interpretation, which assumes that the dream does not create anything new, but merely through the irrational or abnormal processes of the dream-work creates a distorted and condensed version of the rational dream-thoughts. Of course, as I highlighted before, the transfer of the infantile wish onto the dream-thoughts is already a core aspect of the dream content acquiring an irrational character through primary process transformations. Yet, ultimately, what Freud wants to retrieve and restore is not the dream-thoughts but the deep unconscious and the early memories.

There is no exhaustive, complete, and unambiguous dream interpretation. In his Dora and Wolf Man examples, Freud is focused on reconstructing a specific traumatic scene. In the clinical use of dream interpretation, most clinicians do not aim for an exhaustive interpretation of a dream; they use dream reports and the patient's associations as one source—especially valuable but not unique—of material for their interpretive method and therapeutic goals.

In his last summary on dream interpretation, Freud states that the unique value of dreams is that they give access to deep and early memories and also demonstrate "the laws which govern the passage of events in the unconscious" because "the dream-work is essentially an instance of the unconscious working over of preconscious thought processes" (1938, p. 167).

To what extent does *The Interpretation of Dreams* provide us with such laws? Do they account for the main paradox of the unconscious—its timeless stability contrasted with the endless variety and changeability of its manifestations? We have seen that this "working over" involves displacements and transfers of intensities and condensations and mixing of contents. These processes function to allow representation of thoughts and memories, under the special constraints of thinking in the altered state of sleep and the prohibitions of censorship. But, aside from these general and vague goals of discharge under the constraints of censorship, can one speak of specific laws directing "the passage of events in the unconscious"? Freud's ultimate level of explanation is to invoke the primary process with its mobile energy in the service of the pleasure principle.

But can one speak of laws for the primary process, in the sense of predictable regularities and recurrent patterns? The closest that Freud comes to discussing the kinds of links between manifest and latent content is in his references to "intermediate thoughts" and the use of "superficial associations," as contrasted with and a substitute for "deeper legitimate" ones. Or could it be that the only valid law of the primary process is the law of anarchy?

References

Ahbel–Rappe, K. (2006). “I no longer believe”: Did Freud abandon the seduction theory? *Journal of the American Psychoanalytic Association, 54,* 171–199.

Ahbel–Rappe, K. (2009). “After a long pause”: How to read Dora as history. *Journal of the American Psychoanalytic Association, 57,* 595–629.

Balint, M. (1960). Primary Narcissism and Primary Love. *Psychoanalytic Quarterly, 29,* 6–43.

Benjamin, J. (1990). An outline of intersubjectivity: The development of recognition. *Psychoanalytic Psychology,* 7(Suppl.), 33–46.

Beres, D., & Joseph, E. (1970). The concept of mental representation in psychoanalysis. *International Journal of Psychoanalysis, 51,* 1–9.

Bion, W. R. (1967). Notes on memory and desire. *Psychoanalytic Forum, 2,* 272–275, 279–280.

Blamary, M. (1979). *Psychoanalyzing psychoanalysis.* Baltimore, MD: Johns Hopkins University Press, 1982.

Blass, R. (2006). A psychoanalytic understanding of the desire for knowledge as reflected in Freud’s “Leonardo da Vinci and a memory of his childhood.” *International Journal of Psychoanalysis, 87,* 1259–1276.

Blum, H. P. (1996). Seduction trauma: Representation, deferred action, and pathogenic development. *Journal of the American Psychoanalytic Association, 44,* 1147–1164.

Blum, H. P. (2008). A further excavation of seduction, seduction trauma, and the seduction theory. *The Psychoanalytic Study of the Child, 63,* 254–269.

Bodner, G. (2002). From the theory of seduction to traumatic seduction: Incest. *International Journal of Psychoanalysis, 83,* 504–507.

Boston Change Process Study Group (BCPSG) (2007). The foundational level of psychodynamic meaning. *International Journal of Psychoanalysis, 88,* 843–860.

Breuer, J., & Freud, S. (1895). *Studies on hysteria.* In J. Strachey (Ed. & Trans.), *The standard edition of the complete psychological works of Sigmund Freud* (Vol. 2). London, England: Hogarth Press.

Chasseguet-Smirgel, J. (1975). *The ego ideal* (P. Barrows, Trans.). London, England: Free Association Books, 1985.

Crews, F. (1993). The unknown Freud. *New York Review of Books,* pp. 61–66.

Crews, F. (1994a). The revenge of the repressed: Part I. *New York Review of Books, 41*(19), 54–60.

Crews, F. (1994b). The revenge of the repressed: Part II. *New York Review of Books, 41*(20), 49–58.

Crews, F. (1995). *The memory wars/Freud's legacy in dispute.* New York, NY: A New York Review book.

Dunn, J. (1995). Intersubjectivity in psychoanalysis: A critical review. *International Journal of Psychoanalysis, 76*, 723–738.

Eissler, K. R. (1962). On the metapsychology of the preconscious: A tentative contribution to psychoanalytic morphology. *The Psychoanalytic Study of the Child, 17*, 9–41.

Emde, R. N. (2007). Embodiment and our immersion with others: Commentary on Fonagy and Target. *Journal of the American Psychoanalytic Association, 55*, 485–492.

Erikson, E. (1950). *Childhood and society.* New York. NY: W. W. Norton.

Erikson, E. (1954). The dream specimen of psychoanalysis. *Journal of the American Psychoanalytic Association, 2*, 5–56.

Erikson, E. (1956b). The first psychoanalyst. In *Insight and responsibility* (pp. 17–46). New York, NY: Norton, 1964.

Erikson, E. (1962). Psychological reality and historical actuality. *Journal of the American Psychoanalytic Association, 10*, 451–473.

Erreich, A. (2003). A modest proposal: (Re)defining unconscious fantasy. *Psychoanalytic Quarterly, 72*, 541–574.

Fenichel, O. (1941). *Problems of psychoanalytic technique* (D. Brunswick, Trans.). New York, NY: The Psychoanalytic Quarterly.

Ferenczi, S., & Rank, O. (1925). *The development of psychoanalysis.* New York, NY: Nervous and Mental Disease Publishing Company.

Fonagy, P. (1999). Points of contact and divergence between psychoanalytic and attachment theories. *Psychoanalytic Inquiry, 19*, 448–458.

Foucault, M. (1964). Nietzsche, Freud, Marx. In G. Ormiston & A. Schrift (Eds.), *Transforming the hermeneutic context: From Nietzsche to Nancy* (pp. 43–67). Albany, NY: State University of New York Press.

Freud, S. (1887–1902). *The origins of psychoanalysis: Letters to Wilhelm Fliess, drafts and notes, 1887–1902* (M. Bonaparte, A. Freud, & E. Kris, Eds.). New York, NY: Basic Books, 1954.

Freud, S. (1887–1904). *The complete letters of Sigmund Freud to Wilhelm Fliess* (J. M. Masson, Ed. & Trans.). Cambridge, MA: Harvard University Press, 1985.

Freud, S. (1892–1899). Extracts from the Fliess papers. In J. Strachey (Ed. & Trans.), *The standard edition of the complete psychological works of Sigmund Freud* (Vol. 1, pp. 175–280). London, England: Hogarth Press, 1966.

Freud, S. (1894). The neuro-psychoses of defense. In J. Strachey (Ed. & Trans.), *The standard edition of the complete psychological works of Sigmund Freud* (Vol. 3, pp. 43–61). London, England: Hogarth Press, 1962.

Freud, S. (1895). Project for a scientific psychology. In J. Strachey (Ed. & Trans.), *The standard edition of the complete psychological works of Sigmund Freud* (Vol. 1, pp. 281–391). London, England: Hogarth Press, 1966.

Freud, S. (1896a). Further remarks on the neuro-psychoses of defence. In J. Strachey (Ed. & Trans.), *The standard edition of the complete psychological works of Sigmund Freud* (Vol. 3, pp. 157–185). London, England: Hogarth Press, 1962.

Freud, S. (1896b). The aetiology of hysteria. In J. Strachey (Ed. & Trans.), *The standard edition of the complete psychological works of Sigmund Freud* (Vol. 3, pp 189–221). London, England: Hogarth Press, 1962.

Freud, S. (1896c). Heredity and the aetiology of the neuroses. In J. Strachey (Ed. & Trans.), *The standard edition of the complete psychological works of Sigmund Freud* (Vol. 3, pp. 141–156). London, England: Hogarth Press, 1962.

Freud, S. (1898a). Sexuality in the aetiology of the neuroses. In J. Strachey (Ed. & Trans.), *The standard edition of the complete psychological works of Sigmund Freud* (Vol. 3, pp. 261–285). London, England: Hogarth Press, 1962.

Freud, S. (1898b). The psychical mechanism of forgetfulness. In J. Strachey (Ed. & Trans.), *The standard edition of the complete psychological works of Sigmund Freud* (Vol. 3, pp. 289–297). London, England: Hogarth Press, 1962.

Freud, S. (1899). Screen memories. In J. Strachey (Ed. & Trans.), *The standard edition of the complete psychological works of Sigmund Freud* (Vol. 3, pp. 301–322). London, England: Hogarth Press, 1962.

Freud, S. (1900). The interpretation of dreams. In J. Strachey (Ed. & Trans.), *The standard edition of the complete psychological works of Sigmund Freud* (Vols. 4–5). London, England: Hogarth Press, 1958.

Freud, S. (1901a). On dreams. In J. Strachey (Ed. & Trans.), *The standard edition of the complete psychological works of Sigmund Freud* (Vol. 5, pp. 633–686). London, England: Hogarth Press, 1958.

Freud, S. (1901b). The psychopathology of everyday life. In J. Strachey (Ed. & Trans.), *The standard edition of the complete psychological works of Sigmund Freud* (Vol. 6, pp. 1–296). London, England: Hogarth Press, 1960.

Freud, S. (1905a). Fragment of an analysis of a case of hysteria. In J. Strachey (Ed. & Trans.), *The standard edition of the complete psychological works of Sigmund Freud* (Vol. 7, pp. 1–122). London, England: Hogarth Press, 1953.

Freud, S. (1905b). Three essays on the theory of sexuality. In J. Strachey (Ed. & Trans.), *The standard edition of the complete psychological works of Sigmund Freud* (Vol. 7, pp. 130–245). London, England: Hogarth Press, 1953.

Freud, S. (1906). My views on the part played by sexuality in aetiology of the neuroses. In J. Strachey (Ed. & Trans.), *The standard edition of the complete psychological works of Sigmund Freud* (Vol. 7, pp. 269–279). London, England: Hogarth Press, 1953.

Freud, S. (1908). Hysterical phantasies and their relation to bisexuality. In J. Strachey (Ed. & Trans.), *The standard edition of the complete psychological works of Sigmund Freud* (Vol. 9, pp. 155–156). London, England: Hogarth Press, 1959.

Freud, S. (1909a). Some general remarks on hysterical attacks. In J. Strachey (Ed. & Trans.), *The standard edition of the complete psychological works of Sigmund Freud* (Vol. 9, pp. 227–234). London, England: Hogarth Press, 1959.

Freud, S. (1909b). Analysis of a phobia in a five-year-old boy. In J. Strachey (Ed. & Trans.), *The standard edition of the complete psychological works of Sigmund Freud* (Vol. 10, pp. 3–141). London, England: Hogarth Press, 1955.

Freud, S. (1910). Leonardo da Vinci and a memory of his childhood. In J. Strachey (Ed. & Trans.), *The standard edition of the complete psychological works of Sigmund Freud* (Vol. 11, pp. 59–137). London, England: Hogarth Press, 1957.

Freud, S. (1911). Formulations on the two principles of mental functioning. In J. Strachey (Ed. & Trans.), *The standard edition of the complete psychological works of Sigmund Freud* (Vol. 12, pp. 213–226). London, England: Hogarth Press, 1958.

Freud, S. (1912). The dynamics of transference. In J. Strachey (Ed. & Trans.), *The standard edition of the complete psychological works of Sigmund Freud* (Vol. 12, pp. 97–108). London, England: Hogarth Press, 1958.

Freud, S. (1913). Totem and taboo. In J. Strachey (Ed. & Trans.), *The standard edition of the complete psychological works of Sigmund Freud* (Vol. 13, pp. 1–161). London, England: Hogarth Press, 1955.

Freud, S. (1914a). Remembering, repeating and working-through. In J. Strachey (Ed. & Trans.), *The standard edition of the complete psychological works of Sigmund Freud* (Vol. 12, pp. 145–156). London, England: Hogarth Press, 1958.

Freud, S. (1914b). On the history of the psycho-analytic movement. In J. Strachey (Ed. & Trans.), *The standard edition of the complete psychological works of Sigmund Freud* (Vol. 14, pp. 1–66). London, England: Hogarth Press, 1957.

Freud, S. (1914c). On narcissism: An introduction. In J. Strachey (Ed. & Trans.), *The standard edition of the complete psychological works of Sigmund Freud* (Vol. 14, pp. 67–102). London, England: Hogarth Press, 1957.

Freud, S. (1915a). Observations on transference-love (Further recommendations on the technique of psycho-analysis III). In J. Strachey (Ed. & Trans.), *The standard edition of the complete psychological works of Sigmund Freud* (Vol. 12, pp. 157–171). London, England: Hogarth Press, 1958.

Freud, S. (1915b). Instincts and their vicissitudes. In J. Strachey (Ed. & Trans.), *The standard edition of the complete psychological works of Sigmund Freud* (Vol. 14, pp. 109–140). London, England: Hogarth Press, 1957.

Freud, S. (1915c). The unconscious. In J. Strachey (Ed. & Trans.), *The standard edition of the complete psychological works of Sigmund Freud* (Vol. 14, pp. 159–215). London, England: Hogarth Press, 1957.

Freud, S. (1917). Introductory lectures on psycho-analysis. In J. Strachey (Ed. & Trans.), *The standard edition of the complete psychological works of Sigmund Freud* (Vols. 15–16). London, England: Hogarth Press, 1963.

Freud, S. (1918). From the history of an infantile neurosis (The wolf-man). In J. Strachey (Ed. & Trans.), *The standard edition of the complete psychological works of Sigmund Freud* (Vol. 17, pp. 1–122). London, England: Hogarth Press, 1955.

Freud, S. (1919). A child is being beaten (A contribution to the study of the origin of sexual perversions). In J. Strachey (Ed. & Trans.), *The standard edition of the complete psychological works of Sigmund Freud* (Vol. 17, pp. 175–204). London, England: Hogarth Press, 1955.

Freud, S. (1920). Beyond the pleasure principle. In J. Strachey (Ed. & Trans.), *The standard edition of the complete psychological works of Sigmund Freud* (Vol. 18, pp. 1–64). London, England: Hogarth Press, 1955.

Freud, S. (1923a). Two encyclopedia articles. In J. Strachey (Ed. & Trans.), *The standard edition of the complete psychological works of Sigmund Freud* (Vol. 18, pp. 235–259). London, England: Hogarth Press, 1955.

Freud, S. (1923b). The ego and the id. In J. Strachey (Ed. & Trans.), *The standard edition of the complete psychological works of Sigmund Freud* (Vol. 19, pp. 1–66). London, England: Hogarth Press, 1961.

Freud, S. (1924). Neurosis and psychosis. In J. Strachey (Ed. & Trans.), *The standard edition of the complete psychological works of Sigmund Freud* (Vol. 19, pp. 147–153). London, England: Hogarth Press, 1961.

Freud, S. (1925a). A note on the "mystic writing pad." In J. Strachey (Ed. & Trans.), *The standard edition of the complete psychological works of Sigmund Freud* (Vol. 19, pp. 227–232). London, England: Hogarth Press, 1961.

Freud, S. (1925b). Negation. In J. Strachey (Ed. & Trans.), *The standard edition of the complete psychological works of Sigmund Freud* (Vol. 19, pp. 233–239). London, England: Hogarth Press, 1961.

Freud, S. (1925c). An autobiographical study. In J. Strachey (Ed. & Trans.), *The standard edition of the complete psychological works of Sigmund Freud* (Vol. 20, pp. 1–76). London, England: Hogarth Press, 1959.

Freud, S. (1926a). Inhibitions, symptoms and anxiety. In J. Strachey (Ed. & Trans.), *The standard edition of the complete psychological works of Sigmund Freud* (Vol. 20, pp. 75–174). London, England: Hogarth Press, 1959.

Freud, S. (1926b). Psycho-analysis. In J. Strachey (Ed. & Trans.), *The standard edition of the complete psychological works of Sigmund Freud* (Vol. 20, pp. 263–270). London, England: Hogarth Press, 1959.

Freud, S. (1927). Humour. In J. Strachey (Ed. & Trans.), *The standard edition of the complete psychological works of Sigmund Freud* (Vol. 21, pp. 159–166). London, England: Hogarth Press, 1961.

Freud, S. (1933). New introductory lectures on psycho-analysis. In J. Strachey (Ed. & Trans.), *The standard edition of the complete psychological works of Sigmund Freud* (Vol. 22, pp. 1–182). London, England: Hogarth Press, 1964.

Freud, S. (1937). Constructions in analysis. In J. Strachey (Ed. & Trans.), *The standard edition of the complete psychological works of Sigmund Freud* (Vol. 23, pp. 256–269). London, England: Hogarth Press, 1964.

Freud, S. (1938). *An outline of psycho-analysis.* In J. Strachey (Ed. & Trans.), *The standard edition of the complete psychological works of Sigmund Freud* (Vol. 23, pp. 139–207). London, England: Hogarth Press, 1964.

Freud, S. (1939). *Moses and monotheism.* In J. Strachey (Ed. & Trans.), *The standard edition of the complete psychological works of Sigmund Freud* (Vol. 23, pp. 3–140). London, England: Hogarth Press, 1964.

Friedman, L. (1995). Psychic reality in psychoanalytic theory. *International Journal of Psychoanalysis, 76,* 25–28.

Friedman, L. (1996). Overview: Knowledge and authority in the psychoanalytic relationship. *Psychoanalytic Quarterly, 65,* 254–265.

Gabbard, G. O. (1995). Countertransference: The emerging common ground. *International Journal of Psychoanalysis, 76,* 475–485.

Gadamer, G. (1960). *Truth and method.* New York, NY: Crossroad, 1982.

Galatzer-Levy, R. M. (2009). Finding your way through chaos, fractals, and other exotic mathematical objects: A guide for the perplexed. *Journal of the American Psychoanalytic Association, 57,* 1227–1249.

Gill, M. M. (1979). The analysis of the transference. *Journal of the American Psychoanalytic Association, 27*(Suppl.), 263–288.

Gill, M. M. (1982). *Analysis of transference, I: Theory and technique.* New York, NY: International Universities Press.

Gill, M. M. (1994). *Psychoanalysis in transition. A personal view.* Hillsdale, NJ: Analytic Press.

Gill, M. M., & Hoffman, I. Z. (1982). *Analysis of transference, II.* New York: International Universities Press.

Glover, E. (1931). The therapeutic effect of inexact interpretation: A contribution to the theory of suggestion. *International Journal of Psychoanalysis, 12,* 397–411.

Good, M. (Ed.) (2006). *The seduction theory in its second century.* Madison, CT: International Universities Press.

Heimann, P. (1950). On counter-transference. *International Journal of Psychoanalysis, 31,* 81–84.

Holt, R. R. (Ed.) (1967). *Motives and thought: Psychoanalytic essays in honor of David Rapaport.* New York, NY: International Universities Press.

Holt, R. R. (1967a). Beyond vitalism and mechanism: Freud's concept of psychic energy. In J. H. Masserman (Ed.), *Science and psychoanalysis* (pp.). New York, NY: Grune & Stratton.

Holt, R. R. (1967b). The development of the primary process: A structural view. In R. R. Holt (Ed.), *Motives and thought: Psychoanalytic essays in honor of David Rapaport* (pp. 345–383). New York, NY: International Universities Press.

Holt, R. R. (2009). Primary process thinking: Theory, measurement, and research. New York, NY: Jason Aronson.

Jacobson, E. (1954). The self and the object world: Vicissitudes of their infantile cathexes and their influence on ideational and affective development. *The Psychoanalytic Study of the Child, 9,* 75–127.

Jones, E. (1953). *The life and work of Sigmund Freud, I.* New York, NY: Basic Books.

Jones, E. (1955). *The life and work of Sigmund Freud, II.* New York, NY: Basic Books.

Klein, G. (1959). Consciousness in psychoanalytic theory: Some implications for current research in perception. *Journal of the American Psychoanalytic Association, 7,* 5–34.

Klein, G. (1967). Peremptory ideation: Structure and force in motivated ideas. In R. R. Holt (Ed.), *Motives and thought: Psychoanalytic essays in honor of David Rapaport* (pp. 80–128). New York, NY: International Universities Press.

Klein, M. (1952). The origins of transference. *International Journal of Psychoanalysis, 33,* 433–438.

Klein, M. (1961). *Narrative of a child psycho-analysis.* London, England: Hogarth Press.

Laplanche, J. (1970). *Life and death in psychoanalysis* (J. McReaman, Trans.). Baltimore, MD: Johns Hopkins University Press, 1976.

Laplanche, J. (1987). *New foundations for psychoanalysis* (D. Macey, Trans.). Cambridge, MA: Basil Blackwell, 1989.

Laplanche, J. (1992a). Interpretation between determinism and hermeneutics: A restatement of the problem. *International Journal of Psychoanalysis, 73,* 429–445.

Laplanche, J. (1992b). Transference: Its provocation by the analyst. In J. Fletcher (Trans.), *Essays on otherness.* London, England: Routledge, 1999.

Laplanche, J. (1993). A short treatise on the unconscious. In J. Fletcher (Trans.), *Essays on otherness.* London: Routledge, 1999.

Laplanche, J. (1997). The theory of seduction and the problem of the other (L. Thurston, Trans.). *International Journal of Psychoanalysis, 78,* 653–666.

Laplanche J., & Pontalis, J.-B. (1964). Fantasme originaire, fantasmes des origines, origine du fantasme. *Les Temps Modernes, 19,* 1833–1868.

Laplanche, J., & Pontalis, J.-B. (1967). *The Language of Psycho-Analysis,* transl. D. Nicholson-Smith. New York: Norton, 1973.

Laplanche, J., & Pontalis, J.-B. (1968). Fantasy and the origins of sexuality. *International Journal of Psycho-Analysis, 49*:1–18.

Levenson, E. (1972). *The fallacy of understanding.* New York, NY: Basic Books.

Levenson, E. (1981). Facts or fantasies: The nature of psychoanalytic data. *Contemporary Psychoanalysis, 17,* 486–500.

Litowitz, B. E. (2007). Unconscious fantasy: A once and future concept. *Journal of the American Psychoanalytic Association, 55,* 199–228.

Litowitz, B. E., & Litowitz, N. S. (1977). The influence of linguistic theory on psychoanalysis: A critical, historical survey. *International Review of Psychoanalysis, 4,* 419–448.

Loewald, H. (1951). Ego and reality. *International Journal of Psychoanalysis, 32,* 10–18.

Loewald, H. (1960). On the therapeutic action of psycho-analysis. *International Journal of Psychoanalysis, 41,* 16–33.

Loewald, H. (1971a). On motivation and instinct theory. *The Psychoanalytic Study of the Child, 26,* 91–128.

Loewald, H. (1971b). The transference neurosis. *Journal of the American Psychoanalytic Association, 19,* 54–66.

Loewald, H. (1975). Psychoanalysis as an art and the fantasy character of the psychoanalytic situation. *Journal of the American Psychoanalytic Association, 23,* 277–299.

Loewald, H. (1978a). *Psychoanalysis and the history of the individual.* New Haven, CT: Yale University Press.

Lothane, Z. (1999). The perennial Freud: Method versus myth and the mischief of Freud bashers. *International Forum Psychoanalysis, 8,* 151–171.

Lothane, Z. (2001). Freud's alleged repudiation of the seduction theory revisited: Facts and fallacies. *Psychoanalytic Review, 88,* 673–723.

Mahl, G. F. (1970). Expressive behaviour during the analytic process. Unpublished manuscript.

Makari, G. J. (1998a). The seductions of history: Sexual trauma in Freud's theory and historiography. *International Journal of Psychoanalysis, 79,* 857–869.

Makari, G. J. (1998b). Between seduction and libido: Sigmund Freud's masturbation hypotheses and the realignment of his etiologic thinking (1897–1905). *Bulletin of the History of Medicine, 72,* 627–694.

Makari, G. J. (2009). *Revolution in mind: The creation of psychoanalysis.* New York, NY: Harper.

Masson, J. (1984). *The assault on truth: Freud's suppression of the seduction theory.* New York, NY: Farrar, Straus, & Giroux.

Mead, G. H. (1934). *Mind, self, and society.* Chicago, IL: University of Chicago Press, 1967.

Mitchell, S. (1988). *Relational concepts in psychoanalysis: An integration*. Cambridge, MA: Harvard University Press.

Ogden, T. (1979). On projective identification. *International Journal of Psychoanalysis, 60*, 357–373.

Ogden, T. (1994). The analytic third: Working with intersubjective clinical facts. *International Journal of Psychoanalysis, 75*, 3–19.

Perron, R. (2001). The unconscious and primal phantasies. *International Journal of Psychoanalysis, 82*, 583–595.

Piaget, J. (1945). *Play, dreams and imitation in childhood*. New York, NY: Norton, 1951.

Piaget, J. (1964). *Six psychological studies*. New York, NY: Random House, 1968.

Pine, F. (2006). The psychoanalytic dictionary: A position paper on diversity and its unifiers. *Journal of the American Psychoanalytic Association, 54*, 463–491.

Rapaport, D. (1950). On the psychoanalytic theory of thinking. *International Journal of Psychoanalysis, 31*, 161–170.

Rapaport, D. (1951). States of consciousness: A psychopathological and psychodynamic view. In M. M. Gill (Ed.), *The collected papers of David Rapaport* (pp. 385–404). New York, NY: Basic Books, 1967.

Rapaport, D. (1953). Some metapsychological considerations concerning activity and passivity. In M. M. Gill (Ed.), *The collected papers of David Rapaport* (pp. 530–568). New York, NY: Basic Books, 1967.

Rapaport, D. (1958). The theory of ego autonomy: A generalization. *Bulletin of the Menninger Clinic, 22*, 13–35.

Rapaport, D. (1960a). Psychoanalysis as a developmental psychology. In M. M. Gill (Ed.), *The collected papers of David Rapaport* (pp. 530–568). New York, NY: Basic Books, 1967.

Rapaport, D. (1960b). *The structure of psychoanalytic theory. A systematizing attempt*. New York, NY: International Universities Press.

Renik, O. (1992). Use of the analyst as a fetish. *Psychoanalytic Quarterly, 61*, 542–563.

Renik, O. (1993). Analytic interaction: Conceptualizing technique in light of the analyst's irreducible subjectivity. *Psychoanalytic Quarterly, 62*, 553–571.

Renik, O. (1995). The ideal of the anonymous analyst and the problem of self-disclosure. *Psychoanalytic Quarterly, 64*, 446–495.

Renik, O. (1996). The perils of neutrality. *Psychoanalytic Quarterly, 65*, 495–517.

Rosen, V. (1969). Sign phenomena and their relationship to unconscious meaning. *International Journal of Psychoanalysis, 50*, 197–207.

Sadow, L., Gedo, J. E., Miller, J., Pollock, G., Sabshin, M., & Schlessinger, N. (1968). The process of hypothesis change in three early psychoanalytic concepts. *Journal of the American Psychoanalytic Association, 16*, 245–273.

Sandler, J. (1960). On the concept of superego. *The Psychoanalytic Study of the Child, 15*, 128–162.

Sandler, J. (1976). Countertransference and role responsiveness. *International Review of Psychoanalysis, 3*, 43–47.

Sandler, J., & Dreher, A. (1996). What do psychoanalysts want? The problem of aims in psychoanalytic therapy. London, England: Routledge.

Sandler, J., & Rosenblatt, B. (1962). The concept of the representational world. *Psychoanalytic Study of the Child, 17*, 128–145.

Sandler, J., & Sandler, A. (1994). Comments on the conceptualisation of clinical facts in psychoanalysis. *International Journal of Psychoanalysis, 75,* 995–1010.

Schafer, R. (1960). The loving and beloved superego in Freud's structural theory. *Psychoanalytic Study of the Child, 15,* 163–188.

Schafer, R. (1968). *Aspects of internalization.* Madison, CT: International Universities Press.

Schafer, R. (1972). Internalization: Process or fantasy? *The Psychoanalytic Study of the Child,* 27, 411–436.

Schafer, R. (1978). *Language and insight.* New Haven, CT: Yale University Press.

Schafer, R. (1982). The relevance of the "here and now" transference interpretation in the reconstruction of early development. *International Journal of Psychoanalysis, 63,* 77–82.

Schafer, R. (1983). *The analytic attitude.* New York, NY: Basic Books.

Schafer, R. (1992). *Retelling a life: Narration and dialogue in psychoanalysis.* New York, NY: Basic Books.

Schafer, R. (1994). The contemporary Kleinians of London. *Psychoanalytic Quarterly, 63,* 409–432.

Schafer, R. (1997). *Tradition and change in psychoanalysis.* Madison, CT: International Universities Press.

Schimek, J. G. (1973). Signorelli: The parapraxis specimen of psychoanalysis. *Psychoanalysis and Contemporary Science, 3,* 210–230.

Schimek, J. G. (1974). The parapraxis specimen of psychoanalysis. *Psychoanalysis and Contemporary Science, 3,* 210–230.

Schimek, J. G. (1975a). A critical reexamination of Freud's concept of unconscious mental representation. *International Review of Psychoanalysis, 2,* 171–187.

Schimek, J. G. (1975b). The interpretations of the past: Childhood trauma, psychic reality, and historical truth. *Journal of the American Psychoanalytic Association, 23,* 845–865.

Schimek, J. G. (1983). The construction of the transference: The relativity of the "here and now" and the "there and then." *Psychoanalysis and Contemporary Thought, 6,* 435–456.

Schimek, J. G. (1987). Fact and fantasy in the seduction theory: A historical review. *Journal of the American Psychoanalytic Association, 35,* 937–964.

Schimek, J. G. (2002). Unpublished notes, April 11, 2002.

Schmidt, H. (1934). *Philosophisches Wörterbuch. Neunte, neubearbeitete und erweiterte Auflage.* Leipzig, Germany: Kröner.

Schur, M. (1966). Some additional "day residues" of "the specimen dream of psychoanalysis." In R. M. Loewenstein, L. M. Newman, M. Schur, & A. J. Solnit (Eds.), *Psychoanalysis: A general psychology* (pp. 45–85). New York, NY: International Universities Press.

Schwaber, E. (2006). Response. *International Journal of Psychoanalysis, 87,* 17–23.

Smith, H. (2001). Hearing voices: The fate of the analyst's identifications. *Journal of the American Journal of Psychoanalysis, 49,* 781–812.

Smith, H. (2006). On literal misreadings and reconstructed truths. In M. Good (Ed.), *The seduction theory* (pp.). Madison, CT: International Universities Press.

Spence, D. (1982). *Narrative truth and historical truth: Meaning and interpretation in psychoanalysis.* New York, NY: W. W. Norton.

Stein, M. (1981). The unobjectionable part of the transference. *Journal of the American Psychoanalytic Association, 29,* 869–892.

Sterba, R. (1934). The fate of the ego in analytic therapy. *International Journal of Psychoanalysis, 15,* 117–126.

Stern, D. N. (2004). *The present moment in psychotherapy and everyday life.* New York, NY: W. W. Norton.

Stern, D. N., Sander, L. W., Nahum, J. P., Harrison, A. M., Lyons–Ruth, K., Morgan, A. C., Bruschweilerstern, N., & Tronick, E. Z. (1998). Noninterpretive mechanisms in psychoanalytic therapy: The "something more" than interpretation. *International Journal of Psychoanalysis, 79,* 903–921.

Strachey, J. (1934). The nature of the therapeutic action of psycho-analysis. *International Journal of Psychoanalysis, 15,* 127–159.

Thelen, E. (2005). Dynamic systems theory and the complexity of change. *Psychoanalytic Dialogues, 15,* 255–283.

Viderman, S. (1970). *La construction de l'espace analytique.* Paris, France: Denoël.

Wachtel, P. (1980). Transference, schema, and assimilation: The relevance of Piaget to the psychoanalytic theory of transference. In *Annual of psychoanalysis, Vol. 8* (pp. 59–76). New York, NY: International Universities Press.

Waelder, R. (1936). The principle of multiple function: Observations on over-determination. *Psychoanalytic Quarterly, 5,* 45–62.

Waelder, R. (1960). *Basic theory of psychoanalysis.* New York, NY: International Universities Press.

Werner, H., & Kaplan, B. (1963). *Symbol formation.* New York, NY: John Wiley & Sons.

Winnicott, D. W. (1974). Fear of breakdown. *International Review of Psychoanalysis, 1,* 103–107.

Wolff, P. H. (1967). Cognitive considerations for a psychoanalytic theory of language acquisition. In R. R. Holt (Ed.), *Motives and thought: Psychoanalytic essays in honor of David Rapaport* (pp. 299–342). New York, NY: International Universities Press.

Zepf, S. (2006). The concept of psychical reality reconsidered. *Canadian Journal of Psychoanalysis, 14,* 199–213.

Index

E

F

J

K

L

M

R

S

T

U

V

W

Z